SCM STUDYGUIDE TO THE BOOKS OF THE NEW TESTAMENT

Ian Boxall

scm press

British Library Cataloguing in Publication data

A catalogue record for this book is available from the British Library

978 0 334 04047 7

First published in 2007 by SCM Press
13–17 Long Lane
London EC1A 9PN

www.scm-canterburypress.co.uk

SCM Press is a division of
SCM-Canterbury Press Ltd

Typeset by Regent Typesetting, London
Printed and bound in Great Britain by
Biddles Ltd, King's Lynn, Norfolk

Contents

Acknowledgements

This book, and its companion volume *SCM Studyguide to New Testament Interpretation*, are the fruit of teaching and learning from generations of ordinands and undergraduates, first at Chichester Theological College, and subsequently at St Stephen's House, Oxford, and within the wider University of Oxford. I am thankful for their part in making New Testament study such an exciting enterprise; my dedication of this Studyguide to them is a small mark of my appreciation for all that they have taught me.

I am also indebted to my colleagues at both colleges for their encouragement and insight, and to family and friends for their unfailing support. Thanks also are due to Barbara Laing and her staff at SCM Press for their assistance and encouragement.

Unless otherwise stated, biblical quotations are from the New Revised Standard Version.

With gratitude to the students of
Chichester Theological College 1992–1994
and
St Stephen's House, Oxford 1994–2007

Introduction

Purpose of this Book

The purpose of this Studyguide is to introduce the 27 books of the New Testament, and the kinds of issues which studying them raises. Ideally, it is to be used in conjunction with the *SCM Studyguide to New Testament Interpretation*, which reflects more explicitly on the process of interpretation. Nevertheless, each volume is sufficiently self-contained to be usable on its own.

The first three chapters offer some historical orientation. They introduce in turn the worlds of the New Testament authors, and issues relating to historical study of Jesus of Nazareth (the key subject of the New Testament) and Paul of Tarsus (one of its major authors). Succeeding chapters explore the books, either in groups (for example, the Synoptic Gospels, the Catholic Epistles) or as individual texts (for example, Hebrews, Revelation). Though the sequence of chapters is largely canonical, chronological considerations mean that Paul's letters are considered prior to the gospels. A final chapter gives brief consideration to issues raised by the New Testament canon.

Throughout the Studyguide, there are questions for 'reflection', or more practical activities to help you put into practice what has been learnt. Given that interaction is by far the best pedagogic method, they are an integral part of the book and should not be ignored. They are aimed at getting you reading and interpreting the New Testament books as quickly and confidently as possible.

Each chapter contains several suggestions for further reading; brief comments on good commentary series are provided below (fuller bibliographical details are found in the New Testament Introductions mentioned). Those wishing to pursue particular issues in more detail will find assistance in the endnotes.

'Tool Kit' for New Testament Study

The following are useful resources for the student of the New Testament:

- A good **English Study Bible**, with introductions and notes (for further information on different English translations, see chapter 4 of *SCM Studyguide to New Testament Interpretation*).
- A **Greek New Testament**: either the United Bible Societies' *Greek New Testament* or the Nestle–Aland *Novum Testamentum Graece*.
- A **Synopsis of the Gospels** (setting out parallel accounts in the different gospels side-by-side; some just covering the synoptic gospels, some all four). Two good versions are: Kurt Aland, 1982, *Synopsis of the Four Gospels*, United Bible Societies; B. H. Throckmorton, *Gospel Parallels*, Thomas Nelson, various editions.
- A **concordance**: there are a number based on different English translations; on the Greek text, W. F. Moulton and H. K. Geden, 1963, *A Concordance to the Greek Testament*, Edinburgh: T. & T. Clark.
- A good **Bible atlas**: two useful examples are Yohanan Aharoni, Michael Avi-Yonah, Anson F. Rainey and Ze'ev Safrai (eds), 1993, *The Macmillan Bible Atlas*, 3rd edition; New York: Macmillan; Herbert G. May (ed., 3rd edition revised by John Day), 1984, *The Oxford Bible Atlas*, Oxford, New York and Toronto: Oxford University Press.
- A good **New Testament introduction**: among the most accessible, to keep on the shelf and use for reference, are: Raymond E. Brown, 1997, *An Introduction to the New Testament*, New York and London: Doubleday; Luke Timothy Johnson, 1999, *The Writings of the New Testament: An Interpretation*, revised edition; London: SCM Press.
- Scholarly **commentaries**: there are two one-volume commentaries to the whole Bible which are especially valuable to students: Raymond E. Brown, Joseph A. Fitzmyer and Roland E. Murphy (eds), 1995, *The New Jerome*

Bible Commentary, London: Geoffrey Chapman; John Barton and John Muddiman (eds), 2001, *The Oxford Bible Commentary*, Oxford: Oxford University Press. There are a large number of commentary series and stand-alone commentaries covering New Testament books: among these, series of particular note are the Anchor Bible; Black's New Testament Commentaries; Sacra Pagina; Word Commentaries.

- For the serious student, **Bible software** is a valuable aid: one of the best packages for Windows-based computers is *Bibleworks* (for up-to-date information, see www.bibleworks.com). A good package for Mac users is *Accordance* (www.accordancebible.com).

- There are huge numbers of **web resources** relating to the New Testament, of variable quality. One of the best, with links to a large number of other scholarly websites, is Mark Goodacre's *New Testament Gateway* (www. ntgateway.com).

1

The Worlds Which Produced the New Testament

The World and Our Worlds

The New Testament books emerge on the scene of history at particular times (probably the mid- to late first century CE) and in particular places (for example, Ephesus, Corinth, possibly Syrian Antioch and Rome). However much they speak of Israel's God and God's action in Jesus Christ, they each have a historical particularity, bearing the marks of their human authors. Echoes of their time and culture, indications of how they made sense of the world, glimpses of their commitments and priorities, permeate what they write. These books, though familiar, spring from worlds different from our own. Moreover, they were intended to be heard first in worlds different from ours. One of the greatest challenges of New Testament scholarship, indeed, is to make us aware of this gulf, and suggest ways of bridging it.

Note that I speak of the 'worlds' of the New Testament authors, in the plural. I do so advisedly. As interpreters increasingly recognize, there is not simply a great historical and cultural gulf between 'them' in the first century and 'us' in the twenty-first. The New Testament authors live in different cultural contexts, and envisage their world differently, from each other. Compare these two sets of examples:

Example 1
Then some people came, bringing to him a paralysed man, carried by four of them. And when they could not bring him to Jesus because of the crowd, *they removed the roof* (literally 'unroofed the roof') above him; and after *having dug through it*, they let down the mat on which the paralytic lay. (Mark 2.3–4; italics mine)

Just them some men came, carrying a paralysed man on a bed. They were trying to bring him in and lay him before Jesus; but finding no way to bring him in because of the crowd, they went up on the roof and let him down with his bed *through the tiles* into the middle of the crowd in front of Jesus. (Luke 5.18–19; italics mine)

Example 2
Again he began to teach beside *the sea*. Such a very large crowd gathered around him that he got into a boat *on the sea* and sat there, while the whole crowd was beside the sea on the land. (Mark 4.1; italics mine)

Once while Jesus was standing beside the *lake of Gennesaret*, and the crowd was pressing in on him to hear the word of God, he saw two boats there at the shore of *the lake*; the fishermen had gone out of them and were washing their nets. (Luke 5.1–2; italics mine)

Example 1 hints at the very different cultural environments of Mark and Luke. Mark's account of the paralytic's healing presumes the architectural practices of rural Galilee (flat roofs, perhaps made of mud and branches, which could easily be repaired). Luke's world, however, seems to be the urban world of the wider empire. He envisages a tiled roof typical of houses in the eastern Mediterranean.

A similar cultural shift can be detected in Example 2. For Mark, the body of water on which Jesus' disciples fished is a sea: the Sea of Galilee. This is the typical gospel description of the Sea of Kinnereth (Numbers 34.11; from the Hebrew *kinnor* meaning 'harp', perhaps because of its harp-like shape), a freshwater lake approximately 21 km in length and 12 km wide at its widest point. Luke's geographical world, however, is much more expansive. He has sailed the dangerous Mediterranean (see for example Acts 16.11; 20.13–15; 21.1–3), and therefore knows what a real sea is like! By comparison, Kinnereth is no more than an inland lake.

Yet this linguistic difference may conceal even more. In the world Mark envisages (nourished by the Jewish scriptures), 'the sea' has mythological significance. It symbolizes the realm of evil and chaos, which threatens the peace and stability of the created order (cf. Genesis 1; Job 38.8–11; Revelation 13.1; 21.1). It is experienced as a hostile power in need of taming (adding a further dimension to Mark's story of Jesus calming the storm, Mark 4.35–41). Viewed from this perspective, Mark's world may be even richer and more expansive than the world of Luke.

Making Sense of Symbolic Worlds

These are two minor indications of the variant *symbolic worlds* of two first-century evangelists (gospel-writers). The phrase 'symbolic world' is used by scholars to describe that system of shared meanings, cultural assumptions and value-systems by which a group makes sense of reality, and which enables that group to function. As Luke Timothy Johnson puts it:

> A symbolic world is not an alternative ideal world removed from everyday life. To the contrary, it is the system of meanings that anchors the activities of individuals and communities in the real world. Nothing is more down to earth and ordinary than a symbolic world.[1]

In some symbolic worlds, the state impinges on the lives of its citizens, and humans are subject to economic forces. In others, human lives are influenced by the activity of good and malevolent spiritual beings, such as angels and evil spirits. Some may divide humanity into nation-state or transnational union, or according to tribe, extended family or religious affiliation. My world may stretch only to the end of my garden (beyond which is the hostile unknown, 'another world'), or to the extremities of a flat earth, or to the boundaries of an empire like that of Rome or Parthia. A more expansive symbolic world might incorporate a spectacular array of galaxies and universes, or a multiplicity of 'heavens' permitting ever-closer union with God. I (and those of my group) might envisage our world as revolving round the sun, or centred on the city of Jerusalem ('the navel of the earth'), or deriving its energy from the emperor's court in Rome.

Whatever symbolic world we inhabit, there will be a network of customs and rituals which mean something within that world (and may be unintelligible or misleading to someone from another). When I stretch out my hand to another, is that a sign of friendship, or a hostile act? If you stick your tongue out at me, is this an indication of respect, or an insult, or a request for a drink of water? Learning about the customs and rituals of these ancient symbolic worlds is regarded by most New Testament scholars as a fundamental ingredient in responsible interpretation of the New Testament books. When Paul gives advice about marriage in 1 Corinthians 7, can we assume that marriage in his symbolic world has precisely the same web of meanings as in ours? When Jesus talks about one's eye being 'evil' (Matthew 6.23), might one need to understand something of the notion of the 'evil eye' which still influences Mediterranean society?

As we can see in comparing Mark and Luke, symbolic worlds can live side by side, and often in tension with one another. Indeed, given his or her mixed background, geographical movement, or change of status (such as marriage or adoption of a new cult or religious tradition), one individual might inhabit more than one symbolic world. The apostle Paul was a Jew brought up in a significant Greek university city, Tarsus. Moreover, the New Testament claims that he was a Roman citizen. The worlds of Judaism, Hellenism, and Rome must have clashed, or coalesced, in significant ways in his own emerging symbolic world. In addition, his encounter with Christ on the Damascus road seems to have forced a dramatic reassessment of particular symbols and their place within his previous symbolic world (for example, the place of the Jewish Law).

Thus we should expect to find similar tensions in other parts of the New Testament. Indeed, scholars continue to debate whether Judaism or the Graeco-Roman world is the most important context for understanding the emergence of the New Testament writings. A further debate concerns how quickly the Christian movement separated from its original Jewish context/ symbolic world, and whether or not this should be viewed as evolutionary or revolutionary.[2]

Reflection

What are the elements of your 'symbolic world' (or 'symbolic worlds')? What aspects of your culture, ethnic background, education, religious beliefs, experience of travel, have contributed to this symbolic world? How might these differ from the world(s) envisaged by the gospels of Mark or Luke?

Some Resources

What resources are there for reconstructing the two major 'worlds' out of which the New Testament emerged: Judaism and the Graeco-Roman world? Space will not allow for more than a brief outline of these two worlds, and the range of disputed issues about them. Those wishing to 'dig deeper' should consult one of the following excellent yet accessible textbooks:

- Bart D. Ehrman, 2004, *A Brief Introduction to the New Testament*, New York and Oxford: Oxford University Press, Chapters 2 and 4 on the Graeco-Roman context, Chapter 3 on the Jewish context.
- Everett Ferguson, 1987, *Backgrounds of Early Christianity*, Grand Rapids, Michigan: Eerdmans, particularly strong on the wider Graeco-Roman context, including politics, economics, philosophy and religion.
- Christopher Rowland, 2002, *Christian Origins*, 2nd edition; London: SPCK, focuses especially on the Jewish context of the Christian movement.
- E. P. Sanders, 1992, *Judaism: Practice and Belief 63 BCE–66 CE*, London/ Philadelphia: SCM Press/Trinity Press International.

Ehrman and especially Ferguson focus on the wider Graeco-Roman context. I will concentrate here on the Jewish sources. Due to preservation of ancient

Jewish texts by both Jews and Christians, and the occasional rediscovery of lost writings (such as the Dead Sea Scrolls), we have a considerable body of literature springing from the various forms of Judaism around the time of Jesus and the New Testament writers.

Nevertheless, we should not overestimate what we have, some of which is quite fragmentary. The discovery of the Dead Sea Scrolls forced a radical rethink of our understanding of Judaism within first-century Palestine, by uncovering a significant number of distinctive writings hitherto unknown. There may be other areas of ancient Jewish life and practice about which we still know nothing. Moreover, scholars often disagree about how to piece the evidence together, and which texts represent 'mainstream' Jewish life.

The extant literary evidence for Jewish life and practice at the time of Jesus includes the following:

- The *Old Testament* or *Hebrew Bible*, read largely in Hebrew by Jews in the Holy Land, and in Greek (the *Septuagint* (LXX) translation) by Diaspora Jews. LXX contains additional writings, and additions to existing books, which are variously called *deutero-canonical books* or *apocrypha* (literally 'hidden things').
- Aramaic *Targums*, a combination of translation and commentary on the Hebrew text for Aramaic-speaking Palestinian Jews. Though existing Targums are late, they may preserve earlier examples of how a first-century Palestinian Jew heard the Bible read.[3]
- Jewish *pseudepigrapha* (literally 'with a false title'), other Jewish writings (including apocalypses, psalms, testaments, etc.), providing insight into various Jewish groups, both within and outside Palestine. There are three main English collections, by R. H. Charles, James H. Charlesworth, and H. F. D. Sparks.[4]
- The sectarian writings of the Qumran sect ('the Dead Sea Scrolls', discovered in caves near the Dead Sea): two good English translations are those of Geza Vermes and Florentino García Martínez.[5]
- The writings of *Philo of Alexandria*, a Jewish philosopher and biblical exegete who was a direct contemporary of Jesus.[6] These give a glimpse of how one Diaspora Jew, influenced by Greek philosophy, reinterpreted the Jewish tradition.

- The works of *Flavius Josephus*, a Jewish historian and apologist. His *Antiquities* and *Jewish War* are important historical sources for Palestine around the time of Jesus.[7]
- *Rabbinic writings*, of which the *Mishnah* (a collection of laws codified *c*.200 CE) is probably most useful to students of the New Testament.[8] Other later compilations include the *Tosephta*, the Babylonian and Jerusalem *Talmuds*, and the extended biblical commentaries called *Midrashim*. Given their late date in their present form, these need to be used with care as evidence for Jewish beliefs in the first century.

The Narrower Context: Jewish Palestine

The narrower context, at least geographically and politically, is Judaism in Palestine. This was the world of Jesus and his first followers (although a later figure like Paul was a Diaspora Jew). Though the extent of its borders fluctuated somewhat, Palestine in the New Testament period essentially comprised the territory which had been governed by Herod the Great (37–4 BCE), and divided between his sons (Herod Antipas, Archelaus, Herod Philip) on his death.

The northern part was Galilee, where Jesus was brought up and where much of his ministry was focused, with important cities at Sepphoris and Tiberias. This was bordered on the east by the river Jordan, which flowed into the Sea of Galilee before continuing south into the Dead Sea. The southern territory west of the Dead Sea was known as Judea (the territory of the tribe of Judah), whose principal city was Jerusalem, site of the Jewish Temple and place of Jesus' death. In between Galilee and Judea was the hilly region of Samaria, territory of the despised Samaritans. To the west of Samaria and Judea was the coastal plain, containing important Mediterranean ports such as Joppa and Herod's magnificent Caesarea Maritima. Across the Jordan, flanking Samaria and the north-eastern shore of the Dead Sea was Perea, the area in which John the Baptist was probably active. To the north-east of Galilee, were the territories of Gaulanitis (modern 'Golan Heights'), Batanaea, Trachonitis and Auranitis.

Table 1: Rulers of Palestine during Jesus' Lifetime.

Herod Antipas (4 BCE–39 CE)	Galilee
	Perea
Archelaus (4 BCE–6 CE)	Judea
Roman prefects (from 6 CE)	Samaria
Herod Philip (4 BCE–34 CE)	Gaulanitis
	Batanaea
	Trachonitis
	Auranitis

Yet if Palestine was small in terms of geography and political influence, it was certainly not in terms of its symbolic world. Palestinian Judaism, inheriting the symbolic world of the Hebrew Bible, had an expansive view of reality incorporating earth, heaven (or a multiplicity of heavens), and the realm under the earth. Jews in Palestine regularly prayed prayers such as this:

> When I look at your heavens, the work of your fingers,
>   The moon and the stars that you have established;
> What are human beings that you are mindful of them,
>   Mortals that you care for them? (Psalm 8.3–4)

What might be said about this narrower context? First, its geographical territory was strategically located, and politically vulnerable. Buffeted between rival powers, it was regularly fought over and conquered. Nearly sixty years before Jesus' birth, it had come under the political control of Rome, and thus Rome provided the backdrop against which many of the events in Jesus' life and ministry occurred.

> ## To do
>
> Look up the following passages: Matthew 10.2–4; 22.15–22; 27.27–31; Mark 5.1–20; 10.42–5; 15.1–15; Luke 2.1–7; 3.1–2; 7.1–10; 13.1–5; 21.20–4. In each case, note down any evidence for Roman occupation of Palestine. What Jewish attitudes to Rome seem to be reflected here?

Second, Palestinian Judaism prior to Jerusalem's fall in 70 CE was highly diverse. Of course, Jews were distinct from their pagan neighbours. They were monotheists (worshippers of one God) in contrast to the polytheism of the Graeco-Roman world. They also shared a common story: of how this God chose them from among the nations; how he rescued them from slavery in Egypt, and led them into their own land; how he gave them the Law as an expression of his will, which it was their privilege and joy to keep.

Nevertheless, in the first century there were many different ways of being Jewish. Indeed, scholars sometimes speak (somewhat clumsily) of 'Judaisms' rather than 'Judaism'. Much of this diversity reflects different schools of thought or 'sects' (see Table 2). Some are mentioned in the New Testament: the essentially lay Pharisees, noted for their attempts to reinterpret detailed Old Testament laws for contemporary Jewish life, and the more conservative Sadducees, drawn largely from the priestly and aristocratic classes. Both of these groups generally appear in the gospels as opponents of Jesus (a much more positive assessment of the Pharisees is provided by Josephus, himself a Pharisee).[9]

Alongside these, Josephus mentions two other groups or 'philosophies': the Essenes who lived in separate communities throughout the land (of which the group which produced the Dead Sea Scrolls was probably a branch) and what he calls the Fourth Philosophy, which though similar to Pharisaism in outlook was marked by a revolutionary streak motivated by its belief that God alone was master. This stance is reflected in the anti-Roman activities of the *sicarii* or 'dagger-men', bandits like Barabbas (as in Mark 15.7), and the Zealots of the Jewish revolt against Rome which began in 66 CE (for Josephus' descriptions, see his *Jewish War* 2.119–66; *Antiquities* 18.11–23). To these we must add the disciples of Messiah Jesus, who emerged as a reform group *within* Judaism.

There may have been other groups, or variations within these groups, of which we are unaware. We should not, however, assume that all or even the majority of Palestinian Jews belonged to one or other of these groups. Josephus speaks of 6,000 Pharisees and 4,000 Essenes in a total Jewish population estimated at over 3 million.

Other distinctions were due not so much to beliefs and practices as to a person's occupation or social status. Priests were obviously differentiated from laity, with a different role in society. They were assisted in the Temple by Levites. Some (the high priestly families based in Jerusalem) were wealthy and aristocratic, others (for example priests like Zechariah, Luke 1.5) probably not. Scribes (who might belong, for example, to the Pharisee, Essene or Christian group) were skilled in writing, and therefore in interpretation of the Law. Tax-collectors acted as agents of the occupying power, or its client-rulers the Herodians, and therefore attracted antagonism from some of their fellow Jews.

Third, the heart of Jewish Palestine was the Temple in Jerusalem. Most Jews regarded Jerusalem as the only place where cultic worship could be offered (though there was a rival temple at Leontopolis in Egypt, and the Samaritans worshipped on Mount Gerizim). Gloriously restored under Herod the Great, the Temple symbolized the presence of God in their midst. Those who have been on pilgrimage to a sacred shrine can imagine something of the awe and excitement which the first sight of the Temple must have inspired, its marble buildings gleaming in the Middle Eastern sun. This was the centre of the Jewish world, the holiest centre of the holy land.

Indeed, its buildings comprised a series of courts which became increasingly 'holy' as they reached the Temple's centre. Access to each successive court was increasingly restricted: both Jews and Gentiles; Jews only; Jewish males; priests and Levites; priests with responsibility for the incense offering; the high priest (who alone could enter the Holy of Holies, just once a year on the Day of Atonement).

Temple worship centred on a range of animal sacrifices, some offered daily, some annually.[10] Jewish pilgrims from both the land and the Diaspora flocked to the holy city and its Temple for the main pilgrimage festivals: Passover, Pentecost and Tabernacles. Passover, commemorating the liberation of God's people from Egypt, plays a central role in the gospel story, for it was during one Passover pilgrimage that Jesus was arrested and crucified. The theology of this festival, indeed, had an important impact on early Christian attempts to understand Jesus' death and resurrection.

Table 2: New Testament References to Jewish Groups.

And he said to them, 'Therefore every scribe who has been trained for the kingdom of heaven is like the master of a household who brings out of his treasure what is new and what is old.' (Matthew 13.52)

The blind and the lame came to him in the temple, and he cured them. But when the chief priests and the scribes saw the amazing things that he did, and heard the children crying out in the temple, 'Hosanna to the Son of David,' they became angry. (Matthew 21.14–15)

The same day some Sadducees came to him, saying there is no resurrection; and they asked him a question. (Matthew 22.23)

Then Jesus said to the crowds and to his disciples, 'The scribes and the Pharisees sit on Moses' seat; therefore, do whatever they teach you and follow it; but do not do as they do, for they do not practise what they teach.' (Matthew 23.1–3)

When the scribes of the Pharisees saw that he was eating with sinners and tax collectors, they said to his disciples, 'Why does he eat with tax collectors and sinners?' (Mark 2.16)

The Pharisees went out and immediately conspired with the Herodians against him, how to destroy him. (Mark 3.6)

He sat down opposite the treasury, and watched the crowd putting money into the treasury. Many rich people put in large sums. A poor widow came and put in two small copper coins, which are worth a penny. (Mark 12.41–2)

They took Jesus to the high priest; and all the chief priests, the elders, and the scribes were assembled. (Mark 14.53)

At that very hour some Pharisees came and said to him, 'Get away from here, for Herod wants to kill you.' (Luke 13.31)

Then the Pharisees replied, 'Surely you have not been deceived too, have you? Has any one of the authorities or of the Pharisees believed in him? But this crowd, which does not know the law – they are accursed.' (John 7.47–8)

While Peter and John were speaking to the people, the priests, the captain of the temple, and the Sadducees came to them, much annoyed because they were teaching the people and proclaiming that in Jesus there is the resurrection of the dead. (Acts 4.1–2)

Fourth, social divisions were significant. There was a huge gulf between the powerful minority urban elite (in Roman Palestine, client rulers like the Herodians, priestly aristocracy, Roman prefects, and retainers of the elite), and the vast, mainly rural, majority at the bottom of the pyramid. There was nothing in the ancient world like our modern 'middle class'.[11] In early first-century Palestine, the burden of taxation on the peasant population came from three directions: Roman taxation, taxes imposed by the local Herodian client rulers, and tithes and other dues payable by pious Jews to the Temple. In extreme cases, dispossessed peasants, squeezed by the pressures of taxation and confiscation, might resort to banditry (for example, Mark 15.7). Scholars continue to debate the extent of this particular problem in first-century Judea and Galilee.[12]

Whatever the case, hints of the social fragmentation of Jewish Palestine are found in the gospels, notably the parables of Jesus. The world they describe is a world of wealthy, sometimes absentee landowners and dependent tenant farmers, of day labourers in desperate search of work, of debtors struggling to repay often enormous debts (for example, Matthew 18.23–35; 20.1–16; Mark 12.1–12; Luke 7.40–3; 19.12–27). It was within this world that Jesus' proclamation of an alternative reign of God, with its promise of debts forgiven and its vision of egalitarian communities not based on kinship or social status, was first heard.

To do

Look at a map of the first-century Mediterranean and Near Eastern world, in a Bible atlas or study Bible. Where is Palestine located? What size was it (a) during the reign of Herod the Great; (b) under his successors? Who were the major political players in the surrounding area?

History and the Jewish Memory

For a fuller appreciation of the New Testament's Jewish context, one needs to be aware of a number of (relatively recent) historical events which left their mark on Israel's collective memory, and on Jewish theological reflection:

- The exile of the Judeans to Babylon after Nebuchadnezzar's destruction of Jerusalem in 586 BCE. Though some returned to Judea later in the century under the Persian Cyrus, the actual return was far from glorious.
- The hellenizing tendencies of Israel's Syrian overlords the Seleucids, notably Antiochus IV Epiphanes (175–164 BCE), which culminated in the setting up of an altar to Zeus in the Jerusalem Temple in 167 BCE (the so-called 'desolating sacrilege', Daniel 12.11; cf. 1 Maccabees 1.54; Mark 13.14 and parallels). This sparked the Maccabean Revolt, led by Judas 'Maccabeus' (a nickname probably meaning 'hammerer').
- The brief independent Jewish state, under the Hasmonaeans (the brothers of Judas and their descendants), which gave the Jews a taste of relative freedom. The Hasmonaeans eventually assumed both the kingship and the high-priesthood, roles traditionally separate. For some Jews, this was illegitimate, given that they were neither of the royal line of David (they were from the priestly tribe of Levi) nor of the family of Zadok (who had traditionally provided high priests).[13]
- The entry of the Roman general Pompey into Jerusalem in 63 BCE, and the subsequent Roman occupation of the holy land (either directly or through the Herodian client-rulers). Judea and Samaria were under direct Roman rule during Jesus' public ministry, hence his appearance before the prefect Pontius Pilate.

Two further events, occurring after Jesus' death, nevertheless ingrained themselves on the corporate Jewish consciousness during the period in which the New Testament writings were composed:

- The (failed) attempt by the emperor Gaius (Caligula) to have a statue of himself erected in the Jerusalem Temple (this may have been understood by some Jews as a new 'desolating sacrilege': for example, Mark 13.14).
- The destruction of Jerusalem by the Romans in 70 CE, after a long siege. Some Jews seem to have detected strong parallels between this and the Babylonian destruction centuries before.

In their different ways, these events raised theological questions for first-century Jews. If Israel was God's chosen people, why had the exile occurred? Was it because of the people's unfaithfulness, or God's untrustworthiness?

Table 3: Important Events in Recent Jewish Memory.

586 BCE	Fall of Jerusalem to Babylonians and deportation to Babylon
331 BCE	Alexander conquers Palestine (and beginnings of Hellenistic influence)
167 BCE	Defiling of Jerusalem Temple under Antiochus IV Epiphanes ('the abomination of desolation')
164 BCE	Rededication of Temple as part of Maccabean revolt (origins of feast of Hanukkah)
143 BCE	Beginning of Jewish Hasmonaean dynasty (Simon appointed ethnarch as well as high priest)
63 BCE	Pompey takes Jerusalem for Romans, and enters Holy of Holies
40 BCE	Rome proclaims Herod 'king of Judea' (finally installed in 37 BCE)
4 BCE	Death of Herod the Great and division of kingdom between his sons
6 CE	Roman census of Judea and revolt led by Judas the Galilean
6–66 CE	Judea under direct Roman control (apart from reign of Agrippa I in 41–4 CE)
40 CE	Emperor Gaius (Caligula) attempts to set up a statue of himself in Jerusalem Temple
66 CE	Jewish Revolt against Rome breaks out
70 CE	Jerusalem falls to Rome and Temple is destroyed

How should Jews respond to their surrounding culture? By assimilation, or through antagonism? If God had given the holy land to his people, why was it currently under the power of a pagan empire? How would God put that right? What should be the people's response to this situation, and how far should it involve direct action? How is sense to be made of suffering and even death, particularly when it comes as a result of faithfulness to God's Law?

Such questions are bubbling under the surface of the New Testament. John the Baptist's call to national repentance (for example, Mark 1.4–8) should be viewed as one influential Jewish response to these questions. The various hints of 'messianic' hopes (hopes for God to act through an 'anointed' servant, whether a prophet, priest or king) are another. The conversation between Jesus and his disciples at Caesarea Philippi (Mark 8.27–30 and parallels) hints at the range of end-time figures through whom Jews believed God would overcome the current problem. Arguably, the gospel stories of Jesus' passion tap into existing theological responses to evil, suffering and martyrdom. Attempts to make sense of Rome's destruction of Jerusalem in the light of earlier antecedents may be detected in the gospels (such as, Matthew 22.7; Luke 21.20).

Reflection

Look again at the historical events listed above. What questions do these raise for you? Are there particular theological problems which emerge? What are the possible solutions?

The Broader Context: the Graeco-Roman World

The New Testament's wider context is the Graeco-Roman world, a marriage of Greek culture and language with Roman political dominance. Though most of the New Testament authors were probably Jewish, they were familiar with this wider world, which was the world of most of their first audiences. How might one describe the main characteristics of this symbolic world?

First, due to Greek influence since the time of Alexander the Great, it presented a common culture, in which the Greek city or *polis* played a formative role, Greek religion was merged with existing local cults, and Greek language (in a form known as *koinē* or 'common' Greek) facilitated communication and commerce. Although Jesus seems to have avoided the cities (with the exception of Jerusalem), the early Christian mission was essentially urban. We hear of Christian communities in cities such as Syrian Antioch, Ephesus, Pergamum, Athens and Rome. In these cities, we find numerous examples of religious syncretism: the temple to the Anatolian Mother-goddess in Sardis, for example, was assimilated to the Greek cult of Artemis. In terms of language, the New Testament books were all written in *koinē* Greek rather than Latin, even when addressed to Christians living in Rome.

Second, Graeco-Roman religion was also polytheistic. There were gods covering all areas of life, some local, some worshipped throughout the Mediterranean (and keeping them 'on side' was considered vital for society's well-being). For modern Westerners for whom the common experience of religion – whether Christianity, Judaism or Islam – is of belief in one God, this is one of the most striking features of ancient pagan religion. Jews (and Christians as members of an originally Jewish sect) were a minority within the empire for their 'atheistic' refusal to worship the gods of Rome.

However, there is evidence for dissatisfaction with traditional Greek and Roman religion. This manifested itself in the popularity of prophecy, healers and healing shrines (such as the shrines of Asklepios at Pergamum and Corinth), and 'eastern religions' such as the mystery cults of Cybele from Asia Minor and Isis from Egypt, Mithraism, and Judaism (including its Christian offshoot). Among certain philosophers, this dissatisfaction led to a monotheistic-type position, with the Greek Zeus, the Roman Jupiter, or another 'unknown god' (see Acts 17.23) as the supreme God.

Third, Greek culture had strong philosophical traditions. Among the most influential in the New Testament period were the pantheistic *Stoicism*, founded by Zeno of Citium (335–263 BCE; the name Stoic, from the Greek *stoa* or 'porch', refers to the Painted Porch in Athens where Zeno taught), *Cynicism*, an unconventional philosophy traced back to Diogenes of Sinope (c.400–c.325 BCE; their name is derived from the Greek word for 'dog', *kyōn*, reflecting their 'shameless' public behaviour), and *Epicureanism*, named after its founder Epicurus of Samos (341–270 BCE), which taught that the goal of life was pleasure, and that the basic pleasure of the soul was the society of friendship. According to Acts 17.18, Stoic and Epicurean philosophers debated with Paul in Athens. The thought of older philosophers such as Plato (427–347 BCE) also remained influential. While most ordinary people would not have been educated in a particular philosophical school, elements of 'popular' philosophy circulated widely and were absorbed by the surrounding culture.

Stoic ideas of the divine reason or *logos* may be one of the strands (alongside Jewish traditions) present in the Prologue of John's Gospel, which speaks of the *Logos* present with God in the beginning (John 1.1ff.). Paul's teaching to the Corinthians on marriage (1 Corinthians 7) reflects contemporary debates on the subject between Stoic and Cynic philosophers.[14] Some scholars have seen parallels between the equality of Epicurean communities, separated from everyday life and accused of 'atheism', and that of early Christian communities (for example, Acts 2.43–7). Others think that a reinterpretation of Plato's philosophy known as *Middle Platonism* is reflected in the Letter to the Hebrews.

Fourth, particularly with the founding of the empire in the late first century BCE, Roman civilization had brought political cohesion to Greek culture. The rather amusing response to the question 'What have the Romans done for us?' in Monty Python's *The Life of Brian* comprises a long list of benefits to Jewish Palestine, ranging from the wine to public sanitation to the establishment of peace. This is no mere figment of a twentieth-century imagination: excellent Roman roads (covering an estimated 53,000 miles), strong armies with a consequent impact on crime, even a functioning postal system, were benefits from which the early Christians profited. Paul travelled for thousands of miles on Roman roads proclaiming the gospel, and founding churches in Roman colonies such as Philippi and new Corinth as well as in Greek cities.

Indeed, in the Graeco-Roman symbolic world, Rome – through its first emperor Augustus – was hailed as establishing a worldwide peace (the so-called *Pax Romana*). This claim was reinforced by inscriptions, poetry, statuary and public buildings, such as Augustus' Altar of Peace in Rome itself. Nevertheless, there were dissenting voices, some of them found within the New Testament (for example Revelation, which unmasks Rome as a violent, bloody monster: Revelation 13.1–10; 17.3, 7–14). There are even subversive strands within the gospels: when Luke's angel of the Lord announces 'good news of great joy' about the birth of 'a Saviour', accompanied by a heavenly choir singing of peace on earth (Luke 2.10–14), we hear a direct challenge to similar claims made for the 'Saviour' Augustus.

To do

Consult a map of the first-century Mediterranean world in a study Bible or Bible atlas. What was the Roman empire's geographical extent in the first century? What range of peoples had been incorporated into the empire?

The Overlapping Worlds of the New Testament Writers

Given all this, we should probably envisage the symbolic worlds of the individual New Testament writers as created from several overlapping worlds. In the first place, one can detect a coming together of the Jewish (especially Palestinian) world with that of the Graeco-Roman world. This is especially the case in the gospels, which tell the story of the Palestinian Jesus through the lens of the wider Graeco-Roman world. Luke refers explicitly to both worlds when locating Jesus' public ministry chronologically:

> In the fifteenth year of the reign of the Emperor Tiberius, when Pontius Pilate was governor of Judea, and Herod was ruler of Galilee, and his brother Philip ruler of the region of Ituraea and Trachonitis, and Lysanias ruler of Abilene, during the high-priesthood of Annas and Caiaphas, the word of God came to John son of Zechariah in the wilderness. (Luke 3.1–2)

Second, the world of many New Testament writers seems to be an urban one. They live and write in cities. This has a powerful, though often unacknowledged, impact on how the evangelists recount the story of Jesus' essentially rural ministry.

Finally, the worlds of the New Testament writers have radically redefined both Jewish (for example, Torah, Temple, Messiah) and pagan (such as, Emperor, Temples, City) symbols in the light of the Christian story. One finds, for example, dramatic rereadings of Jewish messianic hopes in the light of Jesus' suffering and death. The language of the temple or sanctuary (whether Jewish or pagan) comes to be applied in creative ways to Christian communities rather than to buildings of marble and stone. Fundamental questions are asked about the composition of God's people, in the light of increasing conversions to Christ from among pagans. All this has a powerful impact on the way in which early Christian writers envisage the world.

Further Reading

Everett Ferguson, 1987, *Backgrounds of Early Christianity*, Grand Rapids, Michigan: Eerdmans.

K. C. Hanson and Douglas E. Oakman, 1998, *Palestine at the Time of Jesus: Social Structures and Social Conflicts*, Minneapolis: Fortress Press.

Luke Timothy Johnson, 1999, *The Writings of the New Testament: An Interpretation*, revised edition; London: SCM Press, especially pp. 21–91.

Christopher Rowland, 2002, *Christian Origins*, 2nd edition; London: SPCK.

2

What Can We know About Jesus?

Thinking about Jesus

The central figure of the New Testament is one particular Palestinian Jew, Jesus of Nazareth. Four of the 27 New Testament books relate his life and events surrounding his death, while the others describe his impact upon his followers. As far as we can tell from these four – known as the gospels – the sphere of Jesus' activity was essentially Jewish Palestine (modern-day Israel/Palestine and parts of Jordan), with the occasional foray north into the region around Tyre and Sidon (modern Lebanon). His geographical world, then, was relatively small. He seems to have encountered few non-Jews (the exceptions are worthy of note in the gospel accounts). He died at what – to us at least – seems a tragically early age (probably in his thirties: see Luke 3.23). He left no writings of his own.

Yet this relatively obscure first-century Jew is the central focus of the New Testament. The reason for this centrality is not simply his Jewishness, or his novel teaching, or any miraculous deeds he may have performed. For the New Testament writers, Israel's God acted decisively in Jesus, both during his lifetime and after his death, such that language traditionally reserved for that God could now be applied also to this human being. As Christians would come to proclaim in one of their later formularies: 'begotten, not made, of one being with the Father, through him all things were made' (Nicene-Constantinopolitan Creed).

Thinking about Jesus, then, inevitably involves exploring this relationship between Jesus as he was and Jesus as he is now understood by his followers. For some, there is fundamental continuity between Jesus then and now. For others, there is radical discontinuity between the so-called 'historical Jesus' and the 'mythic Christ' worshipped by Christians.

For many scholars, both Christian and non-Christian, historical study of our sources for Jesus' life lies at the heart of attempts to answer the question 'What can we know about Jesus?' Other scholars object that historical 'questing' for Jesus at best produces negligible results, and at worst is a theologically illegitimate enterprise, attempting to base Christian faith on the shifting sands of the latest historical reconstruction. Anyone browsing the competing – and sometimes mutually exclusive – presentations of 'the real Jesus' on offer in our bookshops may feel some sympathy with this historical scepticism. Nevertheless, there are good grounds both for exploring the possibilities which historical approaches to Jesus might offer, and also for teasing out what might lie behind this broader question: 'What can we know about Jesus?'

Reflection

What do you know about Jesus? What did he do and say? What is important and significant about him? Record your answers, and return to them at a later date to see whether they have changed or developed.

To do

Consult a map of Palestine in the first-century (in a Bible atlas, or study Bible, or using the internet). Locate the following places, to help you get your bearings when studying the gospel accounts:
- Galilee; Judea; Samaria; the Decapolis;
- the Judean desert; the River Jordan; the Sea of Galilee; the Dead Sea;
- Jerusalem; Bethlehem; Jericho; Sepphoris; Tiberias; Nazareth; Capernaum; Bethsaida-Julias; Caesarea Philippi; Caesarea Maritima.

You might find it useful to draw your own map and mark these places on it.

The Challenge of our Sources

Whatever their view of the historical enterprise, most scholars would agree that our sources for knowledge of Jesus are far from straightforward. We have already noted the lack of writings from Jesus himself. But even our earliest sources for his life and teaching are not without historical problems.

The most obvious difficulty is that our main sources – the canonical gospels – are documents of faith, what an outsider might call 'early Christian propaganda'. While there are a few non-Christian references to Jesus from the first century, these do not tell us a great deal, and some may in any case be dependent upon Christians (see Tables 4–5). One of them, the *Testimonium Flavianum* attributed to Josephus, has clearly been reworked by a Christian author, though an original Jewish assessment probably underlies it. The

---

Table 4: Non-Christian References to Jesus.[1]

Christus, from whom the name had its origin, suffered the extreme penalty during the reign of Tiberius at the hands of one of our procurators, Pontius Pilate, and a most mischievous superstition, thus checked for the moment, again broke out not only in Judaea, the first source of the evil, but even in Rome, where all things hideous and hateful from every part of the world find their centre and become popular. (Tacitus, *Annals* 15.44.3)

He drove from Rome the Jews who, stirred up by Chrestus, continually caused unrest. (Suetonius, *Claudius* 25.4)

On the sabbath of the Passover festival Jesus (Yeshu) the Nazarene was hanged. For forty days before execution took place, a herald went forth and cried: 'Here is Jesus the Nazarene, who is going forth to be stoned because he has practised sorcery and enticed Israel to apostasy. Anyone who can say anything in his favour, let him come forth and plead on his behalf.' But since nothing was brought forth in his favour, he was hanged on the eve of the Passover. (bSanh 43a).

[1] Translations from Gerd Theissen and Annette Merz, 1998, *The Historical Jesus: A Comprehensive Guide*, London: SCM Press, chapter 3.

non-canonical or 'apocryphal' gospels are generally dated too late to be of significant value. Exceptions here might include the *Gospel of Thomas*, a collection of Jesus-sayings possibly independent of the canonical gospels (John Dominic Crossan also regards the second-century *Gospel of Peter* as important evidence for the formation of the gospel passion narrative).[15]

Table 5: The Testimonium Flavianum.[1]

Majority Text of Josephus (possible Christian additions placed in italics):

About this time there lived Jesus, a wise man, *if indeed one ought to call him a man*. For he was the one who wrought surprising feats and was a teacher of such people as accept the truth gladly. He won over many Jews and many of the Greeks. *He was the Messiah*. When Pilate, upon hearing him accused by men of the highest standing amongst us, had condemned him to be crucified, those who had in the first place come to love him did not give up their affection for him. *On the third day he appeared to them restored to life, for the prophets of God had prophesied these and countless other marvellous things about him*. And the tribe of the Christians, so called after him, has still to this day not disappeared. (Josephus, *Antiquities* 18.63–4)

[1] Translation from Louis H. Feldman, 1965, *Josephus*, Loeb Classical Library 433; London: William Heinemann, pp. 49–51.

Our main sources, then, are written primarily to promote, or sustain, faith in Jesus as God's Anointed and risen Lord. Their very title ('gospel' = 'good news') expresses this. Of the four canonical gospels, John is the most explicit about its faith-stance:

Now Jesus did many other signs in the presence of his disciples, which are not written in this book. But these are written so that you may come to believe (*or* continue to believe) that Jesus is the Messiah, the Son of God, and that through believing you may have life in his name. (John 20.30–1)

Even if (as recent scholarship has argued) the gospels are Christian examples of the Graeco-Roman genre of *bios* or 'life',[16] this does not undermine their character as propaganda for the Christian faith, since a major purpose of ancient lives was to present the main character as an example to be imitated and honoured. The nature of the gospels means that we cannot straight-forwardly read off 'what happened' from their pages. Indeed, the general consensus among gospel scholars is that they were written between about 35 and 65 years after the events that they describe, in different geographical locations, after a complex period in which the traditions were reflected upon, retold and applied to new circumstances.

The second difficulty is that our sources often disagree with one another, both about the order of events and the precise wording of Jesus' sayings. A couple of examples will suffice. First, the early chapters of Mark recount a series of Jesus' actions, predominantly healings and exorcisms. Matthew's Gospel also highlights Jesus' miracles, yet recounts some of the same events in a different order, as if chronology is less important than thematic ordering. This can be shown from the following two columns (those stories in *italics* are found in Matthew but not in Mark):

Mark 1.14—3.6	*Matthew 4.12—9.34*
Jesus proclaims the kingdom	Jesus proclaims the kingdom
Calling of the first disciples	Calling of the first disciples
Exorcism in Capernaum synagogue	Summary of Jesus' ministry
	SERMON ON THE MOUNT
	Cleansing of leper
	Healing of centurion's servant
Healing of Peter's mother-in-law	Healing of Peter's mother-in-law
Many cured at evening	Many cured at evening
Cleansing of leper	Calming of storm
	Gadarene demoniacs
Healing of paralytic	Healing of paralytic
Call of Levi	Call of Matthew (Levi?)
Dispute about fasting	Dispute about fasting
Plucking grain on sabbath	Jairus' daughter and woman

Man with withered hand   *Healing of two blind men*
                                           Healing of dumb demoniac

A second example concerns the words of Jesus. Many Christians will be familiar with Jesus' words over the bread and the cup at the Last Supper, re-enacted
in the Christian Eucharist. But what precisely did Jesus say at that point?

Matthew 26.26–8	*Mark 14.22–4*	*Luke 22.17–20*
		Then he took a cup, and after giving thanks he said, 'Take this and divide it among your-selves; for I tell you that from now on I will not drink of the fruit of the vine until the kingdom of God comes.'
While they were eating, Jesus took a loaf of bread, and after blessing it	While they were eating, he took a loaf of bread, and after blessing it	Then he took a loaf of bread, and when he had given thanks,
he broke it, gave it to the disciples, and said,	he broke it, gave it to them, and said,	he broke it and gave it to them, saying,
'Take, eat; this is my body.'	'Take; this is my body.'	'This is my body, which is given for you. Do this in remembrance of me.'
Then he took a cup, and after giving thanks	Then he took a cup, and after giving thanks	And he did the same with the cup after supper,
he gave it to them,	he gave it to them, and all of them drank from it.	
saying,	He said to them,	saying,

'Drink from it, all of you; for this is my blood of the covenant, which is poured out for many for the forgivenessof sins.'

'This is my blood of the covenant, which is poured out for many.'

'This cup that is poured out for you is the new covenant in my blood.'

In fact, the evidence is more complicated still. Some manuscripts of Luke omit verses 19b–20 (from 'which is given for you' to 'new covenant in my blood'). This raises the question: which was the original form of Luke, the longer or the shorter version? In addition, there is a parallel in Paul (1 Corinthians 11.23–5), which is closest, but not identical, to the longer form of Luke.

This is an extreme case of a common phenomenon: the evangelists regularly differ in recounting Jesus' words. This comes into sharper focus when the synoptics (where Jesus generally speaks with short, pithy sayings) are compared with John's Gospel (where Jesus' words resemble lengthy meditations). Jesus' words in John's account of the Last Supper, for example, take up 5 chapters out of a total 21 (far longer than the few verses devoted to it in Matthew, Mark and Luke). Notable for their absence in John, however, are Jesus' words over the bread and cup.

This phenomenon makes the task of determining what precisely Jesus said a complex one. It also raises a deeper question. Might not reflection on the significance of Jesus' words – such as the more paraphrastic Johannine version – be more important than a verbatim record of actual words spoken?

To do

Select two stories found in more than one gospel. With the help of a gospel synopsis, compare the different accounts. Are the same stories found in a different location in different gospels? If so, ask yourself why one evangelist might have changed the order. Are there differences between Jesus' words in each? What are they, and how might you account for them?

History, the 'Historical Jesus' and the 'Real Jesus'

Historical study of Jesus is called by scholars 'the quest of the historical Jesus'. In fact, this scholarly historical quest can be divided into several phases – or several 'quests' – beginning with the posthumous publication of Reimarus' *Fragments* in 1774–8 (see Table 6).[17] Some phases are marked by optimism about what historical questing can achieve, though each phase has had its critics. Sometimes this criticism has focused on methods used or claimed results. Modern questers, for example, would accept that their nineteenth-century predecessors were naive in treating Mark's Gospel (believed to be the earliest surviving source) as a chronologically accurate biographical account of Jesus' ministry and growing self-awareness. The criticism of others (such as Martin Kähler and Rudolf Bultmann) runs far deeper, objecting to the whole procedure as theologically illegitimate. As Kähler put it:

> How can Jesus Christ be the authentic object of the faith of all Christians if the questions what and who he really was can be established only by ingenious investigation and if it is solely the scholarship of our time which proves itself equal to this task?[18]

Others might respond that it is important for Christian faith to be able to show historical continuity between Jesus of Nazareth and the 'Christ of faith'. We need to know whether or not the Church went radically wrong in its Christology, for example. While the truth of Christianity cannot be proved by historical research, it could theoretically be falsified (for example, if it showed that Jesus never existed; that he was a charlatan; that the resurrection was based on a fraud). Unless Christianity is to lapse into Docetism – the heresy that Christ only *appeared* to be human – it ought to be prepared to submit itself and its founding figure to historical research.

The terms 'historical' and 'historical Jesus' need some explanation, however. In popular usage, 'historical' is often juxtaposed to 'mythical' or 'unreal'. History tells us 'what really happened', as opposed to interpretations laid upon these 'bare facts'. Such a contrast between 'history' and 'interpretation' has often featured in the quests, particularly as portrayed in media sound-bites.

Table 6: Some Landmarks in the Quests of the Historical Jesus.

Old Quest (1774–1906): The Quest for a Biography of Jesus

Key authors:

Hermann Samuel Reimarus, *Fragments of the Unknown of Wolfenbüttel* (published posthumously, 1774–8)

David Friedrich Strauss, *Life of Jesus Critically Examined* (1835)

Nineteenth-century 'Liberal Lives' of Jesus (e.g. Heinrich Julius Holtzmann)

Critics of Old Quest

Key authors:

Martin Kähler, *The So-Called Historical Jesus and the Historic, Biblical Christ* (1896)

Albert Schweitzer, *The Quest of the Historical Jesus* (German title *von Reimarus zu Wrede*, 1906)

Rudolf Bultmann, *Jesus and the Word* (1934)

New Quest (1953–): The Quest for Continuity between the Kerygma and the Preaching of Jesus

Key authors:

Ernst Käsemann, 'The Problem of the Historical Jesus' (lecture delivered in 1953)

Günther Bornkamm, *Jesus of Nazareth* (1956)

Third Quest: The Quest for the Jewish Jesus and His World

Some dispute as to whether this is distinctive enough to deserve this title.

Key authors:

Geza Vermes, *Jesus the Jew* (1973)

Ben Meyer, *The Aims of Jesus* (1979)

A. E. Harvey, *Jesus and the Constraints of History* (1982)

E. P. Sanders, *Jesus and Judaism* (1985)

John Dominic Crossan, *The Historical Jesus: The Life of a Mediterranean Jewish Peasant* (1991)

John P. Meier, *A Marginal Jew* (3 volumes, 1991–2001)

N. T. Wright, *Jesus and the Victory of God* (1996)

Modern historians, however, generally understand their task to be more complex. History is itself an act of *interpretation*, sifting through evidence, making sense of events, and postulating cause and effect. It is also necessarily limited in what it can offer. Take any past event, or any deceased human figure: we no longer have access to the whole picture, due to our fragmentary sources. We can only piece a picture together from incomplete surviving memories. But not even all that survives will make it into the history books. What percentage of the population of Victorian London, for example, would find their way into a history of that city in the nineteenth century? Recent attempts to write 'marginal history' reflect an attempt to restore the balance, in a discipline which has so often spoken with the voice of the powerful and ruling classes.

It is even more complex with a figure like Jesus, about whom theological claims are made. There are certain aspects of the Jesus tradition on which a historian *qua* historian is not qualified to comment. The miracle stories, which make up a large part of the gospels, are a case in point. One may conclude, on historical grounds, that Jesus performed actions which were understood by his contemporaries as healings or exorcisms. A historian cannot, however, pronounce on whether this was because Jesus was God's agent through whom God's power was at work. Similarly, while a historian might study the resurrection narratives as sources for events in the lives of Jesus' disciples after his crucifixion, she would not be in a position *as a historian* to answer the question: did Jesus of Nazareth rise from the dead?

What, then, is meant by the phrase 'historical Jesus'? For some, the 'historical Jesus' is to be equated with the 'real Jesus', hidden beneath layers of theological interpretation and revealed when these are stripped away. Many historians, however, recognize a difference between the two. John Meier, in *A Marginal Jew*, defines the 'real Jesus' as the 'reasonably complete' portrait of Jesus of Nazareth. This 'real Jesus' is irrevocably lost to historical research, given that what he said and did during the bulk of his life – the thirty or so 'hidden years' prior to his public ministry – has not been preserved. For Meier, the 'historical Jesus' is that fragmentary portrait of the 'real Jesus' constructed from our sources, using the tools of modern historical research. The two are not identical, though the latter is 'a fragmentary hypothetical reconstruction' of the former.[19] This is a good working definition of the phrase 'the historical Jesus'. Still others, however, would take issue with Meier's definition of the 'real Jesus', for it brackets out (at least in practice) faith claims for Jesus. The real Jesus, they object, is Jesus as he is, not some figure of an irretrievable past. Such an objection will be revisited later in this chapter.

Reflection

What do you understand by the words 'history' and 'historical'? Has your understanding been challenged by this chapter so far?

Some Criteria

Historians have developed a series of criteria to assess traditions about Jesus for their likely authenticity. Such assessment is key to constructing the partial portrait which is 'the historical Jesus':

- *Multiple Attestation:* the preservation of a tradition in two or more *independent* sources (for example, in independent gospel traditions; in Paul as well as the gospels), or in more than one literary form (for example, a parable, a conflict story, a prophecy), strengthens its claim to be an authentic reminiscence of Jesus. Conclusions about whether a tradition is multiply attested will depend upon source-critical conclusions such as the existence of Q,[20] and the relationship between John and the synoptics. Examples of multiple attestation include Jesus speaking about God's kingdom (found in Mark, non-Marcan passages of Matthew and Luke, and John, with echoes in Paul), and his saying about divorce (found in both double- and triple-tradition in the synoptic gospels,[21] and in Paul).
- *Embarrassment* (sometimes called 'against the grain'): that which causes a New Testament writer embarrassment is more likely to be authentic than that which is too much 'with the grain'. Examples of embarrassing elements include Jesus' baptism by John, and his crucifixion under Pontius Pilate.

- *Double Dissimilarity* (or 'criterion of uniqueness'): a saying which is dissimilar both to the ideas of Judaism in Jesus' day and to the beliefs of early Christians, has a good claim to be authentic. One example is Jesus' saying 'let the dead bury their own dead' (Matthew 8.22//Luke 9.60). Another is his attitude to fasting in Mark 2.18: this contrasts with the practice of Jewish disciples of John the Baptist and the Pharisees, and also of early Christians (Matthew 6.16–18; *Didache* 8). There are two objections to over-reliance on this criterion. First, our incomplete knowledge of first-century Judaism and Christianity makes it impossible to say with confidence that something is unique. Second, over-emphasizing Jesus' uniqueness draws a wedge between Jesus and Judaism on the one hand, and his later followers on the other.
- *Views shared by Jesus' supporters and opponents:* traditions in which both Jesus' followers and those who oppose him agree with one another, are likely to be authentic. For example, in Mark 3.22 and parallels, hostile scribes agree that Jesus casts out demons (though they disagree with his disciples as to how he is able to do so). Similarly, according to Matthew, both Jesus' followers and the Jewish chief priests agreed that his tomb was empty after his burial (Matthew 28.11–15).
- *Early Attestation:* traditions found in earlier sources (for example, Paul, Mark, the synoptics rather than John) are sometimes thought more likely to be authentic. This criterion is logically flawed, however: the fact that something is found in an earlier, but still theologically motivated, source does not logically make it more primitive. John's Gospel may well be later than Mark's, yet it is now recognized as containing primitive traditions about Jesus not preserved by the latter.
- *Coherence:* sayings and deeds of Jesus which do not pass the criteria already listed, but are in broad terms coherent with sayings or deeds isolated as probably authentic by these other criteria, may be used to supplement the emerging portrait.

As will become clear to anyone engaging in historical study of Jesus, the priority given to particular criteria, and the combination of criteria, will have an impact on the 'Jesus' who emerges. Two additional considerations (both particularly prominent in the so-called Third Quest) are also relevant:

- *Appropriate context:* the portrait of Jesus constructed needs to be intelligible within the context of first-century Palestinian Judaism (the criterion of uniqueness thus has less importance than it did in the New Quest). However 'unique' Jesus was, he was a Jew who proclaimed his message predominantly to Jews.
- *The sense of an ending:* some account should be given of Jesus' crucifixion, and the continuation of the Jesus-movement after his death.

Tom Wright's alternative criterion of *double similarity* (devised as a response to criticisms of the criterion of double dissimilarity) should be viewed in the context of these two considerations: 'when something can be seen to be credible (though perhaps deeply subversive) within first-century Judaism, *and* credible as the implied starting-point (though not the exact replica) of something in later Christianity, there is a strong possibility of our being in touch with the genuine history of Jesus.'[22]

Putting the Criteria into Practice: Jesus as Healer and Exorcist

To illustrate the procedure, let us look at a particular case study: the traditions portraying Jesus as a healer and exorcist. I have chosen these traditions for two reasons. First, anyone reading the gospels will be struck by the sheer volume and range of miracle stories (known as *dunameis* or 'deeds of power' in the synoptics, and 'signs' in John), covering exorcisms, healings, resuscitations and 'nature miracles' (such as the multiplication of loaves and fishes). Out of 424 verses in the first ten chapters of Mark's Gospel, for example, 201 verses (roughly 50 per cent) are taken up in one way or another with Jesus' miracles.

Second, and paradoxically, it is this material which historians have found most controversial. Some have dismissed the miracles out of hand as irreconcilable with a modern scientific worldview, or (in the case of healing miracles) given them a psychological explanation. For others, their apparent similarity to pagan (for example Apollonius of Tyana) and Jewish parallels has led to their treatment as secondary Christian imitations, presenting Jesus as rival wonderworker.

Table 7: Miracle Stories in Mark's Gospel.

Healings	9	(including a raising from the dead)
Exorcisms	4	
Summary statements	5	
Other miracles	5	(calming of storm; two feeding stories; walking on water; fig-tree)

But how do the traditions about Jesus as a healer and exorcist match up to the criteria developed by historians?

- *Multiple Attestation*: Jesus' healing activity is not only attested in a variety of literary types in Mark (healings proper; exorcisms; summary statements about Jesus' activity); there are also non-Marcan healing stories shared by Matthew and Luke (for example the healing of the centurion's servant), and in Luke alone (such as the raising of the widow of Nain's son). John also presents Jesus as a healer, in what is probably an independent tradition (his healings of a paralytic and a blind man have very different settings to their synoptic counterparts, while the raising of Lazarus is unique to him). Further evidence that Jesus was viewed as a healer and miracle worker is to be found in the early chapters of Acts, in speeches which, though perhaps composed in their present form by Luke, are thought by many to contain the early kerygma (Acts 2.22; 10.38). This is further attested in the *Testimonium Flavianum*, which speaks of Jesus as a 'doer of paradoxical works'. In short, there are so many healings and other miraculous actions attributed to Jesus that it would be difficult to imagine him without them.
- *Embarrassment*: at first appearance, the miracle tradition could be regarded as too much 'with the grain' of the evangelists' point of view. On a closer look, however, several fulfil the criterion of embarrassment. Some leave Jesus open to the charge of being a magician: he sticks his fingers in the ears of a deaf and dumb man, and spits on his tongue (Mark 7.31–7; this story is

missing in both Matthew and Luke). There are also stories which play down Jesus' unusual powers: Jesus refuses to use the miracles to impress (for example, Matthew 12.38–42; Mark 8.11–13; Luke 23.6–12); on occasion, his healing power seems diminished (for example, Mark 6.5; 8.22–6). This is in marked contrast to some apocryphal gospels, which portray Jesus as a wonderworker even as a child (notably the Infancy Gospel of Thomas).

- *Double Dissimilarity*: the traditions of Jesus as healer and exorcist do not perform well against the criterion of uniqueness. As the New Testament itself admits (as in Matthew 12.27; Mark 9.38–40), the first-century Jewish world knew of others believed to cast out demons. Jewish healers included charismatic holy men like Hanina ben Dosa.[23] Moreover, healings and exorcisms were attested in the early Church: Paul speaks of gifts of healing and miracles (for example, 1 Corinthians 12.9–10, 28; 2 Corinthians 12.11–12), while the longer ending of Mark expects disciples to function as exorcists and healers (Mark 16.17–18). But this underscores the deficiency of the criterion, isolating Jesus both from his Jewish context and from his followers. If we apply Wright's revised criterion of *double similarity*, then actions attributed to Jesus as healer and exorcist can be shown to make sense within Second Temple Palestinian Judaism (though his particular interpretation of those actions may be unique), and accounting for an ongoing healing ministry within the post-Easter community.
- *Views shared by Jesus' supporters and opponents*: that Jesus was regarded as an exorcist and miracle-worker is one of those few elements in the tradition agreed upon by Jesus' followers and his opponents. The synoptics preserve a tradition (apparently in two independent forms: Mark 3.22–7 and Matthew 12.22–30) where the scribes or the Pharisees accuse Jesus of casting out demons by Beelzebul, 'the ruler of the demons' (cf. John 7.20; 10.20–1). Such an outsider's view of Jesus is also reflected in the passage from the Babylonian Talmud (see Table 4), which accuses him of 'sorcery'.
- *Early Attestation*: although we have noted logical difficulties with this criterion, the healings tradition fits in well with this also. Mark's Gospel, believed by many to be the earliest gospel, is full of miracles. Those who believe in the hypothetical Q source (often dated earlier than Mark) accept that it contains at least one healing story, that of the centurion's servant.
- *Coherence*: at least one aspect of the miracles tradition coheres with other

traditions fulfilling other criteria: their ambiguous nature. Their meaning is not immediately obvious (as the views of opponents make clear). This coheres with the ambiguity of Jesus' teaching in parables, for example (as at Mark 7.17; 10.10).

- *Appropriate Context within Second Temple Judaism:* what removes some of the ambiguity, at least in the synoptic gospels, is the context within which the healings and exorcisms are performed. Set against the backdrop of Jesus proclaiming the kingdom of God, his healings are given an intelligible context within the Jewish world of Jesus' contemporaries. He is the eschatological agent through whom God's kingdom is breaking in. Through his miraculous activity, Jesus' Jewish audiences catch a glimpse of what that kingdom is like: hostile powers are defeated, and sickness and death are overcome.

The New Testament miracle stories perform very well against these criteria. There are good historical grounds for seeing them as part of the earliest gospel strata, and rooted in the ministry of Jesus as remembered by those who witnessed it. This need not lead a historian to conclude that Jesus actually *was* a healer and exorcist: alternative explanations might be given for some or all of the miraculous actions attributed to Jesus. But that Jesus' contemporaries remembered him performing actions which they understood to be healings and exorcisms seems established beyond reasonable doubt.

To do

Apply the various criteria to two of the following gospel episodes/sayings: the temptation of Jesus in the wilderness; Peter's confession; Jesus' teaching about divorce; Jesus' encounter with Zacchaeus in Jericho; the cleansing of the Temple; the crucifixion.

Will the Real Jesus Please Stand Up?

Historical study of our sources for Jesus, then, can yield significant results. It enables us to locate the figure of Jesus in history, and to isolate particular features on which (with varying degrees of probability) a range of historians – Christian, Jewish, atheist, agnostic – can agree. The Third Quest is particularly optimistic about what can be achieved.

Yet a number of criticisms remain. First, the methodology underlying the quests has often regarded the Christian sources as guilty until proved innocent, turning Jesus into something he never was, and even creating deeds and sayings *ex nihilo*. The dice, in other words, have been loaded against Christian claims for Jesus. The traditions have frequently been treated as literary onions, whose outer layers of Christian dogma need to be stripped away in order for the true 'historical Jesus' to emerge. But what might happen if the procedure is reversed, and our sources are presumed innocent until found guilty?

Second, the sheer range of different 'Jesuses' has prompted some scholars to ask what precisely the quests have uncovered: Jesus as he was, or Jesus as the individual questers have wanted him to be, their own reflection, 'seen at the bottom of a deep well'.[24] As Gerd Theissen and Annette Merz have said of the non-eschatological Cynic preacher Jesus (associated with the North American Jesus Seminar), he 'seems to have more Californian than Galilean local colouring'.[25] A greater awareness of one's own stance is called for, as is an expectation that Jesus will be strange, belonging to another world and another time.

But a more positive assessment of the diversity of Jesus reconstructions is possible. Human beings, including Jesus, are intensely complex and multi-faceted, such that one portrait would be insufficient to grasp that complexity. Indeed, a recent book by James Dunn – exploring the oral dimension of the developing Jesus tradition – has argued that there would have been a variety of accounts of the same event from the start, reflecting different aspects of what eyewitnesses saw and understood.[26] This means that the procedure of attempting to strip away layers of 'interpretation' from particular stories and sayings in order to get back to 'the original', may be methodologically flawed.

Finally, sharp criticism has been made of equating the 'historical Jesus' with the 'real Jesus', or even regarding it as a partial reconstruction of the 'real Jesus'. Luke Timothy Johnson argues forcefully that the 'real Jesus' is not that figure of the past recoverable by painstaking sifting of fragmentary traditions. Rather, he is the living being whom Christians claim to encounter in the present.[27] Therefore, the questers' focus only on his pre-crucifixion life is inadequate, at least for Christians. So too is the attempt to 'strip away' layers of interpretation from the tradition. On the contrary, argues Johnson, it is precisely in attending to those later scriptural understandings that we gain a fuller and truer understanding of the 'real Jesus'. None of the New Testament writings gives us the whole Jesus; nevertheless, each provides a crucial perspective on Jesus as he was and as he is, to contribute to the whole. This is in marked contrast to individual scholarly portrayals of the 'historical Jesus', which often claim to have uncovered *the* correct picture of Jesus (as eschatological prophet, for example, or Jewish Cynic preacher, or charismatic holy man), and only as he *was*, prior to his death.

Reflection

Think of a person you know well. How far do you have access to the 'real' person? How far is this hampered if the person is dead? How might this apply to the person of Jesus? What difference might Christian claims of Jesus' resurrection make?

Further Reading

Luke Timothy Johnson, 1996, *The Real Jesus*, New York: HarperCollins.

Jonathan Knight, 2004, *Jesus: An Historical and Theological Investigation*, London and New York: T. & T. Clark International.

E. P. Sanders and Margaret Davies, 1989, *Studying the Synoptic Gospels*, London: SCM Press/Philadelphia: Trinity Press International, chapters 20–2.

Gerd Theissen and Annette Merz, 1998, *The Historical Jesus: A Comprehensive Guide*, London: SCM Press.

3

Studying Paul

Why Begin with Paul?

The decision to begin our discussion of the New Testament books with Paul's letters (Chapter 4) requires some explanation. For it is Jesus, not Paul, who is the central figure of the New Testament. Moreover, chronologically speaking, Jesus' earthly life (*c.*4 BCE–*c.*30 CE) preceded Paul's ministry (*c.*34–*c.*64 CE). However, our main sources for Jesus' ministry – the four gospels – are generally believed to have been written in the last third of the first century, that is, after Paul's letters. They tell us as much about the concerns and questions of late first-century Christians as about the historical ministry of Jesus at the beginning of the century. If we are attempting a broadly chronological survey of the New Testament, therefore, we should begin with Paul.

A word of caution is called for, however. It is difficult to date many New Testament books with any degree of certainty. The letters of Paul are our safest bet, given evidence within the New Testament for the broad chronology of Paul's life. Paul's authentic letters[28] were almost certainly written between the late forties and early sixties. However, while most scholars would date all four gospels relatively late, earlier datings continue to be posited.[29] Similar uncertainty surrounds the dating of other books, especially James, Jude, 1 Peter, Hebrews and Revelation. Though generally dated to the end of the century, there are good grounds for dating some or all of these prior to the fall of Jerusalem in 70 CE.

Nevertheless, I remain convinced of the broad outline of the scholarly consensus: that the letters of Paul are our earliest – or among our earliest –

New Testament writings, and chronologically prior to the canonical gospels. As well as giving us access to Paul and his theological vision, they provide glimpses of early Christian life and practice prior to the gospels. This chapter will introduce the figure of Paul, and Chapter 4 his letters (letters probably written in his name after his death will be treated in Chapter 9).

Which Paul?

Where should we begin with our study of Paul? One possibility is an ancient tomb a couple of miles outside the historic centre of Rome. This is no ordinary tomb. It is surmounted by a Christian altar, enclosed in a large Roman basilica. The basilica is that of St Paul-outside-the-Walls, built over the traditional site of Paul's burial on the Ostian Way, following his martyrdom during Nero's persecution. Here we are presented with an image of Paul the universal apostle and martyr, who preached the gospel at the heart of the empire and whose blood, mingled with that of Peter, provided a solid foundation for the Roman Church. An impressive statue standing to the right of the altar confirms this image of Paul as the fearless proclaimer of God's word.

But how far is this the 'real Paul'? Are there other aspects of him which this vision neglects? Perhaps your own perception of Paul is very different. The search for the 'real Paul', or at least the 'historical Paul' reconstructed from the surviving evidence, raises similar issues to the quest of the historical Jesus. Yet there are two significant differences. First, Christians do not claim for Paul, as they do for Jesus, that he continues to influence them as risen Lord. Second, unlike Jesus, Paul has left us with a considerable body of his own writings. For many scholars, these should be our first port of call if we wish to uncover the 'real Paul'.

Hence, the Paul of the *authentic letters* (those letters generally agreed to come from his own hand) are an important source for 'Paul's own voice'. These focus particularly on his role as pastor of the churches, and avid letter-writer. The authentic letters are the following (more controversially, I would add Colossians and 2 Thessalonians to the list):

Romans
1 Corinthians
2 Corinthians
Galatians
Philippians
1 Thessalonians
Philemon

Nevertheless, we should not neglect the portraits of Paul left by others, which may contribute to a more rounded portrait, or at least need to be judged against what he himself tells us. A number of these are to be found within the New Testament:

- *Paul in the disputed letters:* these probably reveal how Paul came to be perceived by his close followers: at least one (Ephesians) is generally regarded as an impressive meditation on Paul's theological vision; others (1 Timothy, 2 Timothy and Titus, known collectively as the 'Pastoral Epistles') are often accused of 'taming' the radical edge of Paul's gospel.
- *The Paul of Acts:* presenting Paul as continuing Peter's work in bringing the gospel to the Gentiles; Acts presents Paul the intrepid traveller and eloquent public speaker, as opposed to pastor and letter-writer.
- *The difficult Paul:* there are New Testament hints that Paul's relationship with other early Christian leaders was not always harmonious (for example, Acts 9.26–8; 1 Corinthians 9.2; Galatians 2.1–14; Revelation 21.14), or that some considered his message controversial (for instance, Romans 3.8; James 2.14–26; 2 Peter 3.15–16).

In addition, there are later portraits of Paul in the apocryphal writings, which reflect both positive and negative responses to him. For example:

- *Paul in the Acts of Paul and Thecla:* a radical, ascetic Paul, who encourages Christian women to forgo marriage in pursuit of the gospel (some scholars regard the Pastoral Epistles as opposing a similar view, by forbidding a woman to teach and insisting on her role as child-bearer: 1 Timothy 2.12–15).

- *Paul in the Pseudo-Clementines:* a set of Jewish-Christian writings viewing Paul as the arch-heretic of the faith for his views on the Jewish Law.

Reflection

What images do you have of Paul? What might have influenced these different images? Are there any you think 'truer' to Paul than others?

To do

Here are a list of 'facts' about Paul derived from the New Testament. Try and discover which are derived from Paul's own letters, and which from Acts:

- born in Tarsus
- also called Saul
- educated in Jerusalem under Gamaliel
- based in Jerusalem
- converted on the Damascus Road
- engaged in missionary journeys
- a member of the Pharisee party
- a Roman citizen
- sent to Rome on trial, after appealing to Caesar.

Our Sources for Paul's Life and Ministry

All of the above present us with aspects of Paul, as he himself presented them or as others remembered them. Some may be 'truer' to him than others. However, most scholars regard two sources as the most important for reconstructing Paul's life and ministry:

- Paul's own letters
- The Acts of the Apostles.

At first sight, what Paul tells us about himself would appear to be more reliable than the second-hand evidence in Acts (even if we accept the traditional view that the author of Acts was Paul's companion Luke). The letters, after all, give us direct access to the man himself. Acts, on the other hand, is probably written some years after Paul's death, and looks back through rose-tinted spectacles to an ideal apostolic age.

Hence some scholars (such as Jerome Murphy-O'Connor) treat the letters as the primary evidence for Paul, his life and ministry.[30] Whereas Acts presents Paul as the great orator, for example, who debates with Greek philosophers in Athens (Acts 17), and in Lystra is mistaken for Hermes, the spokesman for the gods (Acts 14), we are probably on safer ground to trust Paul's rather different assessment. He reminds the Corinthians that he did not come to them with eloquent words of wisdom (1 Corinthians 2.3), and does not dissent from the views of his opponents that, though his letters are 'weighty and strong', 'his bodily presence is weak, and his speech contemptible' (2 Corinthians 10.10).

Perhaps a more subtle approach is called for, however, for two reasons. First, Paul himself writes for controversial purposes, intending to convince others of his own point of view. He is no less biased than any other author! We need to take this into account when weighing up particular statements he makes. Second, an element of distance, and an independent perspective (such as we find in the later Acts), may provide important insights into Paul which his own letters, written in the heat of the moment, obscure. Take the following passage from Paul's letter to the Galatians:

> But when God, who had set me apart before I was born and called me through his grace, was pleased to reveal his Son to me, so that I might proclaim him among the Gentiles, I did not confer with any human being, nor did I go up to Jerusalem to those who were already apostles before me, but I went away at once into Arabia, and afterwards I returned to Damascus.
>
> Then after three years I did go up to Jerusalem to visit Cephas and stayed with him fifteen days; but I did not see any other apostle except James the Lord's brother. In what I am writing to you, before God, I do not lie! (Galatians 1.15–20)

Here Paul is describing his relationship with the original disciples of Jesus, following his 'Damascus road experience' (when God 'was pleased to reveal his Son to me'). In particular, he is adamant that his contact with the Jerusalem leaders was limited. But how objective is Paul's description?

- Central to Paul's argument in Galatians 1 is his independence from the Jerusalem leaders such as Peter (Paul uses the Aramaic form 'Cephas') and James. Hence, Paul has a vested interest in downplaying the amount of contact with them.
- His denial that he conferred with 'any human being' seems to contradict Acts 9.17–19, where Paul has contact with Ananias and 'the disciples in Damascus' immediately after his experience on the road.
- He provides a theological interpretation of his Damascus road experience, in terms of a prophetic call echoing the prophets Isaiah and Jeremiah (cf. Isaiah 49.1–6; Jeremiah 1.5). A historian wishing to explore this crucial event in his life would therefore compare what Paul says here with other sources for this event (notably the three versions in Acts).

In other cases, it is possible that Acts provides us with a more complete picture of periods in Paul's ministry than Paul's own letters (aimed at addressing issues in the local churches rather than providing a chronology of his life). Take the case of Paul's first visit to Greece, where he founded the important churches at Philippi, Thessalonica and Corinth. Here Acts provides additional information which is not generally contradicted by Paul's own letters:

Acts 16—18	Paul
Philippi (imprisoned)	Shamefully treated at Philippi (1 Thessalonians 2.2)
Thessalonica	Arrives in Thessalonica after Philippi (1 Thessalonians 2.2)
Beroea	

Athens (without Silas and Timothy; tries oratory, doesn't preach cross)	Athens (Timothy sent from there: 1 Thessalonians 3.1–2)
Corinth	Doesn't try oratory (as at Athens?); preaches Christ crucified (1 Corinthians 2.1–2)

In this case there is one point of contradiction: Acts has Silas and Timothy part company with Paul before he arrives in Athens, whereas according to 1 Thessalonians 3.2 he apparently sends Timothy to them *from* Athens (nothing is said here about Silas/Silvanus, although he is mentioned along with Paul and Timothy at 1 Thessalonians 1.1). But the overall impression is of Acts supplementing the rather sketchy picture provided by 1 Thessalonians. These examples suggest that a more creative interplay between Paul's own words and Acts' later portrait may be called for. The concerns and biases of both sources must be borne in mind at every point.

However, our quest for Paul of Tarsus is not simply restricted to literary sources about him. His letters and Acts refer to a large number of places, about which we have considerable evidence (archaeological, literary and inscriptional). These enable us to build up a richer picture of the 'world of Paul' (or, better, his overlapping 'worlds' of Judaism, Hellenism and Roman culture).[31] Of the cities in which he was active, particular reference should be made to Antioch-on-the Orontes,[32] from where he and Barnabas first set out on missionary journeys (Acts 13—14), Corinth,[33] Ephesus,[34] and Rome, the traditional location of his martyrdom during Nero's persecution.[35] The use of the historical imagination, to envisage the workshops on Corinth's Lechaeum Road, or the gleaming marble of the public buildings and temples in Roman Ephesus, adds an important dimension to understanding Paul and interpreting what he wrote.

To do

Compare the account of the so-called 'Jerusalem Council' (Acts 15.1–29) with Paul's account of a visit to Jerusalem at Galatians 2.1–10. List the similarities and the differences between the two accounts. Do you think the two accounts are describing the same event? If not, why not? If so, what different perspectives do the two accounts provide?

Reconstructing Pauline Chronology

The difficulties regarding our sources come into sharp focus when we attempt to reconstruct a chronology of Paul's life. On the one hand, the autobiographical details provided by Paul are few. They need to be extracted carefully from letters concerned with quite different matters, and pieced together in an appropriate order. It is rather like trying to do a jigsaw puzzle of which the vast majority of pieces are missing. On the other hand, though Acts presents a relatively detailed account of Paul's ministry between his 'Damascus road' experience and his arrival in Rome, some elements of this picture are hard to reconcile with snippets Paul himself provides. As examples, we have already noted the issue of Paul's visits to Jerusalem, and the rather different portrait of Paul that emerges from Acts.

In reconstructing Pauline chronology, there will often be a natural preference for Paul's own words. In other cases, Acts might have the edge over Paul. Where Acts does not contradict Paul, but supplements information Paul provides, it may help fill in the 'bigger picture'. Indeed, there are certain external events referred to in Acts alone which provide historical 'pegs' on which to hang details of Paul's life which we would otherwise be unable to date.

Time does not allow for a full-blown discussion of Paul's chronology. In order to flag up some of the issues here, however, a few examples must suffice (one taken from Paul's letters, the others from Acts):

Paul's escape from Damascus: In 2 Corinthians, Paul refers to an event occurring some years previously:

> In Damascus, *the governor under King Aretas* guarded the city of Damascus in order to seize me, but I was let down in a basket through a window in the wall, and escaped from his hands. (2 Corinthians 11.32–3; italics mine)

This seems to refer to the same event as Acts 9.23–5, where again Paul escapes from Damascus in a basket (though to escape the plots of Jews in the city). After the escape referred to in Acts, Paul makes his way to Jerusalem. In Galatians 1.17b–18, Paul also refers to a visit to Jerusalem from Damascus, after his time spent in Arabia (the kingdom of the Nabataeans). This Jerusalem visit, he says, occurred 'after three years', though it is less clear whether this means three years after his Damascus road experience, or after his return to Damascus from Arabia.

The reference to King Aretas provides us with an approximate date for Paul's escape from Damascus, and his first visit to Jerusalem 'after three years'. This Aretas must be Aretas IV, king of the Nabataeans. Aretas IV died c. 39 CE. Moreover, Damascus was under Roman control at least until the death of the emperor Tiberius in March 37 (at which point it may have come under Nabataean control). This enables us to date Paul's escape from Damascus, and his first visit to Jerusalem to meet with Cephas and James, sometime between 37 and 39.

Edict of Claudius: Acts' story of Paul's arrival in Corinth contains the following reference to actions taken against Jews in Rome:

> There [in Corinth] he found a Jew named Aquila, a native of Pontus, who had recently come from Italy with his wife Priscilla, because Claudius had ordered all Jews to leave Rome. (Acts 18.2)

Fortunately, an external reference to this so-called Edict of Claudius has survived in the Roman historian Suetonius, which is also quoted by the fifth-century church historian Orosius (see Table 8).[36] Suetonius seems to have mistaken Christ (Latin *Christus*) for a ringleader he calls Chrestus (corrected by Orosius). While Suetonius does not date this event, Orosius links it to the ninth year of Claudius' reign, which was 49 CE. If we follow Acts, we should date Aquila and Priscilla's departure to Corinth to this time, and Paul's arrival to not much later.

Paul's first visit to Corinth: One additional reference in Acts 18 confirms this approximate dating. Luke tells us that Paul appeared before the proconsul of Achaia, Gallio, apparently towards the end of his 18-month stay in Corinth (Acts 18.11–12). An inscription found at Delphi (the so-called 'Gallio Inscription', see Table 8) makes the most likely date for Gallio's term of office 51/52 CE, suggesting that Paul probably arrived in Corinth in 50.

Table 8: Sources Relevant to Pauline Chronology.

He [Claudius] expelled from Rome the Jews constantly making disturbances at the instigation of Chrestus. (Suetonius, *Claudius* 25)

Josephus refers to the expulsion of Jews by Claudius in his ninth year. But Suetonius touches me more in saying, 'Claudius expelled from Rome the Jews constantly making disturbances at the instigation of Christus.' It cannot be determined whether he ordered only the Jews agitating against Christ to be restrained and suppressed, or whether he also wanted to expel Christians as being men of a related faith. (Orosius, *History* 7.6.15–16)

Tiberius Claudius Caesar Augustus Germanicus, invested with tribunician power for the 12th time, acclaimed Imperator for the 26th time, Father of the Fatherland . . . sends greetings to . . . For a long time have I been not only well-disposed toward the city of Delphi, but also solicitous for its prosperity, and I have always guarded the cult of the Pythian Apollo. But now since it is said to be destitute of citizens, as L. Iunius Gallio, my friend and proconsul, recently reported to me, and being desirous that Delphi should retain intact its former rank, I order you to invite well-born people also from other cities to Delphi as new inhabitants, and to allow them and their children to have all the privileges of the Delphians as being citizens on equal and like basis . . . (Gallio Inscription)

> **To do**
>
> Study the account of Paul's arrest, imprisonment and journey to Rome in Acts 21—8. Pay particular attention to time references, distance between places, and references to the two Roman governors, Felix and Porcius Festus. Using commentaries, study notes and internet searches, try and provide an approximate chronology for these events.

Which Letters did Paul Write?

As noted above, there is broad scholarly agreement that Paul is responsible for at least seven of the letters in the Pauline corpus. Six of these were written to specific churches (Romans, 1 Corinthians, 2 Corinthians, Philippians, 1 Thessalonians) or groups of churches (Galatians), and one primarily addressed to an individual (Philemon, although even this has a wider audience in mind). Rather more controversially, to these seven I would add 2 Thessalonians and Colossians as by Paul himself rather than 'Deutero-Pauline' (that is, from a secondary stage of the Pauline tradition). All nine will be introduced in the next chapter. Ephesians and the Pastoral Epistles (1 Timothy, 2 Timothy and Titus) will be treated separately in Chapter 9 as part of the ongoing Pauline tradition.

How do scholars distinguish between 'genuine' letters and letters like Ephesians and the Pastorals regarded as attributed to Paul by a later writer? Four kinds of arguments are generally employed:

• *Stylistic arguments:* letters differing in style from the broad body of Pauline letters are considered not to be by Paul. In the case of Ephesians, for example, commentators have likened its style to 'a slowly-moving onwards-advancing mass, like a glacier working its way inch by inch down the valley', in contrast to the 'rush of words' in a letter such as Romans.[37] Two caveats need to be stated, however. First, is not an author capable of varying style for different occasions, or changing style over time? Second, the use of an amanuensis might account for some stylistic differences (Colossians

4.18 suggests such a use, for Paul adds: 'I, Paul, write this greeting with my own hand').

- *Linguistic arguments:* the use of vocabulary rarely or never found in the undisputed letters is thought to point to letters being by someone other than Paul. Some would object that we do not possess enough of Paul's writings to make precise judgements as to what is typical Pauline vocabulary, and that we should allow for 'unusual' words (*hapax legomena* is the technical term meaning 'words which occur only once') to be adopted for particular circumstances.

- *Arguments from theological perspective:* letters which seem to promote a different theological perspective from the undisputed letters, or which express a theological development, are regarded as not authentic. Hence the Pastorals envisage a more stable Christian existence, with established institutions, than the undisputed letters; there is an order of 'widows' (1 Timothy 5.3ff.), and Paul's 'faith' has become 'the faith' (e.g. 1 Timothy 1.2; 3.9; 2 Timothy 3.8; 4.7). Ephesians seems to differ from the eschatological perspective of the undisputed letters (compare for example 1 Corinthians 15.24–8 with Ephesians 1.22, where Christ has already had all things placed under his feet).

- *Textual evidence:* this particularly comes into play in relation to the Pastoral Epistles. These are absent from what remains of the Chester Beatty Papyrus (or P[46], a papyrus containing fragments of nine Pauline letters, dated to *c.*200).

Locating Paul's Letters in his Ministry

Given the difficulties involved in reconstructing a chronology of Paul's life, dating his letters is not straightforward. Nevertheless, it is possible (making judicious use of both the letters and Acts) to locate the main letters in a fairly narrow time-band, and to place at least some in chronological sequence.

Autobiographical information provided by 1 Thessalonians would place this letter early (probably the earliest), soon after Paul's departure from Thessalonica. He has either already arrived in Corinth (the Gallio inscription enables us to date this arrival to *c.*50 CE), or is still in Athens when he writes (Acts 18.5 would support the former view). There is a broad correlation between what Paul tells us and the description in Acts 17—18 of Paul's 'second missionary journey' (after Thessalonica, Paul travels to Beroea, then Athens, followed by Corinth). This gives a date of c.50 CE for 1 Thessalonians (an alternative dating, requiring a radical revision of the chronology derived from Acts, is c.41–3 CE) and also 2 Thessalonians, if by Paul.

The relative sequence of other letters can be determined by Paul's references to the 'collection' for the poor Jewish Christians in Jerusalem. 1 Corinthians is written while the collection is underway (1 Corinthians 16.1–4), 2 Corinthians 8—9 presupposes that Corinth has completed the task (2 Corinthians 9.2: 'Achaia has been ready since last year'), while Paul writes to the Romans when he is about to deliver the money to Jerusalem (Romans 15.25–9). This gives us the sequence *1 Corinthians–2 Corinthians–Romans*. If Galatians 2.10 refers to this collection (cf. 1 Corinthians 16.1), then Galatians should also be dated to this period, and earlier than Romans (though there are scholars who would date Galatians much earlier, claiming that this refers to another collection for 'the poor').

Table 9: Possible Dating of Paul's Letters.

c.50	*1 Thessalonians* (written either in Corinth or Athens)
	2 Thessalonians (if by Paul)
c.54	*Galatians* (some date as early as 48–9 CE)
	1 Corinthians (written from Ephesus in the spring: 1 Cor. 16.8)
c.55	*2 Corinthians* (possibly composite; from Macedonia, possibly Philippi)
c.56	*Romans* (from Corinth)
c.61–3	*Philippians* (earlier if from Ephesus or Caesarea)
	Philemon (earlier if from Ephesus or Caesarea)
	Colossians (if by Paul; earlier if from Ephesus or Caesarea)

Other letters are also more difficult to slot in. The dating of those letters written by Paul from prison (Philippians, Philemon and [if authentic] Colossians) depends upon the location of his imprisonment. The main candidates are Ephesus (giving approximate datings of *c*.55–6 CE), Caesarea (*c*.57–9 CE) and Rome (*c*.61–3 CE).

> ## To do:
>
> Consult two or more commentaries on Philippians, looking at the arguments for different datings (connected with the question of where Paul was in prison when he wrote). Which arguments do you find convincing, and which unconvincing? Does consulting a Bible atlas add anything to the debate?

Accessing Paul's Thought

But the study of Paul is not primarily concerned with piecing together the jigsaw of an incomplete chronology, or dating his letters. People study Paul because of his undisputed influence on Christian theology. For many Christians, Paul is the greatest theologian the early Church produced. For others, he is a confused and confusing thinker, or the figure responsible for turning Jesus' kingdom preaching into a new religion Jesus himself would hardly recognize.[38] Either way, what he has to say about God and humanity, Christ and the Church, remains of immense interest to contemporary readers.

However, describing Paul's thought is not straightforward. True, we possess letters written by him, and therefore have his thinking at first hand (unlike Jesus, who left no writings of his own). But the following factors need to be taken into account when attempting to access 'the theology of Paul':

- These letters were originally written in Greek, and most of us are dependent upon English translations (which mean that we are one stage removed from Paul's actual words). Translation inevitably involves interpretation. For example, much ink has been spilt over the meaning of one Greek word used by Paul, *dikaiosunē*. Should it be translated 'righteousness', or 'justice', or 'covenant faithfulness'? Furthermore, ancient Greek manuscripts do not always agree among themselves as to Paul's precise words (signified by a phrase such as 'Other ancient authorities read' in the footnotes of an English Bible). For further discussion of these issues, see chapter 4 of the *SCM Studyguide to New Testament Interpretation*.

- Paul's letters only allow partial glimpses into what he believed. They are written to respond to particular issues within his churches, and so are like the tip of his theological iceberg. Not even Romans, the nearest of his undisputed letters to articulating an overarching vision, gives the whole picture.

- His theological beliefs emerge in response to particular issues within his churches. Hence many argue that we should think of Paul as primarily a 'practical theologian', rather than a systematic thinker. Indeed, John Ashton's recent stimulating book on Paul has questioned whether the category of 'thinker' is appropriate at all, suggesting we should pay more attention to Paul's religious experience.[39]

- But even if we concede that Paul thinks systematically, the ways in which later commentators *describe* that theological thinking are shaped by their own theological vision. The categories they use (such as creation, fall, redemption, the Church) and the letters they treat as primary may tell us as much about them as about Paul himself.[40] Even those who recognize that Paul remains a Jew, proclaiming an essentially Jewish message (a point well argued by N. T. Wright[41]), may occasionally find themselves lapsing into Christian categories to systematize 'Jewish theology'.

- One's starting-point will also affect the way in which one makes sense of Paul's theology. Does one begin with Paul's understanding of God (theology proper), or with humanity and the human condition (anthropology)? Further, is one performing a work of historical reconstruction (piecing together fragments of ancient thought like broken pieces of a first-century pot), or engaging Paul in a dialogue to enable us to speak about God today (essentially the approach of the great German exegete Rudolf Bultmann)?[42]

- There are indications that Paul's thinking developed. This is not surprising, given that his undisputed letters were written over several years during a period of intense missionary activity. Many detect, for example, a shift in Paul's eschatological thinking from 1 Thessalonians through 1 Corinthians to Philippians, as he begins to envisage his own death prior to Christ's coming.

- One aspect of the various 'new perspectives' on Paul, particularly associated with the work of Richard Hays, is that a narrative approach to Paul's thought is the most fruitful. Attention to his 'intertextual' allusions to Old Testament narratives, and the wider Jewish theological framework, is believed to provide the best context within which to explore Paul's theological statements.[43]

Students of Paul need to take such issues into account when grappling with his theology. But such theological grappling, though frustrating at times, is a worthwhile enterprise. Particularly interesting is the way in which Paul redefines the symbols of the worlds he inhabits, in the light of his experience of the risen Christ: whether his Jewish heritage (for example, covenant, Torah) or the wider Greek and Roman worlds (for example, envisaging the Christian community as a 'temple'; acclaiming Christ by titles attributed to the emperor, such as Lord or Son of God). Many note how Paul redescribes the typical Jewish apocalyptic timetable – which seeks to explain what is wrong with our world and how God will act to put it right – in the light of his conviction that the expected 'last days' have already dawned with the resurrection of Jesus from the dead.

Finally, there are always passionate debates going on between New Testament scholars over particular points of interpretation, which means that the study of Paul will never be dull! Among such issues in recent discussion are the following:

- When Paul talks about Christ dying *for us* (Greek *huper hēmōn*: for example, Romans 5.8; 1 Thessalonians 5.10), does he understand this in a substitutionary or a representative way? Does Christ die *instead of* us (as if we were guilty and deserving death, but someone else stepped in and took our place), or *as our representative* (enabling us also to die to sin, so that we can also share his risen life)? Or are both aspects present in Paul's thought?[44]
- How should the Greek phrase *pistis Iēsou Christou* be translated? The New Revised Standard Version (NRSV) translates Galatians 2.16 as 'yet we

know that a person is justified not by works of the law but *through faith in Jesus Christ*' (italics mine; that is, referring to the faith of Christians in Jesus). An alternative, however, which fits a more literal translation of the Greek, would translate the final phrase as 'through the faith/faithfulness of Jesus Christ' (that is, Christ's own faithfulness to the Father's will).[45]

• How should one envisage Paul's 'Damascus road experience'? Christians have tended to speak of this as a 'conversion', highlighting its life-changing effects. But 'conversion' has connotations of changing one's religion, whereas many scholars stress that Paul remained a Jew after this event (albeit now identifying Jesus as Israel's expected Messiah). In the light of Paul's own references to this event (notably Galatians 1.15–16), some prefer to describe it as Paul's prophetic 'call'.[46]

• What does Paul mean when he says that no one can be justified by 'works of the Law' (Greek *erga nomou*)? Is he contrasting, as in Luther's reading of Paul, saving faith with good works (criticizing a legalistic Judaism of 'works-righteousness', a view of Paul and first-century Judaism challenged by the 'new perspective' of E. P. Sanders and others)?[47] Or is he specifically referring to ritual works performed by Jews which marked them out as different from Gentiles (such as circumcision, food laws, sabbath observance and special Jewish festivals)? If the latter, then Paul's real criticism is of Jewish Christians demanding that Gentile converts adopt Jewish practices in order to be full members of God's people.[48]

To do

Browse your library shelves for books on the theology of Paul. Compare the various headings they use to organize Paul's theological thinking. How do they differ? How far do these differences reflect the authors' cultural and theological circumstances? Which way of ordering Paul's thought seems most appropriate to you, and why?

Paul and Jesus

Given that Paul's letters were probably written earlier than the gospels, are they not valuable sources for our knowledge of Jesus? After all, they bring us closer chronologically to Jesus' ministry, being written within about 25 years of his death. But, as so often in scholarly discussion of Paul, matters are not clear-cut.

First, although Paul and Acts agree that he had been a fierce persecutor of Jesus' followers (see Acts 9.1–2; 1 Corinthians 15.9; Galatians 1.13), there is no evidence that he ever met the pre-Easter Jesus. On the contrary, he clearly asserts that his encounter was with the risen Lord (for example, 1 Corinthians 9.1; 15.8). Second, the focus of Paul's preaching appears to be on Christ's death, resurrection and final appearing, not on his earthly life and ministry. He tells the Corinthians that he was determined to know nothing among them 'except Jesus Christ, and him crucified' (1 Corinthians 2.2). He taught the converted Thessalonians to 'serve a living and true God, and to wait for his Son from heaven, whom he raised from the dead' (1 Thessalonians 1.9–10). The Roman Christians are urged to believe in the God who raised Jesus from the dead, 'who was handed over to death for our trespasses and was raised for our justification' (Romans 4.25).

Therefore Christology – what Paul believes about Christ – is the focus of his letters. Paul has encountered him as Lord on the Damascus road, has felt the power of his love and the force of his Spirit.

Nevertheless, it is not true that Paul has no interest in what Jesus said and did prior to his crucifixion. There are explicit references, and other possible allusions (though scholars disagree as to how many),[49] to sayings and actions of the pre-Easter Jesus. These suggest that Paul knew more, and taught more to his converts, than his letters let on. Among the most important examples are the following:

- Paul's conviction 'in the Lord Jesus' that nothing is unclean (Romans 14.14; cf. Mark 7.19);
- Jesus' saying about divorce (1 Corinthians 7.10–11; cf. Matthew 5.32; 19.9; Mark 10.11–12; Luke 16.18);
- Jesus' words over the bread and cup at the Last Supper (1 Corinthians 11.23–5; cf. Matthew 26.26–9; Mark 14.22–5; Luke 22.19–20);
- The saying about the Lord's day coming like a thief in the night (1 Thessalonians 5.2; cf. Matthew 24.43; Luke 12.39; 2 Peter 3.10; Revelation 3.3; 16.15).

The fact that the fourth saying (1 Thessalonians 5.2) is attributed to a heavenly being in the book of Revelation, and that Paul claims he received the third 'from the Lord' (1 Corinthians 11.23), has led some scholars to ask whether these sayings are prophetic oracles originally uttered within Christian liturgical assemblies. This highlights the important hermeneutical question raised in Chapter 2: how far is it possible to separate out 'Jesus as he was' from Christ as he now is experienced within the churches?

One further comment should be made about Paul's understanding of Jesus. On a number of occasions, he hints that what is of prime significance for him and his fellow believers is the pattern of Christ's life and death. That is, the one who laid aside his own status and submitted to the shame of the cross (Philippians 2.6–11), who though rich became poor for our sakes (2 Corinthians 8.9), exemplifies a pattern for his followers to imitate. Indeed, Paul can use almost mystical language which suggests he saw himself, as Christ's *apostle* (the one sent in Christ's name), making the crucified and risen Lord present in the churches, through his own physical weakness:

We [apostles] are afflicted in every way, but not crushed; perplexed, but not driven to despair; persecuted, but not forsaken; struck down, but not destroyed; always carrying in the body the death of Jesus, so that the life of Jesus may also be made visible in our bodies. (2 Corinthians 4.8–10)

We are treated as impostors, and yet are true; as unknown, and yet are well known; as dying, and see – we are alive; as punished, and yet not killed; as sorrowful, yet always rejoicing; *as poor, yet making many rich*; as having nothing, and yet possessing everything. (2 Corinthians 6.8b–10; italics mine; cf. 8.9)

You foolish Galatians! Who has bewitched you? *It was before your eyes that Jesus Christ was publicly exhibited as crucified*! (Galatians 3.1; italics mine)

You know that it was because of a physical infirmity that I first announced the gospel to you; though my condition put you to the test, you did not scorn or despise me, but welcomed me as an angel of God, *as Christ Jesus*. (Galatians 4.13–14; italics mine)

This hints at a whole dimension of Paul's apostolic ministry that has been largely unexplored.

To do

Compare two or more maps of Paul's missionary journeys in Bible atlases or study Bibles. Note any differences between them. Where are Paul's churches located? Can you detect any pattern about these locations? Are there any obvious gaps?

Further Reading

C. K. Barrett, 1994, *Paul: An Introduction to His Thought*, Outstanding Christian Thinkers series; London: Geoffrey Chapman.

Morna D. Hooker, 2003, *Paul: A Short Introduction*, Oxford: Oneworld.

David Horrell, 2006, *An Introduction to the Study of Paul*, 2nd edition; London and New York: T. & T. Clark.

Jerome Murphy-O'Connor, 2004, *Paul: His Story*, Oxford: Oxford University Press.

E. P. Sanders, 1977, *Paul and Palestinian Judaism*, London: SCM Press.

N. T. Wright, 2005, *Paul: Fresh Perspectives*, London: SPCK.

4

Introducing Paul's Letters

Ancient Letters and Paul's Letters

Imagine browsing a library shelf, and stumbling across a box containing a piece of ancient papyrus. When you lay the papyrus out on a desk, you can begin to read its opening words (actually a collection of capital letters in a strange alphabet):

ΠΑΥΛΟΣΔΕΣΜΙΟΣΧΡΙΣΤΟΥΙΗΣΟΥΚΑΙΤ
ΙΜΟΘΕΟΣΟΑΔΕΛΦΟΣΦΙΛΗΜΟΝΙΤΩΑΓΑ
ΠΗΤΩΚΑΙΣΥΝΕΡΓΩΗΜΩΝΚΑΙΑΠΦΙΑΤΗ
ΑΔΕΛΦΗΚΑΙΑΡΧΙΠΠΩΤΩΣΥΣΤΡΑΤΙΩΤ
ΗΗΜΩΝΚΑΙΤΗΚΑΤΟΙΚΟΝΣΟΥΕΚΚΛΗΣ
ΙΑΧΑΡΙΣΥΜΙΝΚΑΙΕΙΡΗΝΗΑΠΟΘΕΟΥΠΑ
ΤΡΟΣΗΜΩΝΚΑΙΚΥΡΙΟΥΙΗΣΟΥΧΡΙΣΤΟΥ

You are looking at the beginning of the shortest surviving letter of Paul (or rather a copy of copies of this original short letter), written to his friend and fellow Christian Philemon, probably in the city of Colossae (Philemon 1–3). This should serve as a stark reminder that Paul's letters are ancient letters, written on ancient materials and in an ancient language, to people of an ancient culture. Indeed, even if you were able to read Greek, you would have some difficulty separating out the individual words and inserting punctuation. The most likely reading, and NRSV translation, is as follows:

Παῦλος δέσμιος Χριστοῦ Ἰησοῦ καὶ Τιμόθεος ὁ ἀδελφὸς
Φιλήμονι τῷ ἀγαπητῷ καὶ συνεργῷ ἡμῶν
καὶ Ἀπφίᾳ τῇ ἀδελφῇ
καὶ Ἀρχίππῳ τῷ συστρατιώτῃ ἡμῶν καὶ τῇ κατ᾽ οἶκόν σου ἐκκλησίᾳ,
χάρις ὑμῖν καὶ εἰρήνη ἀπὸ θεοῦ πατρὸς ἡμῶν καὶ κυρίου Ἰησοῦ Χριστοῦ.

Paul, a prisoner of Christ Jesus, and Timothy our brother,
To Philemon our dear friend and co-worker,
to Apphia our sister,
to Archippus our fellow soldier, and to the church in your house:
Grace to you and peace from God our Father and the Lord Jesus Christ.

As well as illustrating the great gulf between the original recipients of Paul's letters and ourselves, this opening section of Philemon illustrates the distinctive shape of ancient letters. Just as we, often unconsciously, follow a set form in composing a letter (we begin by naming the recipient, for example, 'Dear Gemma', and generally conclude with a greeting and our own name, as with 'Love from Charlie'), so did ancient letter-writers (see Table 10). Paul's letters, not surprisingly, follow such ancient conventions, although his opening and concluding greetings are often more developed and theologically focused (as here, 'Grace [Greek *charis*] to you and peace from God our Father and the Lord Jesus Christ' rather than simply 'Greetings' [Greek *chairein*]).

Table 10: Typical Structure of Ancient Letter.

Opening
• Sender
• To recipient
• Greeting

Main Body

Conclusion:
• Prayer for well-being
• Final greeting

The similarities with such ancient writings raise an important hermeneutical question: how far can these ancient letters speak to us, given that they are personal correspondence addressed to ancient individuals? Indeed, should we be reading these private letters at all? This is an important consideration, as is the related fact that they only allow access to one side (Paul's side) of an ancient conversation, and precise reconstruction of the other side will always be hypothetical. However, there are other considerations to take into account.

First, from the start, these were not purely private letters, but intended for Christian communities. Even though Paul would probably be shocked to discover that his letters were still being read centuries after he penned them, they have a public character. Even Philemon is addressed not simply to the first-century Christian whose name it bears, but also to Apphia, Archippus, and 'the church in your [presumably Philemon's] house'. Thus their subsequent wider treatment as 'letters for the Church' in every age could be viewed as a legitimate development. Such treatment, however, does not excuse contemporary Christians from the difficult task of historical reconstruction.

Second, these letters were intended to be read aloud, publicly, rather than perused silently by an individual. Originally, they would have been read by a reader to the gathered congregation, perhaps in the context of worship (as for example Colossians 4.16; 1 Thessalonians 5.27; cf. Revelation 1.3). Comments from Paul himself suggest that he understood these letters to compensate for his physical absence (as in 1 Corinthians 5.3–4). Modern interpreters sometimes need to *hear* such letters read aloud – and in their entirety rather than in small excerpts – in order to experience something of their original impact.

Third, despite similarities between ancient personal letters and Paul's letters, there are important differences. Most obviously, Paul's are often considerably longer. In my study Bible, Paul's letter to the Romans takes up 23 pages (admittedly with footnotes) as opposed to just over one page for Philemon. Some scholars have therefore argued that Paul's letters are better compared with ancient speeches, or the ideal speeches found in classical rhetorical handbooks. Further discussion of New Testament rhetorical criticism can be found in the *SCM Studyguide to New Testament Interpretation*, chapter 7.[50]

Reflection

What issues do you think are raised by reading ancient letters such as those of Paul? What would you want to bear in mind when attempting to understand them? Is it legitimate to read them at all? If it is, should one do so purely on grounds of historical curiosity? Or might they have something to say to our contemporary world?

Different Ways of Reading

Before we explore the individual letters, further reflection on the task in hand is called for. What has been said so far points to the importance of historical awareness in studying Paul's letters. Failure to take seriously that these are ancient documents, reflecting different perspectives and assumptions from our own, may mean that we miss, or misunderstand, crucial aspects of their message. For example, some historical awareness of the centrality of temple-sacrifice in the lives of first-century Corinthians will help shed light on issues surrounding 'idol meat' (1 Corinthians 8—10).

However, the mention of rhetorical criticism indicates that more is involved in interpreting Paul's letters than historical reconstruction. Even when rhetorical criticism explores how ancient authors composed speeches, it is more interested in the *literary* aspects of these texts than the historical. What is the overall shape of the letter's argument? What kind of rhetorical strategy does Paul employ? Does his argument seek to accuse or to praise, to encourage or to convince his audience to pursue a particular course of action?

Scholars apply other literary approaches to Paul's letters. We have already mentioned intertextuality, associated with the work of Richard Hays, which attends to allusions to and echoes of earlier texts and traditions in a biblical text. In the case of Paul's letters, there is a particular intertextual relationship with the Old Testament. For Hays and others, attention to Old Testament echoes within Paul's letters will reveal far more than focus on explicit Old Testament quotations might suggest. Related to intertextuality are readings of Paul which attend to the narrative substructure of his letters, in which the story of God's dealings with his people in Israel's history is retold to describe the story of God's new people, the Church. Though narrative approaches are more readily applied to the gospels and Acts than to letters, Katherine Grieb's narrative reading of Romans is a fine example of the light such an enterprise can cast on Paul.[51]

However, many students will be studying Paul as part of a degree in theology or religious studies. Hence their primary interest will be in the *theological* dimension of these letters. What do they tell us about the God whom Christians worship, about the Christ in whom this God is believed to have acted, and about the effects of this divine action upon the human race? Renewed interest among scholars in patristic and other pre-Enlightenment methods of reading scripture has heightened this theological dimension. Three new commentary series, concentrating on theological readings of the biblical texts, are worth consulting to get a flavour of a reading strategy which gives priority to theology:

- *Ancient Christian Commentary* (general editor: Thomas C. Oden);
- *The Church's Bible* (general editor: Robert Louis Wilken);
- *SCM Theological Commentary* (general editor: R. R. Reno).

Finally, another kind of historical approach raises rather different questions from that with which we started. Whereas historical criticism tends to stress the huge gulf separating the first century from the twenty-first, reception history of the New Testament (sometimes called *Wirkungsgeschichte*, meaning 'history of influence' or 'effective history')[52] emphasizes the history of reading, interpreting, preaching and praying Paul's letters in the intervening two thousand years. According to reception history, the gulf is not an empty gulf, but one rich in readings of Paul which have made our contemporary readings possible. So both the Lutheran reading of Paul, which reads him through the lens of justification by faith, and the so-called 'new perspective' which criticized this reading, are part of the history of effects of Paul's letters.

Reception history also forces us to explore the rather different readings of Paul in Eastern Christianity, as well as the more popular reception of Paul in preaching, devotional reading and Christian art. In terms of artistic portrayals of Paul, focus has often been on narrative aspects of his story (such as Caravaggio's dramatic *Conversion of St Paul*, or Nicholas Poussin's *Ecstasy of St Paul*, based upon his description of visionary experience in 2 Corinthians 12), although one also finds visual interpretations of Paul the preacher, or Paul the pastor or letter-writer. A more detailed discussion of reception history can be found in chapter 11 of the *SCM Studyguide to New Testament Interpretation*.

To do

Read 1 Thessalonians 2.13–16 (in Greek if you can, or in a number of different English translations). List the questions this passage raises for you, and attempt to provide some answers. Note which of your questions are historical (both historical-critical and reception-historical), which literary, and which theological.

---

1 Thessalonians: The Earliest Letter

1 Thessalonians is almost certainly the earliest surviving Christian writing (a minority of scholars date Galatians earlier). It is a letter to Christians in northern Greece, written within about 20 years of Jesus' crucifixion. Thus, from a historical perspective, it provides a window onto issues faced by a young church at a very early stage. I note a selection of them here, which may help open up other issues (the case of 2 Thessalonians is more complex, and will be addressed briefly below).

First, the relationship between Paul's letters and Acts emerges as an issue. Many scholars accept that, in this case, Acts provides us with important background information, both to Paul's first visit to this city (Acts 17.1–9), and to his subsequent movements from Thessalonica to Athens and then Corinth (Acts 17.10—18.18), from where 1 Thessalonians was probably written. Having been forced to leave Thessalonica, and prevented from returning, Paul dispatches Timothy to them from Athens; on Timothy's return with good news, Paul pens this letter of encouragement (1 Thessalonians 2.17–20). However, though the broad narrative of Acts is probably to be accepted, there are some detailed discrepancies. The impression from Paul's letter is that the Thessalonian Christians were primarily, if not exclusively, converts from paganism (for example, 1 Thessalonians 1.9). This casts doubt on the Acts' account, where Paul preaches in the synagogue in Thessalonica and provokes hostility from the Jews (very much 'with the grain' of a recurring theme in Acts). Paul's letter also has Timothy sent back to Thessalonica from Athens (1 Thessalonians 3.1–2), whereas Acts claims that Paul left Timothy and Silas in Beroea (Acts 17.14–15).[53]

Second, 1 Thessalonians provides a glimpse of Paul's missionary strategy. The locations of Paul's churches referred to are significant: Thessalonica, Philippi, Athens and Corinth. All are strategically located cities, and potential 'hubs' from which the Christian message could spread to the surrounding area. Thessalonica itself was an important Greek city, and capital of the Roman province of Macedonia. Moreover, it was situated on the Via Egnatia, an important Roman road linking Asia Minor with ports on Greece's Adriatic coast. Nor should we envisage Paul as a one-man band. The Pauline mission comprised a complex web of co-workers and other associates. Indeed, 1 Thessalonians is not strictly *Paul's* letter to that church, but from Paul, Silvanus (the Silas of Acts) and Timothy (1 Thessalonians 1.1). Finally, if we leave aside Acts' portrait of Paul preaching in the synagogue, the letter may point to an evangelistic approach which combines methods associated with contemporary philosophers, preaching in private houses, and workshop-based activity ('we worked night and day, so that we might not burden any of you while we proclaimed to you the gospel of God', 1 Thessalonians 2.9).[54]

Third, some scholars believe that the letter contains a summary of the preaching Paul engaged in while in Thessalonica, or part of an early Christian creed. The last two verses of 1 Thessalonians 1 in particular sound like a statement of faith:

> . . . how you turned to God from idols, to serve a living and true God, and to wait for his Son from heaven, whom he raised from the dead – Jesus, who rescues us from the wrath that is coming. (1 Thessalonians 1.9b–10)

Are we given a glimpse here of Paul's early preaching among non-Jews, emphasizing monotheism, the past resurrection of Jesus and his future coming or appearing?

Fourth, one particular passage we have already met has had a significant (and at times dark) reception history, and raises several interpretative issues:

> For you, brothers and sisters, became imitators of the churches of God in Christ Jesus that are in Judea, for you suffered the same things from your own compatriots as they did from the Jews, who killed both the Lord Jesus and the prophets, and drove us out; they displease God and oppose everyone by hindering us from speaking to the Gentiles so that they may be saved. Thus they have constantly been filling up the measure of their sins; but God's wrath has overtaken them at last. (1 Thessalonians 2.14–16)

The antisemitic potential of such a passage is obvious (you may have noted this in your own study of it above). The following three points should be made:

- 'The Jews' is not the only translation: Paul could be comparing the (pagan) compatriots of the Thessalonians with the 'Judeans', historically involved in the arrest of Jesus (that is, a particular geographical group, rather than all Jews).
- Since the original Greek would have had no punctuation, the location of a comma after 'the Jews/Judeans' is a matter of interpretation; hence it could read 'the Judeans who killed both the Lord Jesus and the prophets'.
- Some scholars think that these verses are a later interpolation: they disrupt an otherwise smooth transition between v. 13 and v. 17, and v. 16b sounds like a description of the fall of Jerusalem in 70 CE (though there are no manuscripts which lack these verses).

Finally, 1 Thessalonians 4.13—5.11 has been influential in debates about Paul's 'eschatology' (teaching about the End), and continues to be important among American Dispensationalists (who believe the elect will be 'raptured' or 'caught up' to heaven prior to the 'great tribulation'). Those who have encountered the popular 'Left Behind' novel series, by Tim LaHaye and Jerry Jenkins, will be aware of the importance of this belief in certain Protestant circles.

Mainstream Christianity has read this passage as describing the (future) resurrection of the dead, and addressing a particular pastoral issue in Thessalonica. It seems that Paul's original preaching focused not so much on the resurrection of believers, but on the imminent coming of Christ 'from heaven' (his *parousia*, from the Greek meaning 'coming' or 'presence'). But the deaths of Thessalonian Christians raised an anxious question: would they miss out on what God has prepared? 1 Thessalonians provides Paul's pastoral response, shifting his focus from the parousia to the resurrection. Those who have died will not miss out, but will rise with Christ first, after which 'we who are alive, who are left, will be caught up in the clouds together with them to meet the Lord in the air' (1 Thessalonians 4.17). The Thessalonians' ground for confidence about this future resurrection of the faithful is Christ's own resurrection (now in the past). What is not spelt out (*pace* the 'Rapture' doctrine) is how literally one should understand this language, or whether the elect will be caught up to heaven or reign with Christ on earth.

2 Thessalonians

The question of 2 Thessalonians is more complex. Many scholars dispute the authenticity of this letter, regarding it as written by a follower of Paul some years after his death to address a new situation (indeed, some dispute that it was intended for Thessalonian Christians). They detect a discrepancy between the imminent return of the Lord implied by 1 Thessalonians 4.13— 5.11 ('like a thief in the night', 5.2) and the downplaying of such expectations in 2 Thessalonians 2.1–12. They also point to the schedule of eschatological events implicit in 2 Thessalonians, which contrasts with the warning in the first letter to avoid speculation about 'times and seasons'. Moreover, the close literary relationship between the two might suggest that one is the model for the other. Also, 2 Thessalonians 2.2 and 3.17 point to a need to authenticate this letter as Paul's, in the face of forgeries in circulation.

Others believe that it makes good sense as written by Paul relatively soon after 1 Thessalonians, responding to a heightened sense of crisis. Nor is there necessarily a huge gulf between the eschatological focus of the two letters. It is possible to read 1 Thessalonians as attempting to dampen down over-enthusiasm about the End as well as urging the Thessalonians to be ready, hinting that it is not for them to know 'times and seasons' (compare 1 Thessalonians 5.1–2 with Matthew 24.36–44). A mediating position, taking seriously the corporate greeting from 'Paul, Silvanus and Timothy' in both letters, is that a co-worker of Paul penned the second letter, addressed to the Thessalonians after the situation presumed in 1 Thessalonians had escalated.[55]

A number of other issues are worth noting. First, whatever the conclusions regarding authorship, more recent literary approaches to the New Testament would urge focus on the 'implied author' of this letter (see Chapter 7 of the *SCM Studyguide to New Testament Interpretation*). This implied author – the author suggested by the text itself, irrespective of the real historical author – is 'Paul'. Its historical author intends readers to hear it as a communication from Paul, or bearing his authority. Thus it needs to be read in that light (and also in the light of 1 Thessalonians) in order to be intelligible.

Second, rhetorical criticism of 2 Thessalonians has identified it as an example of *deliberative rhetoric*: that is, a form of rhetorical argument aimed at persuading an audience to take a particular course of action in the future.[56] Analysing the letter in this way highlights tensions between 'Paul' and the addressees: notably the claim that 'the day of the Lord is already here' (2 Thessalonians 2.2).

Third, building on the above rhetorical analysis, the letter (whether by Paul or not) points to a need to dampen down undue eschatological expectation, perhaps due to heightened persecution, and a misunderstanding of 1 Thessalonians:

> As to the coming of our Lord Jesus Christ and our being gathered together to him, we beg you, brothers and sisters, not to be quickly shaken in mind or alarmed, either by spirit or by word or by letter, as though from us, to the effect that the day of the Lord is already here. (2 Thessalonians 2.1–2)

In relation to this, 'Paul' presents an eschatological scenario in which the just God will vindicate his people (currently experiencing sufferings for the sake of the kingdom: 2 Thessalonians 1.5), through the returning Jesus. Certain details of this scenario are particularly obscure, and play a key role in the reception history of the letter: for example, the identity of the 'lawless one' (2 Thessalonians 2.3, 6, 8). The ambiguous, open-ended description of this character has enabled his identification with a host of historical figures, ranging from Roman emperors and fifteenth-century popes to Adolf Hitler and Colonel Gaddafi.

Finally, 2 Thessalonians highlights the relationship between End-time beliefs and Christian conduct. Overemphasis upon the imminence of the End, as is clear from certain Christian stances today, can lead to effective withdrawal from society. In contrast, this letter presents Paul, Silvanus and Timothy as models for Christian imitation, precisely in their roles as people who got their hands dirty, and toiled night and day in order not to be a burden on others. This represents a profound critique of Christians whose sense of the nearness of the End, or the belief that it has already come, causes them to opt out:

> For even when we were with you, we gave you this command: Anyone unwilling to work should not eat. For we hear that some of you are living in idleness, mere busybodies, not doing any work. Now such persons we command and exhort in the Lord Jesus Christ to do their work quietly and to earn their own living. (2 Thessalonians 3.10–12)

Reflection

What difference, if any, would it make if Paul were shown not to be the author of 2 Thessalonians? How convincing are the arguments either way? What does your answer reveal about your own attitude to the New Testament?

Problems in Corinth

We probably know more about the Corinthian church than any other of Paul's churches. This is due in part to archaeological discoveries made in the city, but also to it being such a troublesome community. Hence Paul must deal at great length in 1 and 2 Corinthians with the problems he perceives. One of the main interpretative difficulties is that we only hear one side of a complex and ongoing conversation. It is important to recognize that what we call 1 and 2 Corinthians are all that survive of an ongoing exchange of letters between the Corinthian church and Paul (1 Corinthians is not in fact Paul's *first* letter to the Corinthians!). See Table 11 for one possible explanation of the evidence.

Table 11: Letters between Paul and the Corinthians.

Paul's first letter (alluded to at 1 Corinthians 5.9; some see a fragment of this letter at 2 Corinthians 6.14—7.1)

Letter from the Corinthians (mentioned at 1 Corinthians 7.1, where Paul begins to address the questions it asked; see also 1 Corinthians 7.25; 8.1; 12.1; 16.1, 12); brought to Paul in Ephesus by delegation (1 Corinthians 16.17)

Paul's second letter (our 1 Corinthians), sent from Ephesus with delegation

Paul's third letter, written 'in tears' (now lost? alluded to at 2 Corinthians 2.4; some think this third letter is 2 Corinthians 10—13), written in preparation for 'another painful visit', which didn't materialize

Paul's fourth letter (2 Corinthians 1—9), sent from Macedonia with Titus and another brother, to make the collection (2 Corinthians 8.17–19)

Paul's fifth letter (2 Corinthians 10—13), written in response to a new crisis in Corinth (the arrival of 'super-apostles')

---

1 Corinthians is a letter written in response to two approaches to Paul: the Corinthians' own letter to him (referred to at 1 Corinthians 7.1ff.), and an oral report from 'Chloe's people' (1 Corinthians 1.11, possibly slaves of this otherwise unknown Christian woman, travelling on business between Corinth and Ephesus, from where Paul writes). Literary analysis of the letter's thanksgiving (1 Corinthians 1.4–9), where Paul typically sets out the themes he intends to address in the main body, highlights the following issues:

- 'for in every way you have been enriched in him, in speech and knowledge of every kind' (v. 5: see 1 Corinthians 1—11, with speech particularly

emphasized in 1.18—4.21, and 'knowledge' in 1 Corinthians 8—10);
- 'so that you are not lacking in any spiritual gift' (v. 7a: see 1 Corinthians 12—14);
- 'as you wait for the revealing of our Lord Jesus Christ' (v. 7b: see 1 Corinthians 15).

A useful way into 1 Corinthians is to explore how these themes are developed by Paul, so as to challenge or redefine the understanding some Corinthians have of the centrality of 'speech' (or 'eloquence') and 'knowledge', and to force a rethink of the place of spiritual gifts in the Corinthian church (especially more spectacular gifts such as 'tongues'), through his emphasis upon waiting for 'the revealing of our Lord Jesus Christ'.

From a theological perspective, 1 Corinthians is significant for the importance it places on the 'body'. Some may find this surprising, given the popular perception of Paul as possessing a negative view of 'the flesh', and placing celibacy on a higher level than marriage. Two points should be made here. First, in Pauline terminology, the negative term 'flesh' (Greek *sarx*) refers not to human physicality, but to disordered human nature, weakened by sin: a way of living focused not on God but on self, and therefore closed to fellow human beings. The opposite of this is life in the 'spirit' (Greek *pneuma*, which denotes power as opposed to the weakness of 'the flesh'). By contrast, 'body' (Greek *sōma*) is viewed positively, as a necessity both for individuals (to be fully human, and to relate to other 'bodies') and for communities (the social body). In the ancient world, the social and individual bodies were closely related, and the boundaries of the former were preserved by protecting those of the latter.[57] Paul uses *sōma* in a number of different, sometimes overlapping, ways:

- *individual bodies*, which eat, drink, have sex, etc. (for example, 1 Corinthians 5.3; 6.12–20; 13.3);
- the individual *body of Christ*, which died on the cross, and possibly also his *eucharistic body* (for example, 1 Corinthians 10.16; 11.24, 27–9);
- the *social body*, the Corinthian assembly of Christians, which is 'one body in Christ' (1 Corinthians 10.17; 12.12–31; possibly 10.16; 11.27–9);
- the *resurrection body*, which is of a different kind to the earthly or natural

body which one possesses now (1 Corinthians 15.35–58: Paul talks about a *sōma pneumatikon* as opposed to a *sōma psuchikon*).

The second point is that, where Paul's words sound ascetic, he may well be playing back (and refining) the position of certain Corinthians, as he tries to hold together rival factions who either shun the body or regard it as so unimportant that one can indulge it. The problem here is that the original Greek lacked punctuation, so that it is not always clear where Paul is quoting the views of others, and where putting forward his own view. The NRSV offers this particular interpretation of 1 Corinthians 7.1–2 (note where the quotation marks are placed):

> Now concerning the matters about which you wrote: 'It is well for a man not to touch a woman.' But because of cases of sexual immorality, each man should have his own wife and each woman her own husband.

A useful exercise is to look at other similar passages, to detect where Paul is giving his own view and where quoting the views of others (as at 1 Corinthians 6.12–20; 8.1–6).

Another interpretative question raised by 1 Corinthians is whether Paul's first-century teaching *per se* remains binding, or whether his theological *method* is more significant. This is raised particularly by what he says about marriage and divorce. Here historical awareness is particularly important: a responsible interpretation of 1 Corinthians 7 will involve an exploration of ancient views of marriage and the role divorce played in such societies. To fail to do so may lead us to do violence to the New Testament text.

But the *way* in which Paul addresses the issue is also significant. Faced with a particular pastoral problem – the case of a pagan convert to Christianity, whose pagan partner is unhappy with the changed status – he begins with the inherited teaching of Jesus:

> To the married I give this command – not I but the Lord – that the wife should not separate from her husband (but if she does separate, let her remain unmarried or else be reconciled to her husband), and that the husband should not divorce his wife. (1 Corinthians 7.10–11)

Comparison with the gospels reveals that Paul preserves an adaptation of Jesus' words to a Roman context, where both husbands and wives could initiate divorce (only husbands could do so in Jesus' own world of Jewish Palestine: Matthew 5.32; 19.9). But then Paul takes a further step: how should one interpret Jesus' teaching in a new situation, in which former pagans with pagan partners are now members of the Church? Studying his nuanced response at 1 Corinthians 7.12–16 may provide some surprises (especially v. 15: 'But if the unbelieving partner separates, let it be so; in such a case the brother or sister is not bound').

Significant archaeological work in and around Corinth has also proved illuminating. Excavation of pagan temples, with dining facilities in their precincts, provides some background to the discussion of eating idol-meat in 1 Corinthians 8—10. The discovery of well-to-do private houses (such as the villa from Paul's time excavated in the Corinthian area of Anaploga, whose dining room (*triclinium*) measured 5.5 by 7.5 metres) provides evidence for the physical environment within which the community would have met, shedding light on the divisions and tensions at the Eucharist (1 Corinthians 11.17–34). Excavation of relatively small workshops near the centre of the city, or the market to the north of the archaic Temple of Apollo, brings us close to the working environment – and possible missionary strategy – of Paul the tent-maker. Jerome Murphy-O'Connor's excellent book *St Paul's Corinth* brings together much of the relevant data.[58]

Social-scientific approaches to the New Testament have also helped put flesh on the bones of first-century Corinthian Christianity. Awareness of tensions caused by patronage, the way in which Roman society was dominated by issues of honour and shame, and the kind of social stratification implied by what is said about particular individuals, shed light on a range of issues. For example, a socio-economic dimension may underlie the debate about idol meat, while the failure of Christians to confront the man living with his father's wife (his stepmother? 1 Corinthians 5.1) may be illuminated by knowledge of patron–client relationships. Particularly important in relation to Corinth is the work of Wayne Meeks and Gerd Theissen (see *SCM Studyguide to New Testament Interpretation*, chapter 8).[59]

> **To do**
>
> After reading 1 Corinthians, write an imaginary letter from the Corinthians to Paul, to which 1 Corinthians is his response (there are probable allusions to questions raised in this letter at 1 Corinthians 7.1, 25; 8.1; 12.1; 16.1, 12).

Issues in 2 Corinthians

As Table 11 shows, 2 Corinthians is probably a composite letter. The sharp shift in tone and subject matter at 2 Corinthians 10.1 suggests that 2 Corinthians 1—9 and 2 Corinthians 10—13 represent different Pauline letters. Both almost certainly address situations in the city after the sending of 1 Corinthians. 2 Corinthians 1—9 seems to envisage the restoration of a fractured relationship between the Corinthians and Paul (after a difficult second visit to Corinth, where an unnamed member of the church caused him pain: 2 Corinthians 2.1, 5–6). 2 Corinthians 10—13 directly confronts the activity of rival apostles in Corinth, with whom Paul is being compared unfavourably. Some scholars regard 2 Corinthians 8—9 as a separate letter (or two separate letters) dealing with the collection for Jerusalem. This composite nature (and disagreement as to the chronological order of the fragments) means that 2 Corinthians is difficult to read. Nevertheless, it is among the most rhetorical and lyrical of Paul's surviving letters, raising a range of issues:

• *The nature of apostleship:* How does one recognize an authentic apostle (see Table 12)? In contrast to ancient society's prizing of honour, Paul presents himself and other apostles of Christ as dishonourable and weak. Underlying this is probably the pattern of the crucified Christ. 2 Corinthians 10—13 points to an alternative model of apostleship advocated by rivals in Corinth: apparently emphasizing their Jewish credentials, their visionary experiences, and their powerful rhetoric and impressive physical presence (against which Paul would compare unfavourably). Though he is adamant that his own ministry exhibited the appropriate signs of an apostle ('signs and wonders and mighty works'), Paul's emphasis is upon the revelation of God's power in weakness. There is a hermeneutical problem here: we only gain a picture of these rival apostles' views from Paul's words. Can we be sure that Paul fairly represents his opponents?

- *The relationship between old and new covenants:* One tension running throughout the New Testament is the relationship between the new thing which Christians believe has occurred in Christ and the ancient covenant between God and Israel. Renewed emphasis in recent scholarship upon the Jewish Paul has often wanted to highlight the continuity in Paul's message: he does not turn his back on Judaism, but shows how Christ fulfils Jewish hopes. 2 Corinthians 3 is important for it appears to highlight discontinuity. It presents a contrast between 'the ministry of death, chiseled in letters on stone tablets' (an allusion to the Sinai covenant) and 'the ministry of the Spirit' (2 Corinthians 3.7–8). But this comes in the context of a complex argument, which requires careful study in order to follow its logic.

- *Paul's mysticism:* At 2 Corinthians 12.2–4, Paul speaks of 'a person in Christ' (probably himself) who was 'caught up to the third heaven . . . into Paradise, and heard things that are not to be told'. This may provide us a window onto a first-century version of *Merkavah* mysticism (from the Hebrew word for 'chariot', reflecting the claim of Jewish visionaries to have seen the throne-chariot of Ezekiel 1). There has been renewed interest in recent years in Paul as visionary and mystic.[60] Nonetheless, even if he was privileged to ascend as far as the third heaven (perhaps not even into it, and certainly no further!), Paul was brought down to earth with a jolt. The ultimate revelation he received is that God's power is made perfect in weakness (2 Corinthians 12.9).

Did Paul's letters do the trick? Was he ultimately successful in his dealings with the Corinthians? The constant despatch of letters and series of visits (both of Paul himself and of delegates such as Timothy and Titus) might suggest otherwise. However, two pieces of evidence point to a more positive outcome. The first is the Corinthian letters themselves: presumably preserved by that church and thus for posterity. The second is a letter from the Roman to the Corinthian church (known as *1 Clement*) perhaps forty years after Paul's epistles were dispatched. Responding to the deposition of some Corinthian presbyters, *1 Clement* can appeal to Paul's honoured memory and at least one of his letters (1 Corinthians) in order to resolve this new crisis:

> Take up the epistle of the blessed Paul the Apostle. What did he write to you at the beginning of his preaching? With true inspiration he charged you concerning himself and Cephas and Apollos, because even then you had made yourselves partisans. (*1 Clement* 47.1–3)[61]

Crisis Among the Galatians

Scholars disagree as to where to locate Galatians in Paul's ministry. Some date it as one of the earliest of Paul's letters; for others, it is written during the same period as the Corinthian letters and not long before Romans, while Paul is engaged in the collection for Jerusalem (one reading of Galatians 2.10). Often related to dating is the identity of the recipients. When Paul speaks of 'Galatia', does he mean the tribe of that name (Gauls or Celts who settled in north central Asia Minor, in cities such as Tavium and Ancyra: the so-called 'North Galatian theory')? Or does he mean the Roman province of Galatia (so that the Galatia Christians could be located in those cities mentioned in Acts 13—14: Pisidian Antioch, Iconium, Lystra and Derbe (the 'South Galatian theory'))? Consulting a map at this point will help locate the discussion on *terra firma*.

Either way, Galatians is a circular letter, addressed to a number of churches founded by Paul in the area. In the previous chapter we noted the key role of Galatians 1—2 in discussions of Pauline chronology. No less important, however, is the place of Galatians in Christianity's theological history (it played a crucial role in Reformation debates, for example).

One important interpretative issue centres on the situation which first provoked the letter. Comparison with other Pauline letters highlights the urgency and gravity of this situation. Missing from Galatians is the usual thanksgiving, in which Paul typically gives thanks for the faith of the recipient community. In its place is the following rebuke:

Table 12: 2 Corinthians on Apostleship.

We are putting no obstacle in anyone's way, so that no fault may be found with our ministry, but as servants of God we have commended ourselves in every way: through great endurance, in afflictions, hardships, calamities, beatings, imprisonments, riots, labours, sleepless nights, hunger; by purity, knowledge, patience, kindness, holiness of spirit, genuine love, truthful speech, and the power of God; with the weapons of righteousness for the right hand and for the left; in honour and dishonour, in ill repute and good repute. We are treated as impostors, and yet are true; as unknown, and yet are well known; as dying, and see – we are alive; as punished, and yet not killed; as sorrowful, yet always rejoicing; as poor, yet making many rich; as having nothing, and yet possessing everything. (2 Corinthians 6.3–10)

For they [Paul's opponents in Corinth] say, 'His letters are weighty and strong, but his bodily presence is weak, and his speech contemptible.' (2 Corinthians 10.10)

I think that I am not in the least inferior to these super-apostles. I may be untrained in speech, but not in knowledge; certainly in every way and in all things we have made this evident to you. (2 Corinthians 11.5–6)

Are they Hebrews? So am I. Are they Israelites? So am I. Are they descendants of Abraham? So am I. Are they ministers of Christ? I am talking like a madman – I am a better one: with far greater labours, far more imprisonments, with countless floggings, and often near death. (2 Corinthians 11.22–3)

I have been a fool! You forced me to it. Indeed, you should have been the ones commending me, for I am not at all inferior to these super-apostles, even though I am nothing. The signs of a true apostle were performed among you with utmost patience, signs and wonders and mighty works. (2 Corinthians 12.11–12)

I am astonished that you are so quickly deserting the one who called you in the grace of Christ and are turning to a different gospel – not that there is another gospel, but there are some who are confusing you and want to pervert the gospel of Christ. But even if we or an angel from heaven should proclaim to you a gospel contrary to what we proclaimed to you, let that one be accursed! (Galatians 1.6–8)

Despite disagreement about details, the heart of the problem seems clear: Paul's Gentile Galatian converts have been told that they cannot be full members of the Church unless they adopt certain Jewish practices (which for males includes circumcision: Galatians 5.2). For Paul, this compromises a fundamental plank of his gospel: that in Christ all – both Jew and Gentile – stand before God on an equal basis. Anything which suggests that Gentile converts are second-class members of God's people is anathema.

His vigorous response to the 'agitators' is what makes Galatians so interesting, and topical. It raises a question which still lies at the heart of fierce disagreements between Christians: on what grounds do we decide Christ's will? What are our sources of authority? One can make a good case for Paul's opponents possessing the high ground here. On the necessity of circumcision and other ritual observances for membership of God's people, they could claim scripture on their side. They could make a similar claim for tradition (there is no surviving saying of Jesus stating that Gentiles need not be circumcised). They may also have thought, not unreasonably, that the apostles in Jerusalem held to the same view. In Galatians, then, Paul has to confront the charge that he is the innovator, promoting a novel teaching going against the plain teaching of divine revelation and community practice.

In Galatians, Paul confronts these criticisms point by point. On the basis of his Damascus road experience, he presents his teaching as the direct result of divine revelation rather than due to any human intermediary (Galatians 1). Thus he also sidesteps the objection that Jesus never advocated abandoning circumcision. While distancing himself from the original Jerusalem apostles, paradoxically he claims that they accepted his non-circumcision mission among Gentiles (Galatians 2). Offering a rather novel rereading of the Abraham story (Galatians 3—4), he claims that scripture supports his position. But perhaps what clinched his argument among the Galatians was his appeal to their experience of the Spirit (Galatians 3.2). Given the Jewish belief that the Spirit would be poured out on God's people in the new age, their reception of God's Spirit without being circumcised or observing other 'works of the Law' rendered the latter superfluous.

There is one further question which Galatians raises very acutely. What place should polemics play in religious debate? Some readers may be put off by what they regard as Paul's intemperate language, his caricaturing of religious opponents, even the occasional crude pun (Galatians 5.12). Theirs is a response that must be taken seriously. On the one hand, Galatians reveals Paul at his most passionate, in the heat of debate and desperate to defend what he regards as a gospel of freedom. On the other, Galatians' polemical nature presents a darker aspect of the New Testament writings, reflecting only too clearly the human dimension of their composition.

To do

Examine Paul's arguments in Galatians 3 based on the story of Abraham. Do you find this a convincing account of the story (as found in Genesis)? How might others interpret the Abraham story differently?

Correspondence to the Lycus Valley

Like 2 Thessalonians, the authorship of Colossians is also disputed (although by fewer scholars than Ephesians and the Pastorals). Though arguments from vocabulary and style are often posited against Pauline authorship, the more compelling arguments are theological: aspects of Colossians' thought seem to many to reflect a development of that in Paul's undisputed letters. Examples include its teaching about Christ (which stresses his role in creation, as at Colossians 1.15), the Church (which has a wider, cosmic focus as well as describing the local congregation, compare for example Colossians 1.18 with 4.15–16), and Christian baptism (which is envisaged as both dying *and* rising with Christ, Colossians 2.12).[62] However, the differences can be over-stressed (for example, Colossians 3.4 holds to the 'not yet' aspect of Paul's eschatological teaching reflected in his teaching about baptism in for instance Romans 6). A reasonable case can be made for Colossians being authentic, responding to particular challenges in Colossae and drawing upon the vocabulary of local liturgical traditions.

If we accept the authenticity of Colossians, then it is closely related to the more personal letter to Philemon. Both would be addressed from Paul in prison to Christians living in or near the city of Colossae, on the south side of the broad valley of the River Lycus (a tributary of the more famous Meander), about a hundred miles inland from Ephesus. According to the New Testament, Christianity made significant inroads into this valley, with churches at Colossae, Laodicea and Hierapolis. All three are associated with the Pauline mission (Colossians 4.13, 16), while Laodicea is also one of the seven churches addressed by John of Patmos (Revelation 3.14–22).

Colossians attributes the evangelization of Colossae (and the whole Lycus valley) not to Paul directly (Colossians 2.1), but to his co-worker Epaphras (Colossians 1.7–8; 4.12–13). Indeed, the close relationship between Colossae and Laodicea, some ten miles away, is expressed at Colossians 4.15–16. Again, we have a glimpse of a broad Pauline mission with a network of co-workers moving out from established church centres, in this case probably Ephesus. Ephesus could also be the location of Paul's imprisonment and place of origin for the letter (though Caesarea and Rome are also contenders).

Several interpretative issues are worth noting. First, the situation which provoked Colossians seems to be what scholars call 'the Colossian heresy', glimpsed in the following passage:

> Therefore do not let anyone condemn you in matters of food and drink or of observing festivals, new moons, or sabbaths. These are only a shadow of what is to come, but the substance belongs to Christ. Do not let anyone disqualify you, insisting on self-abasement and worship of angels, dwelling on visions, puffed up without cause by a human way of thinking, and not holding fast to the head, from whom the whole body, nourished and held together by its ligaments and sinews, grows with a growth that is from God. (Colossians 2.16–19)

The picture here suggests a syncretistic combination of Jewish and pagan elements (perhaps reflecting the religious mix of the Lycus valley), with a mystical tinge, of which there are a number of modern parallels. But why is this religious 'mishmash' regarded as so harmful? Moreover, how much of this 'heresy' is reflected elsewhere in the letter? In particular, how far are the positive statements of Paul (or the author) directly responding to elements in this teaching? Building up a picture of this needs to beware of the dangers of mirror-reading.

To do

Read Colossians (it is quite short!), noting down anything you think might refer to the 'false teaching'. What kind of picture emerges? Why might the author have wanted to challenge this kind of teaching? After doing your own work, compare it with scholarly reconstructions in a commentary or New Testament introduction.

A second feature of interest is the possible reuse in Colossians of fragments of early Christian liturgy. Many scholars believe that Paul cites an early Christian hymn at Colossians 1.15–20, perhaps one known to and sung by Christians in the Lycus valley. This familiar hymn, which speaks of Christ's cosmic role (influenced by Jewish traditions about Wisdom as agent of creation and Adam as made in God's image), has been chosen to rebut aspects of the 'Colossian heresy', with certain additions made to it to emphasize Paul's distinctive position. These additions (which arguably break the syntactical flow and hymnic structure) may include focus on Christ's supremacy over heavenly powers, the Church as the locus of Christ's activity, and the centrality of Christ's death in bringing about reconciliation (see Table 13).

A final issue is the emphasis upon Christ's elevation and victory over cosmic powers, variously described as 'thrones or dominions or rulers or powers' (Colossians 1.16), 'rulers and authorities' (2.15), 'elemental spirits of the universe' (2.20). Colossians is at the very least referring to angelic powers here (both benign and malevolent), if not also human authorities. But the overarching claim is that Christ is superior to all those forces which impinge on human lives, and which lead to a sense of enslavement. Indeed, Colossians 2.15 likens Christ's victory to a Roman triumphal procession, in which the vanquished are paraded through the city: 'He disarmed the rulers and authorities and made a public example of them, triumphing over them in it.'

Table 13: The Colossians Hymn (Colossians 1.15–20).

Pauline additions in italics:

He is the image of the invisible God,
the firstborn of all creation;
for in him all things in heaven and on earth were created,
things visible and invisible,
whether thrones or dominions or rulers or powers –
all things have been created through him and for him.
He himself is before all things, and in him all things hold together.
He is the head of the body, *the church.*

He is the beginning,
the firstborn from the dead, so that he might come to have first place in
   everything.
For in him all the fullness of God was pleased to dwell,
and through him God was pleased to reconcile to himself all things,
whether on earth or in heaven,
by making peace *through the blood of his cross.*

Contemporary readers of Paul's letters might want to ask themselves how this language of 'principalities and powers' might be translated into their own context, where human beings still feel threatened by powers apparently beyond their control.

Quite different from Colossians, though written to the same geographical area and mentioning several of the same individuals, is the personal letter to Philemon. Addressed to a prominent Christian called Philemon, along with Apphia (probably Philemon's wife), Archippus and the church in Philemon's house, it provides a glimpse of the close network of small house-churches of which Paul's Christians were comprised.

Paul's letter is apparently preparing the ground for the return of Onesimus, Philemon's slave, who has been with Paul during his current imprisonment. Perhaps Onesimus is the emissary carrying the letter to the Colossians. However, there is a complication which necessitates this short note to Philemon. Many commentators think that Onesimus has run away (though that is not clearly stated in the letter, and other scenarios are possible), and Paul needs to plead on his behalf, first for Philemon to receive him, and then to allow him to return to Paul. The appeal focuses on Onesimus' status as a fellow Christian, and the mutual obligation between Paul and Philemon.

Those reading Philemon in English translation may miss some of the nuances of the Greek original. The name Onesimus in Greek means 'useful', and in verse 11 Paul describes him as formerly 'useless' to Philemon but now 'useful' to both Philemon and Paul. But the precise word Paul uses here for 'useful' is not *onēsimos* but a synonym *euchrēstos*, whose root is very similar to the Greek word for Christ, *Christos*. In other words, Philemon was also once 'without Christ' (playing on the Greek for 'useless', *achrēstos*), but now belongs to him.

The letter to Philemon also raises the issue of Christian attitudes to slavery (though we should bear in mind the diversity of experience and lifestyle among Roman slaves). One way of reading Paul is as a social conservative, who works within the institutions of Roman society rather than challenging them.[63] But even if Paul does not overtly challenge institutions such as slavery, two factors should be borne in mind. First, his stance – like that relating to marriage – is in part determined by eschatological concerns. As he writes at 1 Corinthians 7.31, 'the present form of this world is passing away': the imminence of the End means that social reform is not a priority. Second, albeit implicitly, his conviction that new relationships have been established in Christ is already undermining the structures which sustain slavery: Onesimus is to be received back by his former master 'no longer as a slave but as more than a slave, a beloved brother' (Philemon 16).

One further feature is worthy of comment. The very mundane request for Philemon to 'prepare a guest room for me' (Philemon 22) points to the importance of hospitality in the early Christian movement. This is partly a practical concern: sleeping on the road, or even staying in inns, was extremely dangerous, leaving the traveller prone to violence and robbery. For Christian missionaries like Paul to have a network of safe lodging places was crucial to their success. However, it also has a theological dimension: Paul's vision was for Christians to welcome one another, as Christ had welcomed them

(Romans 15.7). Moreover, Christians shared that older Jewish belief that in offering hospitality some, like Abraham, have entertained angels unawares (Hebrews 13.2; cf. Genesis 18). This one short phrase reveals so much about a Christian sense of love and mutual obligation.

The Broad View: The Story of Romans

Very different from the short personal letter to Philemon, Paul's lengthy letter to the Romans is often regarded as the definitive statement of Paul's gospel, the nearest he provides to a systematic theology. This assessment seems to be reflected in the textual tradition. Some manuscripts lack the words 'in Rome' at Romans 1.7 and 1.15, suggesting that it was depersonalized in order to be circulated more generally as an account of Paul's gospel. In more recent centuries, it has often served as the starting-point for attempts to describe Paul's thought.[64] Romans is certainly a bold statement of the good news, though the lack of substantial teaching about for example the Church, the Eucharist or the Resurrection means that it is not comprehensive.

What makes Romans particularly interesting is that it was composed at a crucial turning point in Paul's apostolic ministry, probably written at Corinth (Romans 16.1, 23; cf. 1 Corinthians 1.14) in the mid- to late 50s. The important autobiographical passage Romans 15.15–33 reveals the following:

- Paul has now (symbolically, at least) completed preaching the gospel in the eastern empire ('from Jerusalem and as far around as Illyricum', Romans 15.19).
- He has now turned his sights westward, wanting to spread the good news to the Gentiles as far as Spain (15.24).
- After unsuccessful attempts, Paul is now planning to visit Rome, a church which he himself has not founded (15.22–4).
- His immediate plan is to go to Jerusalem with the collection for the saints (15.25–9, a collection he has been engaged in for some time among the Christians of Macedonia, Achaia and possibly Galatia).
- He asks specifically for the prayers of the Romans that his collection may be accepted in Jerusalem. (Does he believe that they have particular links with Christian Jews in that city?)[65]

A fuller portrait of the Roman Christians themselves is to be gleaned from Romans 16 (treating this as an integral part of the letter).[66] Attention to the people mentioned, how they are grouped, their names (Latin or Greek), and what is said about their ethnic origin or implied about their social status, suggests a diverse and fragmented set of Christian groups, probably largely based in private houses scattered throughout the city. You might find it helpful to reread Romans 16, listing the various groups. Further information in Romans 14 (where the issue of food, drink and special days emerges) suggests that Paul envisaged tensions within Roman Christianity between those who regarded Jewish practice as central to church life and those for whom it had no significance. In contrast to Galatians, Romans can be read as presenting a conciliatory Paul offering support for the former group.

Yet for many readers, it is the letter's theological vision which is most compelling. Through a series of broad sweeps, and a fair number of tangents, Romans sets out 'the gospel concerning [God's] son' (Romans 1.3). This is the good news of how God has begun to act in Christ to put right a world which is out of kilter, not as God created it to be. The following pointers may be helpful in order for the first-time reader to see the wood for the trees:

- Paul moves from describing the problem (that evil and injustice are present in the world, and human beings are enslaved to powers such as sin), to articulating the solution (the faithful response of Christ), to setting out how Roman Christians are to relate to each other as a result (see Table 14 for the structure of the letter).
- Throughout his argument, Paul makes use of the ancient literary convention of the 'diatribe'. This was the convention of debating with an imaginary conversation partner, who throws up awkward questions and objections to which the author responds. Hence, particularly in the early chapters, phrases such as 'What then are we to say?' (from Paul's imaginary opponent) and Paul's vehement response 'By no means!' regularly occur.
- Paul sees the problem, and the solution to the problem, from a number of different perspectives. Bearing this in mind might help explain the otherwise repetitious nature of Paul's argument (for example, Romans 5, 6, 7 and 8 are describing the solution from four different vantage points:

a new humanity in Christ; Christian baptism, which involves a ritual 'death' to the old self; freedom from the Law, used by sin to enslave human beings; life in the Spirit, God's power which makes possible a more human way of living).

- Paul's consideration of the place of Israel in God's unfolding plan (Romans 9—11) is probably not an appendix to the real argument, but integral to it. It is an attempt to show that, despite appearances (the large influx of Gentiles into the Church and the apparent failure of the mission to Israel), God remains trustworthy. One feels in these chapters that Paul is agonizing on paper, trying to understand the present situation while remaining utterly convinced that 'all Israel will be saved' (Romans 11.26). In particular, he lists Israel's privileges, the gifts showered on God's people which have not been revoked or taken back (Romans 9.1–5; 11.29). These chapters have come to play a particularly important role in Christian–Jewish dialogue. They are key, for example, to Vatican II's Declaration on the Relation of the Church to Non-Christian Religions, *Nostrae Aetate* (28 October 1965).[67]

- Recent interest in intertextuality has highlighted how Paul's letters tap into ancient Old Testament narratives, often by quite subtle allusions and echoes. Mention has already been made of Katherine Grieb's *The Story of Romans*, subtitled 'A Narrative Defense of God's Righteousness'. Grieb's book shows how Romans can be read as a series of interlocking stories, drawn from the Hebrew scriptures, themselves embedded in that greater story of what God has done for both Israel and the nations in the Messiah Jesus. Moreover, the story is deliberately open-ended: will the members of the different Roman house churches receive one another, as Christ has received them? It is for the Christian audiences in first-century Rome, and indeed readers and audiences in every age, to provide a satisfactory ending.

Table 14: A Possible Structure for Romans.

1.1–15	**Introduction**
1.1–7	Salutation
1.8–15	Thanksgiving
1.16—11.36	**The good news**
1.16–17	Summary of gospel
1.18—3.20	The problem: Jews no less than Gentiles are under sin's power
3.21–31	God's solution in Christ
4	Scriptural proof: Abraham's story
5—8	Four ways of looking at what God has done:
	5 Adam and Christ: two ways of being human
	6 The effects of baptism
	7 Life under the Law and freedom from the Law
	8 Life in the Spirit
9—11	The mystery of Israel
12.1—15.13	**Ethical exhortations**
	How, on the basis of Romans 1—11, Roman Christians are to live together as God's new humanity in Rome
15.14–33	**Paul's travel plans**
16	**Commendation of Phoebe and list of greetings**

To do

Read Romans 3.21–6, paying special attention to verses 24–5. Work out the different images Paul uses here to describe God's action in Christ. From which contexts are the images derived? What does each of them suggest about humanity's problem, and its solution? If you are stuck, you might like to consult a commentary or two, but only do so as a last resort.

Paul's Last Will and Testament?

Romans was written from Corinth, preparing for a visit Paul hoped to make to the capital. One reading of his letter to the Philippians would place it after his arrival in Rome, now a prisoner for the Lord (cf. Acts 28.16–31; as for the other 'letters from prison', Ephesus and Caesarea are proposed as alternative locations). This would fit the references to 'the whole praetorian guard' (Philippians 1.13) and 'those of the emperor's household' (4.22). If Paul is in Rome, then it may be that Philippians, rather than Romans, functions as Paul's testament. In this letter he writes to a church – significantly located in a Roman colony – for whom he has great affection, uncertain as to whether he will see them again. It is a letter of thanksgiving, expressing gratitude for their gift delivered by Epaphroditus (4.18), who is now returning to them after serious illness (2.25–30). Nevertheless, Paul is aware of difficulties facing the Philippian Christians, including external pressure (1.28–9), internal disagreements (4.2–3) and a threat from rival teachers similar, if not identical, to those encountered in Galatia (3.2–3).

We should not underestimate the significance of Paul's imprisonment, and the rather different perspective on the world this loss of freedom would have cultivated. Richard Cassidy's study of Paul and Roman imprisonment offers fascinating insights into this aspect of Paul's ministry.[68] Moreover, in Paul's case, death is a distinct possibility. This may have led to some radical rethinking of his eschatological teaching, as he contemplates his own death prior to the Lord's return. He can now speak of his desire 'to depart and be with Christ' (1.23), even though he acknowledges that remaining 'in the flesh' in order to return to Philippi may be more necessary.

Again, the pattern of Christ crucified emerges as fundamental for Paul's understanding of the Christian life, no doubt accentuated by his personal sufferings and those of the Philippians. This is particularly so in his use of what looks like an existing Christian hymn (2.6–11), in the context of an appeal to the Philippians to model Christ's humility in their dealings with one another. Commentators have offered quite different readings of the Christology presupposed in this hymn. For many, it describes Christ's *kenosis* or self-emptying, describing a divine being who becomes incarnate as a human (as implied in the NRSV translation). For others, like Jerome

Murphy-O'Connor and James Dunn, it presents an Adam Christology.[69] Christ, unlike Adam, did not 'snatch at' being equal with God but accepted his human status 'in the image and likeness of God', and therefore found himself being exalted:

> Who, being in the image of God,
> did not consider being equal to God something to be grasped at,
> but made himself of no account,
> taking the form of a slave,
> becoming like all human beings. (Philippians 2.6–7)

Whichever interpretation one prefers, what is important is that Christ's humility becomes the pattern for Christian existence: followed by Paul, now in chains at the risk of death, and by Epaphroditus, who has risked his own life in Paul's service (2.30). It is a particularly poignant reminder, perhaps towards the end of Paul's life, of how far the vision of Christ suffering, crucified and risen not only captivated Paul of Tarsus, but formed the heart of his urgent mission to Gentile communities across the first-century Mediterranean world. As Paul puts it in this most affectionate of letters:

> Yet whatever gains I had, these I have come to regard as loss because of Christ. More than that, I regard everything as loss because of the surpassing value of knowing Christ Jesus my Lord. For his sake I have suffered the loss of all things, and I regard them as rubbish, in order that I may gain Christ and be found in him . . . I want to know Christ and the power of his resurrection and the sharing of his sufferings by becoming like him in his death, if somehow I may attain the resurrection from the dead. (Philippians 3.7–11)

> ## To do
>
> Read through Philippians in one sitting. Note any apparent disruptions in the texts, and places where Paul seems to be drawing to a close. Does this make sense as a single letter to the Philippians? Or are there grounds for treating it as a compilation of two or more letters? As a letter whose sections are now in the wrong order?

Further Reading

James D. G. Dunn (ed.), 2003, *The Cambridge Companion to St Paul*, Cambridge: Cambridge University Press.

Bruce J. Malina and John J. Pilch, 2006, *Social-Science Commentary on the Letters of Paul*, Minneapolis: Fortress Press.

Calvin J. Roetzel, 1982, *The Letters of Paul: Conversations in Context*, 2nd edition; London: SCM Press.

Stanley K. Stowers, 1986, *Letter-Writing in Graeco-Roman Antiquity*, Philadelphia: Westminster.

5

The First Three Gospels

Introducing the Synoptic Gospels

Paul's letters provide a glimpse into the worlds of the earliest Christian communities. Yet they also present the profound theological vision of one prominent leader in the early Church. This same mixture of theological vision and contemporary community concern is found in a group of writings probably written in the last third of the first century CE (*c*.65–95 CE). The four gospels, although telling the story of Jesus of Nazareth, do so through the lens of later generations of Christians. As we saw in Chapter 2, they are not straightforward accounts of Jesus' life. Rather, they are the result of complex reflection on and interpretation of his significance, by people who believed he was Israel's Messiah and risen Lord, in the light of their own interests, concerns, and difficulties. A more extensive discussion as to why the New Testament contains four 'lives of Jesus' can be found in the *SCM Studyguide to New Testament Interpretation*, chapter 5.

The fourth of these books, the Gospel according to John, will be the subject of the next chapter. This chapter is concerned with the first three, attributed to Matthew, Mark and Luke. Though similar to ancient 'lives', these texts (as the name given to them suggests) are essentially proclamations of the 'gospel' or 'good news' (Greek *euangelion*). Their particular concern is to convince people of, or confirm people in their existing conviction about, the truth of Jesus Christ. The material they incorporate was probably circulating in small independent units, much of it orally rather than in written form, over several decades. This would have allowed for the material to be reshaped as it was applied to new circumstances, to fall into set patterns, and to be interpreted differently in different geographical and cultural contexts. With the notable exception of the Passion story, it is possible that much of the chronological sequence in the gospels is due to the evangelists' own arrangement, rather than traditional memory of where events occurred in relation to one another. These are complex texts, with a complex history.

Moreover, in their current form, the gospels present us with overlapping worlds. On the level of the narrative, they relate the story of Jesus of Nazareth, whose ministry was largely confined to rural Jewish Galilee, and the Judean city of Jerusalem, in the first three decades of the first century CE. But the gospel writers tell their stories decades after the events they describe, probably in quite different geographical locations and cultural contexts, almost certainly urban rather than rural, and with significantly different audiences in mind. The gospels, then, are stories of the early first century overlaid with the stories of the intervening years, and especially the evangelists' own cultural stories. Viewed historically, they are like overhead projector transparencies layered on top of each other, enabling us to view all layers simultaneously. Thinking of their literary features, they are like rich tapestries in which a variety of threads and colours are woven together to create dramatic new patterns.

To do

Consult a map of the Mediterranean world in the first century. Locate the following places, all of which have been proposed as possible locations for the writing of the gospels: Syrian Antioch; Alexandria; Ephesus; Rome. You might find it useful to draw your own map and mark these places on it.

But why separate out the first three gospels (Matthew, Mark and Luke) from the Fourth Gospel, attributed to John? This question deserves serious attention, given the unfortunate way in which John has been bracketed out from historical study of Jesus. The main reason is their similarity in structure, content and even wording, which leads most scholars to believe that there is some literary relationship between them. Hence they are known as the 'synoptic gospels' (from the Greek meaning 'seeing together'). In what has become the consensus view since the nineteenth century, Mark is the earliest, and was used as a major source by Matthew and Luke (an alternative, known as the 'Griesbach' or 'Two Gospel' hypothesis, is that Matthew is the earliest, Luke the second, and both were conflated by Mark). For many scholars who hold to Marcan priority, Matthew and Luke worked independently of each other. The significant amount of non-Marcan material they share is accounted for by their independent use of a now-lost source, known as Q (from the German *Quelle* = 'source'). A significant minority of scholars, however, make a good case for Luke being dependent upon Matthew as well as Mark.

Reflection

Is it a problem for you that there are four gospels in the New Testament? In what ways might this fact be an advantage, and in what ways a disadvantage? What issues does it raise for the interpreter of the New Testament? For the historian? For the believing Christian?

Beginning to Read

What kind of questions emerge when one begins to read a gospel? By way of example, we shall look at the opening section of Mark. In the NRSV translation, Mark 1.1–13 reads as follows:

> 1 The beginning of the good news of Jesus Christ, the Son of God. 2 As it is written in the prophet Isaiah,
>
> 'See, I am sending my messenger ahead of you,
> who will prepare your way;
> 3 the voice of one crying out in the wilderness:
> "Prepare the way of the Lord, make his paths straight."'
> 4 John the baptizer appeared in the wilderness, proclaiming a baptism

of repentance for the forgiveness of sins. 5 And people from the whole Judean countryside and all the people of Jerusalem were going out to him, and were baptized by him in the river Jordan, confessing their sins. 6 Now John was clothed with camel's hair, with a leather belt around his waist, and he ate locusts and wild honey. 7 He proclaimed, 'The one who is more powerful than I is coming after me; I am not worthy to stoop down and untie the thong of his sandals. 8 I have baptized you with water; but he will baptize you with the Holy Spirit.'

9 In those days Jesus came from Nazareth of Galilee and was baptized by John in the Jordan. 10 And just as he was coming up out of the water, he saw the heavens torn apart and the Spirit descending like a dove on him. 11 And a voice came from heaven, 'You are my Son, the Beloved; with you I am well pleased.'

12 And the Spirit immediately drove him out into the wilderness. 13 He was in the wilderness forty days, tempted by Satan; and he was with the wild beasts; and the angels waited on him.

In order to understand a passage such as this, one might first ask about its structure and component parts. For ease of interpretation, this longer passage can be broken up into the following units:

- verses 1–3: the 'beginning', as set out in the quotations from the Old Testament;
- verses 4–8: introducing John the baptizer;
- verses 9–11: the story of Jesus' baptism by John;
- verses 12–13: the story of Jesus' testing in the wilderness.

Here are some questions which emerge from a first reading of this passage (there may well be others which occur to you):

- What precisely is the 'beginning' of the good news of/about Jesus Christ? Is it only verse 1, as a kind of title to the book? Or the prophecy attributed to Isaiah in verses 2–3? Or the whole section 1.1–13, as the preparation for the main story in which Jesus proclaims the kingdom of God? Or is the whole book simply the 'beginning', suggesting that Christians are still performing the 'good news' of Jesus Christ in their lives?

- What associations might the word 'good news' evoke for ancient readers (and indeed for modern readers)? Is Mark thinking of the prophetic proclamation of good news in the Old Testament (such as Isaiah 40.9)? Or is he consciously evoking, and subverting, the Roman imperial 'good news' which saw the emperor as Saviour and bringer of peace?
- How can one account for the variant readings in the ancient Greek manuscripts? For example, the words 'Son of God' are missing from some versions at Mark 1.1, while others change 'in the prophet Isaiah' at 1.2 to 'in the prophets'. Which are the original readings, and why might a scribe have altered the text (whether deliberately or accidentally)?
- In the Old Testament quotations in 1.2–3, who are the 'messenger' and the one whose way is prepared? Who is the voice, and whose way does it prepare?
- Given the prophetic quotations, what are we to infer from the fact that two individuals are then introduced: first John the baptizer (1.4–8), and then Jesus of Nazareth (1.9–11)?
- Does John's strange clothing, and his rather ascetic diet, mark him out as a particular kind of person? Is there anyone else in Israel's history dressed in this way?
- What kind of event is the baptism of Jesus (1.9–11)? What effect does the descent of the Spirit have on Jesus? Does the heavenly voice shed light on what is happening?
- How does this event fit into the gospel as a whole? Is the term 'baptism' used elsewhere in Mark (a concordance is a useful tool for answering such questions), and what does it symbolize? Does anyone else speak like the heavenly voice?
- How does this event relate to the baptism of Christians, a question often addressed visually by artists (see, for example, Piero della Francesca's *The Baptism of Christ* in London's National Gallery: www.nationalgallery.org.uk, NG665)?
- How do I respond to the two main characters here? Is there anything in the text which might suggest how I ought to respond?
- What was Jesus doing in the wilderness (1.12–13), and how does Mark interpret the event? Are the 'wild beasts' hostile or friendly, and how might our answer affect our understanding of the episode?

Some of these questions are concerned with textual issues (variant readings in the ancient manuscripts), some historical, some literary, and some theological. Moreover, some express specific focus on details in the passage, while others are more interested in how it connects to the wider narrative. Primary focus may be on the author's role in shaping the material for ancient audiences, on the shape of the text now before our eyes, or on possible ways in which readers might respond, in the light of their context and inherited ways of hearing the story. A further dimension is provided by the ways in which Matthew and Luke tell the story differently. If they are using Mark, as most scholars think, then they are his earliest surviving commentators. Consulting a gospel synopsis will make the task of comparing the three versions easier (see the Introduction for some suggestions).

Visiting an Art Gallery

The emergence of redaction criticism in the second half of the twentieth century, and especially the growth of narrative and other literary approaches in the past two decades, have refocused attention on the distinctiveness of each gospel. Redaction critics, with their more historical concerns, are interested in the distinctive voices of the evangelists: how they have edited ('redacted') their material. Narrative critics are more interested in the shape of the resulting text, the story it tells and the effect it has on readers (with particular interest in the 'implied readers').

Hence reading the synoptic gospels (and also John) can be likened to a visit to an art gallery. In a gallery, you may be confronted with different portraits of the same subject, reflecting the artists' cultural heritage, artistic school or tradition, and particular insight. This is particularly the case with religious art. On a visit to the National Gallery, for example, you could see more than twenty different representations of Christ's nativity. These would represent the work of artists from the thirteenth to the seventeenth centuries, and as wide-ranging in style as Botticelli's *Mystic Nativity*, Geertgen tot Sint Jans' *The Nativity at Night*, and Nicholas Poussin's *Adoration of the Shepherds*.

Similarly, the various gospels paint quite different portraits of Jesus. Attention to little details, editorial comments, or the different ordering of events and broad sweep of the narrative, will bring into focus Matthew's distinctive view of Christ, or the particular texture of Luke's narrative.

Take a portion of the Marcan passage we have just considered: the story of Jesus in the wilderness (Mark 1.12–13 and its parallels in Matthew 4.1–11 and Luke 4.1–13). Mark's portrait is brief and matter-of-fact, and both Matthew and Luke substantially expand the story. For example, by the subtle addition of the words 'He fasted' and 'and forty nights' to Mark's 'forty days', Matthew clothes Jesus in the mantle of Moses and Elijah, figures of Israel's past who both fasted for that length of time (Deuteronomy 9.18; 1 Kings 19.8). It is important in the portrait Matthew paints that Jesus walks in the steps of – and occasionally trumps – the great authority figures of Israel's memory. In Luke's canvas, the battle between two rival kingdoms, that of God and the devil's alternative realm, is accentuated. On the one hand, he stresses the gentle leading of the prophetic Spirit, with which Jesus is now filled following his baptism (Luke 4.1; contrast the more violent 'the Spirit immediately drove him out' or 'chucked him out' of Mark 1.12). On the other, the frustration of the devil is highlighted at the climax to Luke's story: 'When the devil had finished every test, he departed from him *until an opportune time*' (Luke 4.13; italics mine).

Mark's Story

Let us return to Mark's Gospel, and try and sketch some of the contours of his story. The opening verses, as we have seen, speak of John the baptizer preparing the 'way' or 'road' (Greek *hodos*) for the Lord, and this provides something of a motif for the remainder of the book. The word occurs no fewer than 16 times, with a particular concentration (eight occurrences) in Mark 8—10. The reason for this is the prominence of one particular 'road' or 'way' in Mark's story: the road from Caesarea Philippi (Mark 8.27–30), through Galilee to Jerusalem. For Jesus, this road to Jerusalem is the road to his suffering and death. This is the setting for Mark 8—10, and provides the context for Jesus' teaching to his disciples taking up their cross and following him on this road of suffering (Mark 8.34).

This provides us with a basic pattern for Mark's story (see Table 15).

After an initial prologue setting the scene and introducing two key characters (John the baptizer and Jesus: Mark 1.1–13), we hear of Jesus' preaching of the kingdom, mainly in Galilee in northern Israel. Yet the episodic nature of the various stories, and the regular use of the word 'immediately', give a rushed, urgent feel to this part of the narrative. It is as if the author, or narrator, is in a hurry to get to the climax of the story in Jerusalem.

Mark 8.27—10.52 recounts the journey there, punctuated by three predictions which highlight the necessity of Jesus' sufferings, and his disciples' inability to receive this (Mark 8.31; 9.31; 10.33–4). This journey-narrative plays on the ambiguity of the word *hodos*: it is both the physical road that Jesus must walk, and the way or pattern of life that he has chosen, and which his followers are called to imitate. The story climaxes in Jerusalem, where Jesus teaches, provokes controversy, is arrested by the religious authorities, and put to death by the Romans. Yet the story does not finish there: after his death and burial, Mark recounts a further episode in which some women followers find his tomb empty, and are told by a young man in white that Jesus has been raised and is going ahead of them to Galilee (Mark 16.1–8).

But where precisely does Mark's story end? In most English translations, there will be a gap in the text after 16.8, where some ancient manuscripts finish. Two alternative endings (the 'shorter ending', and the 'longer ending' comprising verses 9–20) are found in other manuscripts, though their very different style and vocabulary points to their composition by later hands, dissatisfied with the ending as it stood. This raises further questions. Was the original ending lost, or is the book unfinished? Particularly appealing is the view that Mark intended this open ending at 16.8. It invites the reader to enter into the story, and complete it in a more satisfactory way than the three women, who 'said nothing to anyone, for they were afraid'.

A related feature of Mark's Gospel is the portrayal of Jesus as a suffering Messiah. Quite unexpectedly given contemporary messianic expectations, the good news of Jesus Christ, the Son of God, is that he is the suffering Son of Man. Although he is an impressive healer and exorcist, it is as the Messiah who must suffer, be rejected, be killed and be raised, that Mark's Jesus comes into his own. Indeed, the first time that he publicly admits to being the Messiah is when he stands as a humiliated prisoner before the high priest in Jerusalem (Mark 14.62). If you want to see what it means to be the

Messiah, says Mark, and if you want to know what it might mean to follow him, then you must look at the cross.

Table 15: Structure of Mark's Gospel.

Mark 1.1–13	Prologue: the beginning of the good news
Mark 1.14—8.30	Proclamation of the kingdom in Galilee
Mark 8.31—10.52	The road to Jerusalem and the cross
Mark 11.1—15.47	Ministry in Jerusalem, passion and death
Mark 16.1–8	Epilogue: discovery of empty tomb
[Mark 16.9–20	Marcan appendix (and alternative endings)]

Other aspects of Mark's portrayal have been highlighted by redaction critics and by the more holistic readings of narrative critics. Among these the following provide an indication of Mark's distinctive story:

- *Jesus the enigma:* Jesus is not simply the suffering Son of Man; he is a deeply enigmatic figure, whom people regularly fail to understand. He is unpredictable, occasionally angry (for example, Mark 11.15–19), regularly puzzling. His message is disturbing and ambiguous; indeed, his teaching in parables is aimed at preventing people from understanding (4.12). Those who think they have begun to grasp him and his teaching, like Peter (as at 8.29–30), are suddenly wrong-footed. The warning to those who think of themselves as 'insiders' is that they might find themselves 'outsiders'.
- *Secrecy:* Related to this portrait of Jesus is the motif of secrecy, famously discussed by William Wrede in his 1901 classic *Das Messiasgeheimnis in den Evangelien* (English translation *The Messianic Secret*).[70] Jesus often diverts attention from himself (so 8.23), urges demons to be quiet about his identity (as at 3.12), and commands his disciples to say nothing about what they have seen until after his resurrection (for example at 9.9). Scholars disagree vehemently, however, as to the purpose (or purposes) of this secrecy motif.

- *The portrayal of the disciples:* Despite their initially positive portrayal, Jesus' own disciples, particularly the Twelve, increasingly fail to understand Jesus' enigmatic message. In the second half of the gospel, they are among the most hostile to the idea that the Messiah must suffer (indeed, Jesus calls Peter 'Satan' at 8.33!), and ultimately all desert him in his darkest hour (14.50). Yet there are more promising hints that this is not their final response (for example, 13.9–13; 16.7). For some scholars, Mark is using the disciples in order to correct misguided Christologies which give little place to the cross; for others, the text presents the disciples as characters in which implied readers will recognize themselves, their own potential failure, and the possibilities for change.[71]
- *Crossing boundaries:* Mark's Jesus is regularly crossing boundaries, both social and geographical. He offends traditional piety by touching the ritually unclean (so Mark 1.41), challenging interpretations of the sabbath laws (as at 2.23–8) or eating with sinners prior to repentance (for example 2.15). He also crosses that boundary separating God's holy people Israel from the Gentiles: first, by crossing the sea (4.35–41), and then by travelling north to Tyre and Sidon, where he is persuaded to act on behalf of a Syro-Phoenician woman (7.24–30).
- *Opposition:* Partly because of his transgression of boundaries, Jesus increasingly provokes opposition from his contemporaries. People from a number of Jewish groupings (such as Pharisees, Herodians, Sadducees) and occupations (for example, scribes, priests) object to his actions and challenge him in debate. One such collection of 'controversy stories' (Mark 2.13—3.6) culminates in the sinister editorial comment: 'The Pharisees went out and immediately conspired with the Herodians against him, how to destroy him.' This is picked up in Mark's passion narrative, where the chief priests, elders and scribes seek to have Jesus arrested.
- *Marginal Figures:* While the religious establishment is increasingly hostile to Jesus, and his own disciples fail to understand, other characters are able to understand what the good news might mean. These tend to be marginal figures, on the fringes or even beyond the boundaries of Israel's society: the ritually unclean, sinners, a pagan woman, a blind beggar. This unlikely band find their voice in the Roman centurion at the cross: the first human being in Mark to echo the heavenly voice in declaring Jesus 'Son of

God' (15.39). Whether he is speaking ironically, or failing to understand fully what this title might mean (the Greek could mean 'Truly this man was *a* son of God'), he becomes the vehicle of the narrator in articulating the truth about Jesus.

What kind of date and historical setting might account for Mark's Gospel? Dating of the gospels remains an inexact science. Nevertheless, a date in the late 60s is a reasonable assessment (particularly if there are echoes of the turbulent times after Nero's death, and the early years of the Jewish revolt against Rome, in Mark 13). Some scholars would date Mark after the fall of Jerusalem in 70 CE (though Mark 13 is not so obviously referring to those events as passages in Matthew and Luke).

As for Mark's location, two possibilities remain popular with scholars. The first would locate the evangelist in Rome, in the years after Nero's fierce persecution in that city following the fire of 64 CE, during which some Christians literally did 'take up their cross and follow' Jesus (Mark 8.34). Against such a background, the 'good news' of a suffering Messiah who is vindicated beyond death at the hands of Roman authorities would have a particular appeal. This is an appropriate scenario, and would account for the presence of Latin loanwords and idioms in the gospel, but it is not conclusive. An alternative scenario would locate Mark closer to the action of the Jewish revolt (and indeed of Jesus' own ministry): in Galilee, where Mark 16.7 suggests the future to be located, or in the wider area of Syria–Palestine.

To do

Read the following examples of Mark's 'sandwich' technique (sandwiching one story in between two halves of another, so that the two interpret one another): Mark 3.20–35; 5.21–43; 6.7–30; 11.12–26. In each case, write down what light you think the sandwiching sheds on the meaning of the two stories.

Matthew's Story

Most scholars think that Matthew's Gospel was written a decade or so after Mark, using Mark as one of its main sources (the events of 70 CE may well be reflected in Matthew 22.7). If so, then the author of Matthew can be viewed as the first commentator on Mark. He keeps the basic framework of Mark's story (Galilean ministry, followed by a journey to and activity in Jerusalem, culminating in Jesus' passion and death, and the discovery of the empty tomb), and approximately 90 per cent of Mark's content, but expands it significantly with additional material. He prefaces the appearance of John and Jesus with two chapters of narratives describing Jesus' origins and events surrounding his early life (these will be discussed further in Chapter 7). He is also one of those readers of Mark dissatisfied with Mark's ending. Hence he adds stories of appearances of the risen Jesus to his disciples (Matthew 28.9–20).

He also reorders material thematically rather than chronologically (as in the collection of miracle stories in Matthew 8—9), and uses repetitions (such as doublets of the same stories) and numerical patterns (especially sets of three) effectively. This makes Matthew's book all the more memorable: most Christians would remember Matthew's version of the Lord's Prayer ('Our Father, who art in heaven . . . ', Matthew 6.9) and the first Beatitude ('Blessed are the poor in spirit . . . ', Matthew 5.3) rather than Luke's alternatives. Matthew is an accomplished teacher.

But perhaps most striking is Matthew's addition of substantial blocks of teaching material. Mark claims that Jesus taught 'with authority' (for example Mark 1.22). Matthew spells out in greater detail the content of that teaching, arranging much of it systematically into five discourses (possibly paralleling the five books of Moses):

- Sermon on the Mount (Matthew 5—7)
- Missionary Discourse (Matthew 10)
- Parables Discourse (Matthew 13)
- Discourse on Life in the Community (Matthew 18)
- Eschatological Discourse (Matthew 24—5).

Thus Jesus is presented as the teacher *par excellence*, who resembles Israel's great teacher Moses (though occasionally trumping him). His rescue from a wicked king at his birth parallels the birth of Moses (Matthew 2.16–18; cf. Exodus 1—2); like Moses he comes out of Egypt (Matthew 2.19–23); when he interprets the Law in his Sermon on the Mount, there may be echoes of Moses' reception of the Law on Mount Sinai (Matthew 5.1; cf. Exodus 19.3); the shining of his face in Matthew's Transfiguration story echoes the shining of Moses' face on the mountain (Matthew 17.2; cf. Exodus 34.29–35). Yet Matthew's Jesus is more than a Moses figure, as Matthew's wide range of christological titles attests (such as Son of God, Son of Man, Son of David, Lord, Messiah, Wisdom).

Reflection

In his rewriting of Mark, Matthew tends to tie up loose ends, and replace ambiguity with clarity. What are the strengths and weaknesses of this representation of Jesus? Which do you prefer: the enigma and ambiguity of Mark, or the tidiness and clarity of Matthew? What do you think are the reasons for your preference?

The picture of Jesus in Moses' clothing highlights a wider feature of Matthew's story: the emphasis upon Jesus' Jewish credentials. Indeed, after Mark's rather radical Jesus who crosses sacred boundaries, Matthew has re-Judaized Jesus. In his teaching, he envisages that his followers will practise fasting (6.16), wear phylacteries (though not broad ones!) and prayer-shawls (though without long fringes, 23.5!), and keep the sabbath (24.20). His reworking of Mark also suggests he considers his audiences still bound by Jewish food laws. The relevant passage in Mark (part of Jesus' discussion about washing hands before eating) reads as follows:

He said to them, 'Then do you also fail to understand? Do you not see that whatever goes into a person from outside cannot defile, since it enters, not the heart but the stomach, and goes out into the sewer?' (*Thus he declared all foods clean.*) (Mark 7.18–19; italics mine)

In the parallel at Matthew 15.17, the editorial comment 'Thus he declared all foods clean' is conspicuous by its absence! Matthew, unlike Mark, does not understand Jesus' words as permitting non-kosher food such as pork.

Such a Jewish portrayal of Jesus provokes the question: for whom was Matthew writing? What kind of setting should we envisage for this gospel? In the ancient Church, Matthew was often viewed as a gospel written for the Jewish people, while Luke was the gospel for the Gentiles. In more recent scholarship (building upon W. D. Davies' influential book *The Setting of the Sermon on the Mount*),[72] the writing of Matthew has often been set against the background of Jewish developments after the loss of the Temple in 70 CE. Scholars speak of 'emerging Pharisaic Judaism', 'Jamnian Judaism' (after the Palestinian town Jamnia or Yavneh in which the Pharisees gathered under Yohanan ben-Zakkai), or 'formative Judaism' post-70 CE as the debating partner with which Matthew is engaged.[73] Both the Pharisees as the largest surviving party after 70 (often seen as the main antecedents of later rabbinic Judaism),[74] and Christian Jews like Matthew, are engaged in reconstructing a form of Judaism to survive the events of 70. Such a reading of Matthew's Gospel remains valid as insight into the context out of which Matthew emerges, despite criticisms from Richard Bauckham and others of the tendency to view the gospels as written for narrowly defined audiences.[75]

Matthew's Gospel is thus presenting his distinctly Christian Jewish view of what this might look like, consciously engaging with Pharisaic developments, such as increased focus on Torah as opposed to Temple, deeds of loving kindness as opposed to sacrifice, the increasing importance of the title 'rabbi', and the need to overcome internal dissent by strengthening community boundaries. In Matthew's alternative account, it is Jesus who takes the central role of Torah, not only definitively interpreting it (Matthew 5.21–48), but supplanting it as the locus of God's presence (as at 18.20). Like leading Pharisees such as Yohanan ben-Zakkai, Matthew's Jesus regards Hosea's prophecy 'I desire mercy and not sacrifice' as authoritative (Matthew 12.7, quoting Hosea 6.6), and regards almsgiving, prayer and fasting as central to religious practice (Matthew 6.1–18). In contrast to 'formative Judaism', Matthew's Jesus is adamant that the leaders of his community are not to be called 'rabbi' (Matthew 23.8). Finally, Matthew seems to write out of a situation of persecution of Jesus' followers by the synagogue authorities (for example, Matthew 5.10–12; 10.17, 23), perhaps reflecting the trend towards quashing internal dissent.

Where this evangelist might be located remains a matter of dispute, although Antioch in Syria is often proposed (Matthew's Gospel is known to Ignatius of Antioch early in the second century). Certainly the text seems to presuppose an urban environment, perhaps bilingual (though with Greek predominating), where Christians are living in close proximity with Pharisees and their synagogues, and continuing to observe some Jewish practices, but also have an eye towards a mission to Gentiles.

The Beginning of Luke's Story

The Gospel according to Luke also seems to be dependent upon Mark, though containing rather less of Mark's content than does Matthew (famously omitting Mark 6.45—8.26, for example). He also shares a good deal of material, mainly sayings of Jesus, with Matthew (variously explained by their independent use of Q and by Luke using Matthew). But Luke is far more than a compilation of various predecessors. He is an accomplished literary artist who weaves his material into sophisticated patterns. Moreover, he is a memorable storyteller, who captures his readers' imagination. The annunciation to Mary, the story of the shepherds, the parables of the Good Samaritan and the Prodigal Son, and the moving narrative of the Emmaus road, all come to us through the pen of Luke.

However, there is another more significant way in which Luke's Gospel differs from the other two synoptics: it is probably the first volume of a two-volume work, Luke–Acts. This fact is obscured in our New Testaments, which separate Luke from the Acts of the Apostles (John's Gospel standing between them). But many believe that the two books belong together, with similar themes and motifs running like threads between them:

- The spread of the gospel from an original Jewish to a wider Gentile world.
- The reconstitution of the ancient people of God, to include Gentiles and to account for a division within Israel.

- The prominence of the Holy Spirit, first in Jesus' ministry and then in the Church's mission.
- The importance of prayer, at key moments in Jesus' ministry and at strategic turning points in the Church's life.
- A prominent role for outcasts and the marginalized, both within and beyond Israel's boundaries.
- The offer of forgiveness of sins, with an emphasis upon repentance.
- The centrality of Jerusalem as the holy city where Christ must suffer, and as the focus for the renewed people of God.

Again, unlike Matthew and Mark, Luke is quite explicit in setting out his purpose, in a four-verse prologue:

Since many have undertaken to set down an orderly account of the events that have been fulfilled among us, just as they were handed on to us by those who from the beginning were eyewitnesses and servants of the word, I too decided, after investigating everything carefully from the very first, to write an orderly account for you, most excellent Theophilus, so that you may know the truth concerning the things about which you have been instructed. (Luke 1.1–4)

The elegant literary Greek of this prologue is somewhat ambiguous in places, but makes a number of points relevant to interpreting Luke:

- Luke seems somewhat dissatisfied with the work of his predecessors (which includes written accounts or 'narratives'), and is attempting something better.
- He has engaged in careful research, providing the ground for later claims that Luke is a historian.
- His chief witnesses are both 'eyewitnesses and servants (or ministers) of the word'. Two things follow from this: (a) Luke is not himself an eyewitness (traditionally he has been identified as a Gentile companion of Paul, as at Colossians 4.14); (b) he bases his work not simply on those who saw Jesus (such as Caiaphas or Pilate), but those who also preached the story of Jesus as good news.

- Luke's account is 'orderly' and well-structured: this does not necessarily mean, however, that it is in *chronological* order (and its order does differ in places from Mark's or Matthew's).
- Theophilus (probably the patron who paid for Luke's work to be published) seems to be a Christian, who needs assurance about the faith he has adopted (the verb translated 'instructed' in verse 4 may well refer to instruction in the faith or 'catechesis').

The memorable story begun by Luke in his first volume picks up on the motif of the road or journey prominent in Mark. For Luke, however, it assumes new proportions. Jesus' journey from Galilee to Jerusalem dominates no fewer than ten of Luke's 24 chapters (Luke 9.51—19.28), astounding for a journey which would have taken just a few days! The significance of this journey is underlined by Luke's solemn introduction: 'When the days drew near for him to be taken up, he set his face to go to Jerusalem' (Luke 9.51). On the level of Luke's narrative, this is a pilgrimage journey, in which Jesus and his disciples are joined by an increasing number of pilgrims heading to Jerusalem for Passover. Like pilgrims before and since, Luke knows that the journey is often as life-changing as the arrival at the pilgrim-shrine. Hence, it becomes the opportunity for the disciples (and Luke's readers) to be gradually changed by Jesus' teaching, which dominates this section of his gospel. We owe to Luke the insight that the Christian life is itself a journey, in which believers take up their cross 'daily' (Luke's addition at 9.23) in order to follow Jesus.

Yet this Jerusalem journey also echoes Israel's ancient Exodus journey whose beginning Passover commemorates. In Luke's addition to the Transfiguration story, Moses and Elijah speak with Jesus about 'his departure (Greek *exodos*), which he was about to accomplish at Jerusalem' (Luke 9.31). In the Jerusalem journey, Jesus relives the experience of the ancient people, as he gathers a new Exodus generation around him, and completes that Exodus through his suffering and death. Finally, this journey to Jerusalem becomes a springboard for other transforming journeys: the journey from Jerusalem to Emmaus, for example (Luke 24.13–35), or Paul's missionary journeys, which bring God's grace to the wider Gentile world.

One further issue relating to Luke's Gospel is worth raising: what is its stance vis-à-vis the Roman world? Luke–Acts has often been read as a pro-Roman text, keen to show the authorities that Christians represent no threat to the stability of the empire. Scholars point to Luke's positive portrayal of Roman officials (for example, centurions at Capernaum, Jerusalem and Caesarea). Nevertheless, there are more subtle features which could offer a subversive critique of Roman imperial ideology. One example is Luke's story of Jesus' birth, when set against claims made for the ruling emperor at that time, Augustus. Augustus was acclaimed as 'Saviour', and to him was attributed the establishment of peace (the *Pax Romana*) across the Mediterranean world. A famous inscription referring to Augustus' birth, found in a number of cities of Asia Minor, gives a flavour of these claims:

> the birthday of the god [the Saviour Augustus] heralded the beginning of good news [or *gospels*] for the whole world

Against this background, the message of the angels in Luke's nativity account assumes a further resonance:

> But the angel said to them, 'Do not be afraid; for see – I am bringing you good news of great joy for all the people: to you is born this day in the city of David a Saviour, who is the Messiah, the Lord. . . . ' And suddenly there was with the angel a multitude of the heavenly host, praising God and saying,
>   'Glory to God in the highest heaven,
>   and on earth peace among those whom he favours!'
>   (Luke 2.10–11, 13–14)

To do

Read the story of Jesus in the Nazareth synagogue at Luke 4.16–30. Note down any themes and phrases which seem to you important about this story. How many of these are themes distinctive to Luke (see above)?

Reading Synoptically

Having sketched out in broad terms the distinctive voices of the three synoptic gospels, the last section of this chapter will give you an opportunity to explore how this might work at the micro-level. The following example (in the RSV translation) has been chosen because it is contained in all three synoptic gospels, and is given a distinctive interpretation in each (the extra material common to Matthew and Luke is in italics, and points of difference in this extra material are in bold):

Matthew 12.38–42	Mark 8.11–12	Luke 11.29–32
Then some of the scribes and Pharisees said to him, 'Teacher, we wish to see a sign from you.'	The Pharisees came and began to argue with him, seeking from him a sign from heaven, to test him.	
But he answered them,	And he sighed deeply in his spirit, and said,	When the crowds were increasing, he began to say, 'This generation
'An evil and adulterous	'Why does this generation	is an evil generation;
generation seeks for a sign	seek a sign?	It seeks a sign;
but no sign shall be given to it *except*	Truly, I say to you, no sign shall be given to this generation.'	but no sign shall be given to it *except*
the sign of **the prophet** *Jonah. For as Jonah* **was** **three days and three** **nights in the belly of** the whale, *so shall the* *Son of man be* **three** **days and three nights** **in the heart of the earth.** *The men of Nineveh will*		*the sign of Jonah.* *For as Jonah* **became a** **sign to the men of** **Nineveh,** *so will the* *Son of man be* **to** **this generation.**

arise at the judgement
with this generation and
condemn it; for they
repented at the preaching
of Jonah, and behold,
something greater than
Jonah is here.
The queen of the South
will arise at the
judgement
with this
generation and condemn
it; for she came from
the ends of the earth
to hear the wisdom of
Solomon, and behold,
something greater than
Solomon is here.

The queen of the South
will arise at the
judgement
with the men of this
generation and condemn
them; for she came from
the ends of the earth
to hear the wisdom of
Solomon, and behold,
something greater than
Solomon is here.
The men of Nineveh
will arise at the
judgement with this
generation and condemn
it; for they repented at
the preaching of Jonah,
and behold, something
greater than Jonah is
here.

The following are among the questions raised by studying these three accounts synoptically:

• What does this passage suggest about the relationship between the gospels? Is Mark's shorter version earlier, or later? Is the material shared by Matthew and Luke due to one being the source for the other, or to their independent use of Q?

- At what point in each gospel does this scene come? How does it fit into the wider narrative?
- Who is Jesus speaking to in each of the three accounts? How might one account for the differences?
- In Matthew's account, the scribes and Pharisees address Jesus as 'Teacher'. Who else calls Jesus 'Teacher' in Matthew's Gospel? Do his disciples ever do so?
- Is it a problem that in Mark Jesus refuses any sign, whereas in Matthew and Luke he promises the sign of Jonah?
- What does Matthew understand by the sign of Jonah? What does Luke understand by it? How might this fit into their distinctive messages?
- Who are 'the men of Nineveh', and who is 'the queen of the South'? What Old Testament narratives are being evoked here?
- What attitude are the implied readers to have towards 'signs'?

Further Reading

Stephen C. Barton (ed.), 2006, *The Cambridge Companion to the Gospels*, Cambridge: Cambridge University Press.

Mark Goodacre, 2001, *The Synoptic Problem: A Way through the Maze*, London and New York: Sheffield Academic Press.

E. P. Sanders and Margaret Davies, 1989, *Studying the Synoptic Gospels*, London: SCM Press/Philadelphia: Trinity Press International.

Graham Stanton, 2002, *The Gospels and Jesus*, 2nd edition; Oxford: Oxford University Press.

6

John: The 'Spiritual Gospel'

The Eagle has Landed

Moving from the synoptics to the Gospel of John is like moving into another world. Its profound meditation upon the incarnation of the Word or Logos, its offer of eternal life in and through that Word-made-flesh, and its division of the cosmos into light and darkness, give John's narrative an almost mystical feel. Clement of Alexandria, writing in the late second century, famously described the Fourth Gospel in this way:

> But last of all, John, perceiving that the external facts had been made plain in the Gospel, being urged by his friends, and inspired by the Spirit, composed a spiritual Gospel. (Clement, cited in Eusebius, *Historia Ecclesiastica* 6.14.7)[76]

For Clement, the three synoptics present the 'external facts' or 'bodily things' (*ta sōmatika*). John, however, complements them by taking us more deeply into the events, drawing out their spiritual significance.

To use another analogy, adopted by St Jerome (*c.*340–420), John is symbolized by the eagle (one of the four creatures around the heavenly throne in Revelation 4). His theology gives us the eagle's view, just as the grandeur of his language soars eagle-like above the earth. This is the perspective encountered in his very first words, which take us not to John the baptizer by the Jordan (as Mark), nor even to Jesus' conception and birth (as Matthew and Luke), but to the very dawn of creation, echoing the opening words of the Bible itself:

> In the beginning was the Word,
> and the Word was with God,
> and the Word was God.
> He was in the beginning with God.
> All things came into being through him,
> and without him not one thing came into being. (John 1.1–3)

Yet for all its spiritual profundity, and its heavenly vantage-point, John's book is arguably also the 'earthiest' of the gospels. First, it locates the revelation of God firmly within the human life of Jesus of Nazareth, and presents earthly realities – water, bread, wine, even mud – as vehicles of divine healing and life. But more significantly, John's Gospel emerges out of the cut-and-thrust of ferocious debates – and a certain amount of name-calling – between the followers of Jesus and a group John calls 'the Jews' or 'the Judeans' (Greek *hoi Ioudaioi*). This 'spiritual gospel', then, is also a highly polemical gospel. Reading it, one cannot help but feel that the eagle has well and truly landed.

The Distinctiveness of John

We will begin by exploring some of the Fourth Gospel's distinctive features. Even a cursory reading of John will reveal a significant gulf between his presentation of Jesus and those of Matthew, Mark and Luke (which for all their differences share a family resemblance). We have already noted the contrast between John's exalted beginning – with God, prior to creation – and the openings of the synoptic gospels. Other differences between John and the synoptics include the following:

- *Dualism:* John's Gospel paints the world in dualistic terms: light and darkness; truth and falsehood; heavenly and earthly; life and death. This is not a thoroughgoing theological dualism, for God remains the Creator (as at 1.1–5), and the powers of darkness are not his equal match (as at 12.31). Nor does it rule out human beings moving from the darkness to the light (as at 9.1–7), or indeed vice versa. Rather this seems to be a 'dualism of decision': John's audiences are presented with two sharp alternatives, only one of which is positively described (many find this one of the Fourth Gospel's most problematic aspects).
- *Miracle Stories:* although John shares with the synoptics an interest in Jesus' miracles, he describes far fewer, and deals with them at greater length. John refers to them as 'signs', or (on the lips of Jesus) 'works' (as at 5.36), and they are often performed in order to elicit faith (as at 2.11) rather than as a response to faith. As 'signs', they point beyond themselves, to who Jesus is, and what the life he offers is like.
- *Words of Jesus:* although there are some longer speeches attributed to Jesus in the synoptics (for example, Matthew 5—7; Mark 13), they normally portray Jesus talking in short, pithy sayings about the kingdom of God. In John, Jesus speaks in long, meditative discourses, normally about himself and his relationship to the Father. Notable among his words in John are the so-called 'I am' sayings (for example, 'I am the bread of life', 6.35; 'I am the light of the world', 8.12).
- *Parables:* whereas the synoptic Jesus regularly speaks in parables, these are all but lacking in John's Gospel. The nearest we find to parables in John are the figures of the Good Shepherd in John 10 and the Vine in John 15.
- *Christology:* John's Jesus is the one who has come down from heaven, a stranger who hardly seems to belong here. He is the unique Son of the Father (unlike Paul, John does not call believers 'sons of God', but 'children', Greek *tekna*). He not only speaks in a distinctive way; he has divine foreknowledge (as at 2.24–5), as one who has come from the Father and has seen what the Father does. This 'foreignness' makes his words and actions all the more enigmatic.
- *Special vocabulary:* John's Gospel has a number of favourite words (some of them also found in the Johannine Epistles). We have already noted the dualistic 'light' and 'darkness', 'truth' and 'falsehood'. Others include:

'life' or 'eternal life' (John's distinctive way of speaking about salvation, 'life in its fullness'); 'glory' (the presence of God found in Jesus); 'the world' (humanity at enmity with God).

• *Misunderstanding and irony:* John regularly employs ambiguous Greek phrases, which characters misunderstand. Nicodemus is told, for example, that he must be born *anōthen*. This Greek word could mean 'again' (Nicodemus' understanding, 3.4), but Jesus means it as 'from above', that is, in a heavenly way, by water and the Spirit (3.5–6). Again, Jesus offers the Samaritan woman *hudōr zōn* (4.10). The woman misunderstands him to be speaking of 'fresh water' or 'spring water' (hence her comical response at 4.11: 'Sir, you have no bucket'); Jesus is speaking of 'living water'. Other characters ironically say more than they mean: for example, the high priest says of Jesus that it is better for one man to die for the people, articulating a theological interpretation of Jesus' death (11.50–2).

Table 16: The Johannine Signs.

1. Wedding at Cana (2.1–11): lack of wine

2. Healing of Official's Son (4.46–53): at point of death

3. Healing of Paralytic (5.2–9): ill for 38 years

4. Multiplication of Loaves (6.1–14): lack of food

[5. Walking on Water (6.16–21)]

6. Healing of Man born Blind (9.1–12): in state of darkness from birth

7. Raising of Lazarus (11.17–44): dead for four days

Moreover, there are significant differences in content and chronology. For example, although John also recounts John the baptizer's activity, we are not told that he baptizes Jesus, nor does he disappear from the scene before Jesus begins his ministry. On the other hand, it is from the baptizer's circles, down by the river Jordan, that Jesus' first disciples emerge, including Andrew, Simon Peter's brother (John 1.35–42; contrast the call of the first disciples in Matthew 4.18–22//Mark 1.16–20; Luke 5.1–11). Unlike the fairly simple synoptic division between Jesus' Galilean ministry and his final days in Jerusalem, John has Jesus moving backwards and forwards between Galilee and Jerusalem throughout his gospel, and describes activity in the wider territory of Judea. Given the expectation on pious male Jews to attend pilgrimage festivals in Jerusalem, it is possible that John is more historically correct here than his synoptic counterparts.

There are other chronological differences. John locates Jesus' driving out of money-changers from the Temple towards the beginning of his ministry (John 2.13–22), not at the end as in all three synoptics. The timing of Jesus' crucifixion is also different: not during the Passover festival, as in the other gospels, but on the day before, the 'Day of Preparation' (John 19.31). This enables John to present Jesus as the true Paschal Lamb, given that it was on the afternoon of this day that the Passover lambs were slaughtered.

> ### Reflection
>
> What are the implications of John differing from the synoptics in his chronology? Does it matter? Should one attempt to reconcile their respective chronologies? Or is theological vision more important than chronological precision? If you were to prefer one chronology, on what grounds would you choose between them?

Why the Differences?

A number of explanations (not necessarily mutually exclusive) have been given for John's distinctive language and imagery. Among the commonest are the following:

- *Different Traditions:* though there may be some overlap with synoptic-type traditions, a number of scholars explain the differences by John's use of independent traditions.[77] Sometimes, though not always, this is tied up with the identity of the 'disciple whom Jesus loved' as the author or source behind the tradition.
- *Cultural Background:* the distinctiveness is often explained in terms of the

theological or philosophical milieu of the evangelist or the tradition on which he draws. Bultmann famously posited Gnosticism, drawing on later Mandaean texts in his commentary on John.[78] Other suggestions include the wider Hellenistic world. More recent commentators, in the light of the Dead Sea Scrolls and study of other Jewish sectarian literature, have located John more firmly within 'dissenting Judaism' of the late Second Temple period.[79]

- *Audience:* some have seen the needs of the intended audience as accounting for the distinctiveness of John's language. For example, an appeal to the wider religious world might have influenced John's Logos theology (speculation about the divine Logos being widespread in Greek thought). A similar universal appeal may be reflected in the use of archetypal symbols such as water and light.

If one can speak of a scholarly consensus, it would seem to be that we do not need to look beyond the world of first-century Jewish Palestine to find the seeds for John's distinctive language and imagery. The division of humans, and human communities, according to their association with either the light or the darkness, for example, can be found in the Qumran scrolls (for example 1QS 1 and 3). Moreover, the 'bitter squabbles' attested in the gospel between disciples of Jesus and 'the Jews' point to the intra-Jewish nature of the debate.

This does not necessarily mean that the Fourth Gospel was composed in its present form in Palestine (traditionally, it has been linked with Ephesus, for example), nor that it does not also reflect attempts to engage with the wider non-Jewish world. However, the origins of this gospel, and the tradition which it represents, seem well-rooted in the diverse and often volatile soil of Jewish Palestine in the early to mid-first century CE.

To do

Read John 3.16–21. Note down any distinctive Johannine words and themes. Are there any words or phrases which are unclear? If so, look them up in a commentary on this passage.

Literary Difficulties

Mention has just been made of John's Gospel 'in its present form'. John's distinctive themes, vocabulary and style might lead one to conclude that it is all of a piece, like the seamless robe removed from Jesus prior to his crucifixion (John 19.23). However, there are clues that this gospel is the end result of a complex literary process, leading one famous scholar to liken it to a patchwork 'coat of many colours'.[80] These include the following:

- The Prologue has a poetic, hymn-like quality (interwoven with more prosaic statements about John the baptizer, for example John 1.6–8), leading some to suggest that it was missing in an earlier edition of the gospel.
- John 6 breaks the narrative flow between John 5 and 7 (note especially the sharp disjunction between 5.47, where Jesus is in Jerusalem, and 6.1, where he crosses the Sea of Galilee).
- John 6 also seems to have been re-edited, to draw out further layers of the 'bread of life' symbolism (for example, the explicit eucharistic references at 6.53–6).
- John 15—17 breaks the continuity between John 13—14 and 18 (see for example 14.31 and 18.1), and chapters 15—16 repeat material found in chapter 14.
- John 21 (with its post-resurrection story of a miraculous catch of fish, a feeding and the rehabilitation of Peter) looks like an addition, added to an original ending at 20.30–1. It concludes with a second ending (21.24–5), with its own assessment of the beloved disciple's role.

These features have been attributed variously to dislocation (pages of an early codex being put together in the wrong order, or being reordered by an editor), poor redaction of disparate sources, and the final editing of an 'ecclesiastical redactor' adding more 'orthodox' touches to a non-mainstream gospel (for example the sacramental references in John 6). In particular, a good case has been made by a number of recent Johannine scholars such as J. Louis Martyn, Raymond Brown and John Ashton for the Fourth Gospel having undergone several editions and redactions to achieve its present form. These would have been produced either by the evangelist himself or by members of his community in basic sympathy with his theological outlook, responding to new challenges.

> ## To do
>
> Read John 21, asking yourself what it adds to a gospel ending at John 20.31. Note down your answers. What purpose might this addition serve? What might have prompted someone (the evangelist or another author) to add it? Are there indications that it is the work of more than one hand?

Exploring John's Story

For all its literary complexity, and the profundity of its theology, the basic structure of John's story is relatively simple. After the Prologue, the story falls into two parts, often referred to as the Book of Signs (John 1—12) and the Book of Glory (John 13—20/21). In the Book of Signs, Jesus is revealed to his own people, attested by a number of witnesses such as John the baptizer. It is so called because of the miracles or 'signs' which permeate this section, through which Jesus reveals his glory. Inroads are also made into the Samaritan world, through a woman of Samaria who becomes an evangelist to her own people (John 4.1–42). This section of the gospel culminates in some Greeks (thought by many scholars to be representatives of the non-Jewish world) coming to see Jesus (12.20–2).

The Book of Glory, which begins at 13.1, can be subdivided into two. John 13—17, often known as the Farewell Discourses, describe Jesus' words and actions at the Last Supper (though lacking any words over the bread and the cup). Here we have a sense of Jesus focusing his revelation on his disciples, behind closed doors, preparing them for his departure. John 18—20 then parallels the synoptics by describing Christ's passion, death, the discovery of the empty tomb and resurrection appearances. Even here, John provides his own distinctive perspective on these familiar events, drawing out their theological significance and meditative potential.

We have already noted the chronological differences between John and the synoptics, with John departing from the neat synoptic pattern of a Galilean ministry followed by one journey to Jerusalem. If there is an organizing factor to Jesus' travels in this gospel, it is liturgical. John's narrative is structured around the Jewish festival calendar:

- Passover (2.13), when Jesus casts the merchants out of the Jerusalem Temple;
- an unnamed Feast of the Jews (5.1), when Jesus heals a paralysed man on a sabbath;
- a second Passover (6.4), when Jesus feeds the multitude in Galilee;
- the Feast of Tabernacles or Booths (7.2), when Jesus returns to Jerusalem;
- the Feast of Dedication (10.22), while Jesus is still in Jerusalem;
- a third Passover (12.1), when Jesus' arrest, passion and death occur.

But the Fourth Gospel does not simply use these festivals to orientate Jesus' ministry chronologically. It also presents Jesus as the one who fulfils the hopes and expectations they evoke. Those of us less familiar with Jewish festivals may miss some of the allusions John makes. John's original audiences, however, would have understood them well. Passover associations, for example, included God feeding his people with manna in the wilderness (evoked by Jesus' feeding of the five thousand in John 6) and the liberation of God's people through the death of the Passover lamb (linked to the death of Jesus, the true Passover Lamb in John 19).

Similarly, two major rituals performed in first-century Jerusalem during Tabernacles or Sukkoth were the lighting of lamps in the Court of the Women, and the daily procession of water from the Pool of Siloam. Those from a Jewish background hearing John would appreciate the significance of Jesus declaring himself the Light of the World during Sukkoth (8.12), and standing up on the last day of the festival to proclaim: 'Let anyone who is thirsty come to me, and let the one who believes in me drink' (7.37–8a).

> **To do**
>
> Find out what you can about the Feast of Dedication (Hanukkah) and its associations. In the light of your research, read John 10, especially 10.22–39; note down any possible allusions to Hanukkah, and what John's narrative might mean as a result.

'The Jews' in John

The Fourth Gospel's focus upon Jesus' fulfilment of Jewish festivals and other institutions (such as the purification rites and the sabbath) has its darker side. John's Jesus might be understood not simply as fulfilling what these celebrations promise, but actually replacing them. This ambiguity is thrown into sharper relief by the gospel's negative portrayal of a group called in Greek *hoi Ioudaioi*, normally translated into English as 'the Jews'. John's Gospel presents a 'them and us' mentality, in which Jesus and his disciples, and even the crowds, are generally to be distinguished from *hoi Ioudaioi*. Translated as 'the Jews', this can sound decidedly odd: Jesus, his mother, John the baptizer, Jesus' followers cease to be 'Jewish', despite their obvious ethnic origin and religious observance. Examples include the following:

This is the testimony given by John when the Jews sent priests and Levites from Jerusalem to ask him, 'Who are you?' (John 1.19)

After this Jesus went about in Galilee. He did not wish to go about in Judea because the Jews were looking for an opportunity to kill him. (John 7.1)

The Jews did not believe that he had been blind and had received his sight until they called the parents of the man who had received his sight and asked them, 'Is this your son, who you say was born blind? How then does he now see?' (John 9.18–19)

Then after this he said to his disciples, 'Let us go to Judea again.' The disciples said to him, 'Rabbi, the Jews were just now trying to stone you, and are you going there again?' (John 11.7–8)

'Little children, I am with you only a little longer. You will look for me; and as I said to the Jews so now I say to you, "Where I am going, you cannot come."' (John 13.33)

However, this Johannine tendency ceases to be simply odd, and becomes decidedly dangerous, when the Fourth Gospel is read in a context where Judaism and Christianity have become separate religions, and Christians the dominant majority with political influence over a Jewish minority. The reception history of John's Gospel provides enough examples of anti-Jewish readings and their dark consequences to make this issue a serious one for responsible interpreters. How is one to deal with the portrayal of *hoi Ioudaioi* in the Fourth Gospel?

First, contextualizing the passages is crucial to interpretation. In some cases, the phrase simply describes Jewish practices (for example 'a festival of the Jews'), without necessarily having negative connotations. When describing a particular set of characters in the narrative, however, *hoi Ioudaioi* generally refers to a group separate from, and hostile to, Jesus and his disciples. Moreover, these seem to be in a position of authority and leadership. However, there are two exceptions. On the one hand, John provides a few positive usages. Jesus himself is identified by the Samaritan woman as a *Ioudaios* (4.9), and he tells her that 'salvation is from the Jews' (*ek tōn Ioudaiōn*, 4.22). Moreover, throughout the Passion Narrative, Jesus is acclaimed as 'king of the Jews' (*ho basileus tōn Ioudaiōn*, as at 19.3). Though the usage is ironic, John leaves us in no doubt that Jesus is indeed a king, with a crown (of thorns), regal attire (a purple robe), and a royal throne (the cross). On the other hand, perhaps the most negative passage is addressed not to *hoi Ioudaioi* in general but to a subgroup. The sinister charge 'You are from your father the devil' (8.44) is made specifically against '*hoi Ioudaioi* who had believed in him' (8.31). It is unclear whether they still believe in him (the Greek perfect tense would suggest so), or have now fallen away from faith (taking the perfect as a pluperfect), hence being the particular target of John's animosity.

Second, the issue of translation is significant. Given the general application of the term to those with authority, some commentators suggest we should translate *hoi Ioudaioi* quite specifically as 'the Jewish leaders'. If this is what John means, however, one might ask why he is not more specific (as he can be, for example at 7.48; 11.46–7). An alternative suggestion, recognizing that the Greek word *Ioudaios* and the English word Jew are both derived from the tribe of 'Judah', is that *hoi Ioudaioi* be translated 'the Judeans': either those from that geographical area (though see 6.41, where *hoi Ioudaioi* are in Galilee) or ideologically committed to Judea and its Temple-focused economy. If one opts for the traditional translation 'the Jews', one needs to be aware of the wider contextual issues mentioned above.

Third, the environment within which the Fourth Gospel emerges is important for interpretation. We are almost certainly hearing the story of Jesus told from the much later perspective of separation from the synagogue (as at 9.22), after the bitter experience of family splits, mutual suspicion, and possible persecution of Christian Jewish missionaries by synagogue authorities (as at 16.2). Thus the language of John is the polemical language of a threatened minority against the majority of which they were recently a part (John Ashton describes them as 'fierce family rows').[81]

However, this does not allow us to disengage ourselves from the dark reception history of John's *hoi Ioudaioi* passages, which has fed into later centuries of European antisemitism. There is a direct line between John 8.44, for example, and a German children's book produced under the Nazis: *Der Vater der Juden is der Teufel* ('The Father of the Jews is the Devil').[82] Awareness of this history, and ways in which it is still perpetuated today, must play a part in contemporary interpretation of John's *hoi Ioudaioi* passages. Christians who continue to hear John's Passion Story during the liturgy of Holy Week have a particular responsibility to ensure awareness of the tragic consequences of this reception history, and to keep the above contextual issues at the forefront of contemporary preaching and catechesis.

To do

Read the story of Jesus' arrest and crucifixion in John 18—19. Note all the references to 'the Jews' (*hoi Ioudaioi*), and the different ways in which this phrase is used. Are all of them negative? Is there justification for identifying them with the Jewish leadership? How might you explain the portrayal of 'the Jews' in this section to a Jewish friend?

Was there a Johannine Community?

Imagine an elderly man, full of memories of distant events, pondering over those events in the light of the wisdom of his years. As his earthly life begins to ebb away, he commits these memories to writing. Such is the traditional image of John the evangelist (identified since the second century with John the apostle), composing his gospel in Ephesus towards the end of the first century.

As we have seen, recent scholars have posited a more complex process of composition, with two or more editions and several hands at work. In this view, the 'author' of the gospel is less a physical author who composed all 21 chapters than the 'authority figure' whose testimony the Fourth Gospel preserves. Scholars often distinguish between this beloved disciple (the unnamed 'disciple whom Jesus loved'), the evangelist who preserved his tradition in a written gospel, and other redactors belonging to the same Christian community, responsible for the gospel's final editing. Indeed, there is a strong emphasis upon community memory, preserving and reflecting more deeply on the traditions springing from the beloved disciple.

Since the second half of the twentieth century, scholars have often spoken of a 'Johannine Community' as the group around the beloved disciple, responsible for the production of the Fourth Gospel and other Johannine writings (the three Letters of John, and in some reconstructions also the book of Revelation). In this view, John's Gospel presents a kind of allegory of the history of this community – from its origins within the wider Jewish community to its fierce expulsion from the synagogue and beyond – under the guise of the story of Jesus. A pioneer of this kind of reading strategy was J. Louis Martyn, in his 1968 book *History and Theology in the Fourth Gospel*.[83]

John 9 (the story of the man born blind) provides Martyn with his way into this 'two-level' reading. Though containing a synoptic-like healing story, it quickly develops into a debate about sabbath observance, and then a full-blown drama in which the characters are divided into various groups, according to their attitude towards Jesus. On the side of Jesus are the disciples and the blind man; the Pharisees and *hoi Ioudaioi* are against him; there are also people sitting on the fence such as the neighbours of the man, the witnesses to the healing, and the blind man's own parents. Most significant for Martyn is a puzzling verse, which he takes as evidence for a fierce expulsion of followers of Jesus from the synagogue:

> for the Jews had already agreed that anyone who confessed Jesus to be the Messiah would be put out of the synagogue. (John 9.22)

Having read John 9 in this way, Martyn applied this reading strategy to other sections of the gospel, developing a three-stage theory of the history of the Johannine Community. Martyn's work has been developed, and refined by others, notably Raymond Brown and John Ashton.[84] Brown's 1979 reconstruction also drew upon the evidence of the Johannine Epistles (which he regarded as later than John's Gospel), positing a four-stage history of the Johannine Community from its origins in Judaism to a community schism over christological beliefs.

More recently, this kind of allegorical reading has faced significant criticism. The collection edited by Richard Bauckham famously challenged approaches to all four gospels which regarded them as composed for the evangelists' own communities.[85] The arguments of Bauckham and his colleagues need to be taken seriously, and have forced Johannine scholars to sharpen up their arguments. But not all have been persuaded that their arguments undermine the 'Johannine Community' thesis. First-century religious groups were quite capable of producing texts – and not just letters – for internal consumption, while the Johannine Epistles point to groups of first-century Christians who shared a distinctive 'Johannine' vision and vocabulary, even if they were not in total isolation from other types of Christians. Nevertheless, the 'Johannine Community' question, and the wider hermeneutical question about the legitimacy of such 'two-level' reading strategies for John, continue to be on the agenda of scholarly study of this most fascinating of gospels.[86]

Further Reading

John Ashton, 1991, *Understanding the Fourth Gospel*, Oxford: Clarendon Press, new edition 2007.

Raymond E. Brown, 1979, *The Community of the Beloved Disciple*, London: Geoffrey Chapman.

Warren Carter, 2006, *John: Storyteller, Interpreter, Evangelist*, Peabody, Massachusetts: Hendrickson.

Ruth Edwards, 2003, *Discovering John*, London: SPCK.

D. Moody Smith, 1995, *The Theology of the Gospel of John*, New Testament Theology; Cambridge: Cambridge University Press.

7

From the Cradle to the (Empty) Grave

Beginning at the End

It may seem puzzling to begin a chapter on the narratives of Jesus' birth, death and resurrection, not with the beginning of his earthly life, but with its end. Yet most New Testament scholars believe that this is the order in which these stories were written. If we look at our earliest Christian sources – the letters of Paul – as well as traditions about the original Jerusalem community in Acts, the heart of the early Christian preaching seems to have been on the death and resurrection of Jesus:

> For I decided to know nothing among you except Jesus Christ, and him crucified. (1 Corinthians 2.2)

> For I handed on to you as of first importance what I in turn had received: that Christ died for our sins in accordance with the scriptures, and that he was buried, and that he was raised on the third day in accordance with the scriptures, and that he appeared to Cephas, then to the twelve. (1 Corinthians 15.3–5)

> Grace to you and peace from God our Father and the Lord Jesus Christ, who gave himself for our sins to set us free from the present evil age, according to the will of our God and Father. (Galatians 1.3–4)

It will be reckoned to us who believe in him who raised Jesus our Lord from the dead, who was handed over to death for our trespasses and was raised for our justification. (Romans 4.24–5)

Therefore let the entire house of Israel know with certainty that God has made him both Lord and Messiah, this Jesus whom you crucified. (Acts 2.36)

This chapter will therefore consider these earliest stories first: stories, woven together from Christian memory and experience, tradition and interpretation, describing what happened to Jesus at the end of his earthly life. It will explore some of the issues raised by the narratives of Jesus' suffering and death (the Passion Narratives), and the strange events described after his death (the Resurrection Narratives). Aspects of the stories surrounding Jesus' birth and upbringing (the Birth or Infancy Narratives) will then be considered. These stories seem to have emerged later in the gospel tradition: they are found in Matthew and Luke but not in Mark, and also – in more developed forms – in later apocryphal writings such as the *Infancy Gospel of Thomas* (not to be confused with the better-known *Gospel of Thomas*).

To do

Read 1 Corinthians 15.3–8, believed to contain one of the earliest Christian creeds (perhaps learned by Paul from Jerusalem). Note the various elements of this creed: what does it consider important? What is said, and what isn't? How are Christ's death and resurrection being understood at this early stage? What is the significance of the names mentioned in relation to appearances of the risen Jesus?

The Emergence of the Passion Story

Judging by the reaction of Jesus' first disciples to his arrest, the passion and death of Jesus seems to have been unexpected. Indeed, there is little evidence that first-century Jews expected a Messiah who would suffer and die. Yet from an early stage, Christians felt the need to remember what happened to Jesus in the last days of his earthly life, and to make sense of those events theologically. The early creed just mentioned claims that 'Christ died for our sins in accordance with the scriptures' (1 Corinthians 15.3). This interprets Jesus' death as a sacrifice, foretold in the Old Testament. Scholars are uncertain as to which scriptures are envisaged, although the description of the Suffering Servant in Isaiah 53 is a prime candidate. Here we have an example of early Christians, in the light of Jesus' suffering and death, rereading old passages in a new way. Similarly in Romans, Paul interprets a line from Psalm 69 as referring to Christ's passion (Romans 15.3: 'The insults of those who insult you have fallen on me'). Interestingly, Psalm 69 is one of those key psalms (along with Psalm 22) alluded to throughout the gospel Passion Narratives.

How early a narrative account of these events emerged is a debated point. Certainly many point to Mark's Gospel as evidence for an early written form of the Passion Narrative. The contrast between the loosely connected, episodic nature of the bulk of Mark's Gospel, and the coherence of his passion story (Mark 14—16) with its precise time references and links between scenes, is a major piece of evidence. One might also point to the fact that John's Passion Narrative, for all its differences and apparent independence of the synoptics, shares with them a basic framework and sequence of events. This may be evidence for variant forms of the passion story prior to the composition of the gospels. Some point to the importance of scriptural reflection for the development of the passion tradition; others to the testimony of eyewitnesses (though certain elements of the story, such as Jesus' private prayer in Gethsemane, are not easily accounted for in this way). Still others have looked to Christian worship – specifically the liturgical commemoration of Christ's death during the Jewish Passover celebration – as the context within which the Passion Narrative might first have developed.[87]

However one accounts for their origin, the Passion Narratives have continued to move and fascinate both believers and unbelievers across the centuries. Artists as diverse as El Greco, Matthias Grünewald and Salvador Dali have attempted to paint scenes from this story; composers such as Johann Sebastian Bach and John Stainer have enabled them to be performed musically; while their dramatic potential has fed into the Holy Week Liturgy, the Oberammergau Passion Play, and Mel Gibson's *The Passion of the Christ*. Scholars too have approached them from several different angles, addressing the variety of issues they raise:

- *Historical questions:* How far do these narratives deliver a reliable presentation of the events? Who was ultimately responsible for the death of Jesus (the Romans, or the Jewish authorities, or both)? On what day was Jesus crucified: during Passover (as in the synoptics), or the day before Passover began (as in John)? Was there a practice, as the gospels claim, of a prisoner being released at Passover? How historical are the accounts of Jesus' trial before the Sanhedrin (which seem to contradict Jewish law governing capital trials)?
- *Issues of tradition and redaction*: Given the variations between the four accounts, is it possible to trace the development of the pre-gospel tradition, or (by comparing the accounts and positing literary relationships between them) how the evangelists have redacted their material? This is particularly the case with the portrayal of the Jewish leaders, who seem to take on a more sinister role in the later gospels. For example, Matthew's account has heightened their negative role through his insertion of the story of Judas and the blood money (Matthew 26.14–16; 27.3–10), and explicitly calls the testimony they seek against Jesus 'false testimony' (Matthew 26.59; cf. Mark 14.55).
- *Use of the Old Testament:* The Passion Narratives seem to be shaped by creative interplay between historical memory and Old Testament scripture, reflecting early attempts to make sense of Jesus' suffering and death. Scholars debate the extent to which they represent 'prophecy historicized' (so for example John Dominic Crossan) or 'history remembered' (so Raymond E. Brown).[88] Certainly the theme of fulfilment of scripture runs like a thread through all four gospels. Psalms which speak of righteous suffering (such as Psalms 22 and 69) have played a key role, generally through allusion rather than explicit citation (as in the dividing of Jesus' garments by the Roman soldiers, and the giving of vinegar and gall). Echoes of Isaiah's Servant Songs have also been detected. Sometimes, there are explicit quotations from the Old Testament (notably in John's account, for example John 19.24, 28, 36–7).

- *Theological issues:* How do the individual evangelists understand God to be at work in the dreadful events of Jesus' last hours? What meaning is there in Jesus' suffering and death? This theological concern is partly tied up with the evangelists' use of the Old Testament, as they use scripture as their hermeneutical lens. But it is reflected in their overarching vision of these events, and the interpretation of Jesus they convey. Attention to how the evangelists recount the same events differently, and present the same Jesus under different categories, is important for understanding the deeper significance of these narratives.
- *Didactic function:* Finally, as generations of Christian congregations and readers have realized, characters in the Passion Narratives have a didactic function beyond their historical involvement in the events. These stories are full of characters who teach the audience something about themselves and their own response to Christ: the weak but familiar character of Peter; the tragic figure of Judas; the fidelity of the female disciples, who remain when all the men have fled; the wavering Pilate, torn between the truth about Jesus and the pressure of the crowd; the unexpected response of Pilate's wife, who receives a dream about Jesus, and declares his innocence (Matthew 27.19).

> ## To do
>
> Read the first part of Mark's passion account (Mark 14), identifying the various characters and their reaction to Jesus. Note which characters inspire empathy (a desire to identify with them), which more distant sympathy, and which antipathy. Try rereading the chapter, through the eyes of the latter group, and note your reactions.

Four Perspectives on the Death of Jesus

So far we have been thinking about the Passion Narratives in broad terms. But how might things look at the micro-level? A good example is the four-fold account of the death of Jesus (Matthew 27.45–54; Mark 15.33–9; Luke 23.44–8; John 19.28–37). Here, as elsewhere in the passion story, Mark and

Matthew are very close, both in content and wording (so close that it is very easy to see where they diverge). Luke has some overlap with Matthew and Mark, though also significant differences. Apart from the basic shared framework, John is quite different from his synoptic counterparts, providing his own distinctive interpretation of events. You might find it helpful to compare these four accounts in a synopsis. The following observations are worth noting:

- Despite the close similarities between Mark and Matthew, Matthew diverges from Mark at four significant points: (1) he changes Mark's *Eloi* to *Eli* (Matthew 27.46: closer to the Hebrew of Psalm 22.1, and making the mishearing as 'Elijah' more intelligible); (2) he has 'let go the spirit' (*aphēken to pneuma*, Matthew 27.50) to Mark's 'expired' (*exepneusen*, Mark 15.37), making possible an interpretation in terms of the Holy Spirit; (3) he has an additional section (Matthew 27.51b–53) describing End-time events such as an earthquake and the opening of tombs following Jesus' death; (4) the centurion who confesses Jesus as 'Son of God' in Mark is joined by other guards in Matthew (Matthew 27.54).
- Luke agrees with Mark and Matthew in the basic framework (the time of Jesus' crucifixion; the darkness; Jesus speaking before his last breath; the confession of the centurion). But he puts his distinctive mark on the material: (1) he interprets the darkness as due to an eclipse of the sun (Luke 23.45a); (2) he relocates the tearing of the Temple curtain to before Jesus' death (Luke 23.45b), perhaps so as not to detract attention from that death when it is described; (3) the dying words of Jesus are not from Psalm 22 ('My God, my God, why . . . ?') but from Psalm 31.5 ('Father, into your hands I commend my spirit'); (4) the words of the centurion are slightly different, declaring Jesus to be 'innocent' (Luke 23.47); (5) he adds the reaction of the crowd, who go away from the crucifixion in a state of penitence ('beating their breasts', 23.48).
- John, as so often, tells the story in a very distinctive way. He shares two things in common with the synoptics at this point: that Jesus was offered vinegar to drink, and that he spoke words immediately prior to his death. But here the similarities end: (1) for John, Jesus himself requests a drink ('I am thirsty', John 19.28), and in order that the scriptures might be ful-

filled (this may be an allusion to Psalm 69.21: 'and for my thirst they gave me vinegar to drink'); (2) the sponge full of vinegar is placed not on a reed but on hyssop (perhaps to identify the dying Jesus as the true Passover Lamb, see Exodus 12.22); (3) Jesus speaks only one Greek word as he dies, in sharp contrast to Jesus' words of desolation in Mark and Matthew: *tetelestai*, variously translated 'It is completed', 'It is finished', and 'It is accomplished'; (4) he uniquely continues with a scene involving the body of the dead Jesus (John 19.31–7), in which the soldiers refrain from breaking his legs (again an allusion to the Passover lamb, Exodus 12.46), but instead pierce his side with a lance, prompting blood and water to flow.

All four evangelists, then, through their shaping of the (already interpreted) tradition and their inherited sources, paint their own distinctive portraits of the suffering and dying Jesus. Mark, with his dark portrayal (reflected in the darkness of the sky, and Jesus' abandonment by all his male disciples), presents a Jesus who has experienced the depths of human despair and alienation. Matthew echoes this sense of darkness, but also sees the eschatological significance of the cross. For him, this is a death which has changed the world forever, inaugurating the expected New Age. Luke, perhaps with wider Graeco-Roman audiences in mind, portrays a serene martyr-figure, who goes calmly to his death dispensing forgiveness. Finally, John's capacity to see the glory, even in the suffering and humiliation of crucifixion, offers an interpretation of Christ's death as the seal on a life completed. John's Jesus has done all that the Father sent him to do.

Reflection

What might be the value of four different accounts of Jesus' death? Do you prefer one over the others, or do all four contribute something vital? How do you understand the death of Jesus (for example, its meaning, the historical circumstances surrounding it, its impact on human culture and art)?

Table 17: Themes in the Crucifixion Scene.

Mark/Matthew	Luke	John
Themes:		
Desolation/ abandonment	Forgiveness and trust; martyr's death	Victory and completion
Last Words:		
	'Father, forgive them, for they do not know what they are doing.'	'Woman, here is your son.' 'Here is your mother.'
	'Truly I tell you, today you will be with me in Paradise.'	'I am thirsty.'
'My God, my God, why have you forsaken me?'	'Father, into your hands I commend my spirit.'	'It is finished.'

The Empty Tomb

For the evangelists, as for the other New Testament writers, Jesus' death is not the end. All four follow the crucifixion account with a brief story of his burial, watched by some of his female disciples. They then recount how these same women (at least one, though normally a group) discover Jesus' tomb empty when they return after the sabbath. Three of the gospels, and the various additions to Mark, also describe appearances of the risen Jesus to individuals and groups. These Resurrection Appearance stories are different types of stories to the Empty Tomb narratives, and will be discussed separately below.

The narratives of the Empty Tomb (Matthew 28.1–8; Mark 16.1–8; Luke

24.1–12; John 20.1–13) are like rich tapestries of interpreted memory and theological reflection, in which every word seems carefully chosen. They continue to be a focus of stimulating debate. First, when, and how, did they emerge? More significantly, how central is belief in an empty tomb to Christian faith?[89]

The discovery of the empty tomb is not explicitly mentioned by Paul in 1 Corinthians 15, leading some scholars to conclude that it was a late addition to the tradition (originating with Mark, whose motif of the women's silence at 16.8 serves to explain why it had not been heard of before). Certainly, the Empty Tomb narratives contain legendary features, such as the stone being rolled away, and (in one account) a dramatic earthquake. However, they are rather reserved when it comes to the resurrection itself, which is never directly described (compare the much more legendary account in the apocryphal *Gospel of Peter*).

On the other hand, the central role of the women, whose testimony would have been considered invalid according to Jewish law, has convinced many of the antiquity of these stories. A later author, it is claimed, is unlikely to create a story whose validity depends upon the testimony of invalid witnesses. Rather, it is more probable that the voices of the original women have been written out of the 'official list' of resurrection witnesses in 1 Corinthians 15.

Second, the discrepancies between the accounts need some explanation. They are all the more striking given that (a) there is substantial agreement between all four evangelists, unlike the Appearance stories; (b) there is almost certainly a literary relationship between the three synoptics (in the usual explanation, Matthew and Luke are drawing upon Mark). Discrepancies between the four include the following:

- *The number and identity of the women:* they vary between one (Mary Magdalene) in John to a group of five or more (Mary Magdalene, Joanna, Mary the mother of James, and 'the other women') in Luke. Mark knows of Mary Magdalene, Mary the mother of James, and Salome; Matthew has Mary Magdalene and 'the other Mary', probably 'the mother of James and Joseph' (Matthew 27.56).
- *Their time of arrival at the tomb:* in the darkness before dawn (John, probably Matthew), at dawn (Luke), or after sunrise (Mark).

- *Their purpose in coming:* to anoint the body (Mark, despite Jesus' body having been pre-anointed by the woman at Bethany, Mark 14.8), to bring spices (Luke), or simply to see the tomb (Matthew).
- *How the stone was rolled away:* Mark, Luke and John simply state that it had been removed, posing a question; Matthew attributes it to an angel of the Lord, accompanied by an earthquake.
- *Whether any of the male disciples also went to the tomb:* none are mentioned by Matthew or Mark, while John has both Peter and the beloved disciple go, and some manuscripts of Luke refer to a visit by Peter.
- *Who/whom they saw at the tomb:* a young man in white (Mark), interpreted as an angel of the Lord by Matthew, two men in dazzling clothes (Luke), or two angels in white (John).
- *What was said to them:* the words of the man/men vary from a simple 'Woman, why are you weeping?' (John) to more detailed questioning and a proclamation of the resurrection (Matthew, Mark and Luke); in Matthew and Mark, the women are entrusted with a message to the disciples to go to Galilee; Luke has a reference to Galilee, but lacks the command to go there.
- *The women's response:* they say nothing to anyone (Mark), or they (Matthew and Luke; Mary alone in John) go and tell the disciples (Luke: 'the eleven and all the rest').

Some appeal to differing oral traditions and community memories may help account for variations, even between those gospels in literary relationship with one another (the synoptics). Nevertheless, we should probably attribute many of these discrepancies to theological reasons. The four evangelists understand the meaning of the empty tomb differently. The women's silence in Mark continues his secrecy motif (at just the point when the disciples should not keep silent!), and asks searching questions of the audience about their own response. Matthew's introduction of an earthquake continues the eschatological motif introduced at the crucifixion. These are earth-shattering events, through which the New Age breaks in.

The words of the two men in Luke ('Remember how he told you, while he was still in Galilee . . .', Luke 24.6) avoid the need for the disciples to go to Galilee. Thus they prepare for Luke's resurrection appearance stories, set in and around Jerusalem, the holy city so central to his narrative. John's timing of the discovery, 'while it was still dark', reflects his vision of the light shining in, and overcoming, the darkness. Again, John's focus on Mary Magdalene is in line with his concentration on individual women throughout his gospel who seem to have a symbolic function (for example, the mother of Jesus, the Samaritan woman). In this case, echoes in John 20 of the Song of Songs suggest that Mary is playing Bride to Jesus' Bridegroom.

A third area of scholarly discussion relates to the function of the Empty Tomb narratives. These stories are sometimes treated as proof of the resurrection of Jesus. Within the wider narratives of the gospels, however, they function rather as a question mark. The discovery of the empty tomb is ambiguous, prompting the question: why was the tomb empty? Did the women go to the wrong tomb by mistake, misled perhaps by the semi-darkness of early morning? Did someone steal the body? That is the initial conclusion that Mary Magdalene draws at John 20.2: 'They have taken the Lord out of the tomb, and we do not know where they have laid him.' Matthew 28.11–15 attests a story circulating among Jews of Matthew's day, which claimed that Jesus' own disciples took the body. Or was the tomb empty because God had raised Jesus from the dead (the Christian claim)? The empty tomb by itself, apart from the interpretation of its emptiness by the man/angel/men/angels, simply poses a question open to several different answers.

To do

Read aloud Matthew's account of the discovery of the empty tomb (Matthew 28.1–8). Write down the features of Matthew's version which stand out, and the questions they raise for you. Try and answer these questions yourself, before comparing your answers with a commentary.

Stories of Resurrection Appearances

There are even wider variations between the stories describing appearances of the risen Jesus to his followers (see Table 18). Although some of the stories in the different gospels seem to be variations of the same event (compare for example Luke 24.36–49 and John 20.19–23), it is not easy to harmonize all the accounts neatly.

Table 18: Resurrection Appearance Stories.

Matthew	Mark	Luke	John
	[16.7 points to appearances in Galilee]		
	Longer Ending:		
Appearance to women near tomb	Appearance to Mary Magdalene		Appearance to Mary Magdalene at tomb
	Appearance 'in another form' to two, walking into the country	Appearance to two disciples on road to Emmaus	
		Reference to an appearance to Simon (Peter?)	
	Appearance to Eleven at table; commission	Appearance to disciples in Jerusalem	Appearance to disciples in Jerusalem
			Appearance to Thomas in Jerusalem
Appearance on a mountain in Galilee			
			Appearance by Sea of Tiberias (Galilee)

There are, for example, two separate geographical traditions about the appearances. Matthew knows only of an appearance to the disciples in Galilee (though there is a brief appearance to the women near the tomb), and a Galilee appearance is also implied in Mark 16.7 (though the 'Longer Ending', Mark 16.9–20, seems to draw on Jerusalem traditions). Luke locates his appearance stories in and around Jerusalem. John knows of both traditions: John 20 locates them in Jerusalem, while John 21 describes an appearance in Galilee (but 21.4 implies that the disciples are seeing the risen Lord for the first time).

The relationship between the various appearance stories is further complicated by the list given by Paul at 1 Corinthians 15.5–8, which includes some not mentioned in the gospels, though it lacks any reference to location:

1. Cephas (Peter)
2. the Twelve
3. more than five hundred
4. James (the Lord's brother?)
5. all the apostles
6. Paul (referring to Paul's 'Damascus road' experience)

But if we should resist the attempt to harmonize all these stories into a neat account of 'what happened', this does not necessarily lead us to treat them as fictional creations. Rather, for many readers they are the complex result of eyewitness testimony to surprising events experienced by the first disciples, interwoven with community reflection, born of the Church's ongoing experience of the risen Lord. Attempts to 'peel away' layers of interpretation, to uncover 'facts' beneath, will always be speculative and tendentious. Such attempts do not always take seriously enough that original experiences are themselves already interpretations.

Approaching the stories as they stand (as opposed to reconstructions of earlier versions) raises enough issues to make study of them rewarding and interesting. Among the features of these stories are the following:

• *The Nature of the Resurrection:* The Appearance stories articulate, in narrative form, the evangelists' understandings of the resurrection (compare

Paul's more conceptual articulation in 1 Corinthians 15). A number of them echo Old Testament stories of theophanies (manifestations of the divine): the emphasis is upon Christ taking the initiative (as in Matthew 28.18), coming to the disciples unannounced and unexpected (so Luke 24.15). He is no longer constrained by physical barriers such as walls and doors (for example John 20.19), yet he is not a ghost (Luke 24.39: he is more real, more powerful, rather than insubstantial as a phantom would be). In at least one case, he eats fish (Luke 24.42, which may be an apologetic motif to rule out rival understandings of the resurrection). Luke's understanding is interesting, not least because he seems to distinguish appearances of the risen Lord prior to Jesus' ascension after forty days (Acts 1.3) from later encounters, such as Paul's Damascus road experience. Luke describes the latter as a vision (Acts 9.1–9); for Paul, it is of the same order as the first disciples' experience (1 Corinthians 15.8).

- *Continuity and Discontinuity:* They contain a crucial dynamic between *continuity* and *discontinuity*: it is the same Jesus who suffered and died (he bears the scars of the crucifixion: for example, Luke 24.39; John 20.20), but he has been transformed (hence his disciples do not at first recognize him: for example, Luke 24.16; John 20.14; 21.4), and become the object of worship (so Matthew 28.17).

- *Experience of the Community:* The stories seem to have been shaped by the ongoing experience of the Church in the intervening decades between the events they describe and the composition of the gospels. They reflect the Christian claim that the risen Lord, as life-giving Spirit (1 Corinthians 15.45), is still encountered in Christian gatherings. In particular, the experience of Christ's presence at the Eucharist has left its mark: the two disciples at Emmaus recognize him in the breaking of the bread (Luke 24.30–1, 35); the risen Jesus feeds his disciples with bread and fish beside the Sea of Tiberias (John 21.12–13). The implication is that the risen Christ continues to make his presence felt to subsequent generations, in and through the Eucharist.

- *Commissioning Narratives:* A number of the resurrection appearance stories contain a commission, by which the risen Lord sends out his disciples to continue his mission. This points to the central experience of the resurrection in driving the Church out into the world. The precise wording of the commission varies from gospel to gospel, and tends to reflect the theological interests and vocabulary of the individual evangelist:

> Go therefore and make disciples of all nations, baptizing them in the name of the Father and of the Son and of the Holy Spirit, and teaching them to obey everything that I have commanded you. (Matthew 28.19–20a)

> Go into all the world and proclaim the good news to the whole creation. The one who believes and is baptized will be saved; but the one who does not believe will be condemned. (Longer Ending of Mark, Mark 16.15–16, possibly influenced by Matthew)

> Thus it is written, that the Messiah is to suffer and to rise from the dead on the third day, and that repentance and forgiveness of sins is to be proclaimed in his name to all nations, beginning from Jerusalem. (Luke 24.46–7)

> Receive the Holy Spirit. If you forgive the sins of any, they are forgiven them; if you retain the sins of any, they are retained. (John 20.22b–23)

To do

Find an artist's representation of a resurrection appearance (useful websites include www.nationalgallery.org.uk and www.wga.hu). Try and identify which scene is being depicted, and which gospel is the main influence. Ask yourself how the resurrection is being understood, and how any characters are presented. Are there any symbols or other features in the picture needing explanation? What can you discover about the background to the artist and this painting which might shed light on its meaning?

Forward to the Beginning

In terms of order of writing, we now move forward to the beginning of the story. Whereas Mark begins his narrative with the emergence of John the baptizer and the adult Jesus, Matthew and Luke both add stories of events surrounding his birth and childhood (commonly referred to as the Infancy Narratives).[90] For some, the significant variations between the two are conclusive evidence for their independence (for example proponents of the Two Source theory). For others, the fact that both have Infancy Narratives at all, and that there are fixed points of agreement despite their differences, supports the conclusion that Matthew and Luke have some literary relationship. The contents of their respective Infancy Narratives are as follows (with points of contact in italics):[91]

Matthew	Luke
Genealogy of Jesus (traced to Abraham)	[Luke 3.23ff. *Genealogy of Jesus* (traced to Adam)]
	Annunciation to Zechariah (of birth of John the baptizer)
Annunciation to Joseph (*of birth of Jesus*; in Bethlehem?), *during period of betrothal*	*Annunciation* to Mary (*of birth of Jesus*; in Nazareth), *during period of betrothal*
	Mary visits Elizabeth Birth and circumcision of John
Birth of Jesus in Bethlehem and visit of Magi	*Birth of Jesus in Bethlehem* (Mary and Joseph travel from Nazareth) and visit of shepherds
Flight into Egypt and slaughter of innocents	Circumcision and presentation of Jesus
Family move to *Nazareth*	followed by return to *Nazareth*

The points of contact may point to a common core of infancy tradition, or even Luke using Matthew (though diverging from him for theological purposes). But there are differences even between some of the overlaps. The annunciation of Jesus' birth is made to a different parent in each gospel: Joseph in Matthew, Mary in Luke. The relationship between Mary and Joseph and Nazareth has a different explanation in the two: in Matthew, they apparently live in Bethlehem, and settle in Galilean Nazareth in order to escape Herod's son Archelaus; in Luke, Nazareth is their home. The two genealogies are also quite different: Matthew has 40 generations between Abraham and Jesus inclusive, while Luke has 56, with several different names.

What kind of stories are these? Some scholars regard them as drawing upon existing sources, including traditions springing from eyewitnesses (Luke, for example, is traditionally regarded as having known Mary). For others, these are imaginative creations of the evangelists, woven out of christological beliefs and Old Testament texts. The truth may be somewhere in between: a complex interweaving of traditions, with some historical kernel, popular piety, and theological reflection. Their prominence in Matthew and Luke, but not in Mark, points to a growing popular Christian interest in the early years. This trajectory finds fuller development in texts such as the *Infancy Gospel of Thomas*, where the child Jesus performs miracles such as making clay sparrows fly, and raising the dead.

The message which these two sets of stories convey is important. The first part of Matthew's Infancy Narrative, for example (Matthew 1) attempts to hold together Jewish traditions about Jesus' descent from David (thus locating him in the royal line, eligible to be Davidic Messiah) and Abraham, the father of the nation, with a tradition that he was conceived of a virgin, without the involvement of a human father. Matthew finds scriptural warrant for the latter in a prophecy from Isaiah, quoted by him in the Greek Septuagint (in the Hebrew, the word translated a 'virgin' by the LXX means simply 'young woman'):

'Look, the virgin shall conceive and bear a son,
and they shall name him Emmanuel'
which means, 'God is with us'. (Matthew 1.23, quoting Isaiah 7.14 LXX)

In the second part (Matthew 2) a succession of stories present Jesus as reliving the experience of Moses and the people of Israel. Like Moses, Jesus is rescued as a baby from a wicked king intent on destroying the male children; like Moses, Jesus is associated with Egypt. This is the beginning of a Moses typology which will run throughout Matthew's story. But Jesus, as Son of God, also re-enacts the story of 'God's son' Israel. He goes down into Egypt, and comes back out of Egypt into the promised land (the quotation from Hosea cited at Matthew 2.15, 'Out of Egypt I have called my son', originally referred to Israel at the Exodus: Hosea 11.1). But whereas the wilderness generation was disobedient, Jesus is the perfectly obedient Son of God, who relives Israel's experience faithfully.

Two further noteworthy threads run throughout Matthew's Infancy Narrative. The first is his positive portrayal of Gentile characters, notably the magi. Although not explicitly called Gentiles, their occupation (*magoi*: astrologers or magicians from the East) and two of their gifts (gold and frankincense: Isaiah 60.6) make their pagan origin clear. In Matthew's story they come in search of the new-born king, with a spirit of acceptance contrasted sharply with the reaction of Herod, the king of Jesus' own nation, 'and all Jerusalem with him' (Matthew 2.3). Thus we have a hint – right at the beginning of the story – of those tragic events at the end of Jesus' earthly life, when Jerusalem will call for his crucifixion, in contrast to the Gentile Pilate and Pilate's wife.

The second thread concerns the fulfilment of scripture. We have already noted two of Matthew's distinctive 'formula citations' (quotations from the Old Testament introduced by the formulaic phrase: 'This was to fulfil what had been spoken by the Lord through the prophet . . .'). These formula citations are scattered throughout his gospel, and Matthew shows explicitly how events in Jesus' life are foretold in prophecy. They are particularly concentrated in the Infancy Narrative: the others focus on his birth at Bethlehem (Matthew 2.6 = Micah 5.2), sorrow at the slaughter of the innocents (Matthew 2.18 = Jeremiah 31.15) and his association with Nazareth ('He will be called a Nazorean/Nazarene', Matthew 2.23, a puzzling one, since it does not conform to any clear Old Testament passage).[92]

In his Infancy Narrative, Luke lives up to his reputation as an artist, creating a veritable literary masterpiece. Indeed, his infancy stories (painting memorable scenes of the two annunciations, the visitation, and the nativity with the adoration of the shepherds) have been especially favoured by artists (you might like to consult websites such as www.nationalgallery.org.uk and www.wga.hu to locate some examples). Luke's literary structure for these first two chapters is like a two-panelled diptych, in which scenes connected with the conception and birth of Jesus on the right-hand panel are paralleled by similar scenes relating to John the baptizer on the left-hand. From the beginning of their stories, John and Jesus are intimately related, though Luke is equally clear that Jesus is the superior.

This literary creativity is also reflected in Luke's style for these two chapters. After his prologue, Luke's Greek consciously imitates the Septuagint, such that first-century readers would hear Luke 1.5—2.52 as 'old-fashioned', biblical Greek. The effect would be startling: Luke is describing fairly recent events (about John and Jesus) in terms traditionally used to describe how God acted many centuries before. As God once did, so now God is doing again!

Particularly influential for Luke seem to have been stories in the historical books, such as the story of Samuel:

> There was a certain man of Ramathaim, a Zuphite from the hill country of Ephraim, whose name was Elkanah son of Jeroham son of Elihu son of Tohu son of Zuph, an Ephraimite. He had two wives; the name of the one was Hannah, and the name of the other Peninnah. Peninnah had children, but Hannah had no children. (1 Samuel 1.1–2)

> In the days of King Herod of Judea, there was a priest named Zechariah, who belonged to the priestly order of Abijah. His wife was a descendant of Aaron, and her name was Elizabeth. Both of them were righteous before God, living blamelessly according to all the commandments and regulations of the Lord. But they had no children, because Elizabeth was barren, and both were getting on in years. (Luke 1.5–7)

> She [Hannah] made this vow: 'O Lord of hosts, if only you will look on the misery of your servant, and remember me, and not forget your servant, but will give to your servant a male child, then I will set him before you as a nazirite until the day of his death. He shall drink neither wine nor intoxicants, and no razor shall touch his head.' (1 Samuel 1.11)

'You will have joy and gladness, and many will rejoice at his birth [John the baptizer], for he will be great in the sight of the Lord. He must never drink wine or strong drink; even before his birth he will be filled with the Holy Spirit.' (Luke 1.14–15)

Hannah prayed and said, 'My heart exults in the Lord; my strength is exalted in my God. My mouth derides my enemies, because I rejoice in my victory . . .' (1 Samuel 2.1)

And Mary said, 'My soul magnifies the Lord,
and my spirit rejoices in God my Saviour,
for he has looked with favour on the lowliness of his servant.' (Luke 1.46–48a)

Now the boy Samuel continued to grow both in stature and in favour with the Lord and with the people. (1 Samuel 2.26)

And Jesus increased in wisdom and in years, and in divine and human favour. (Luke 2.52)

A final aspect of Luke's story is the theme of gospel reversal. It is reflected in the Lucan canticles (the Benedictus, Magnificat and Nunc Dimittis), which continue to be used – out of their Lucan literary context – in Christian liturgy. Mary's canticle is particularly expressive:

He has brought down the powerful from their thrones,
and lifted up the lowly;
he has filled the hungry with good things,
and sent the rich away empty. (Luke 1.52–3).

It is also reflected in the lowly origins of the Christ, forced to be laid in a manger at his birth, because there was no room at the inn or guest room (*kataluma*, Luke 2.7), and the politically subversive terms in which that child is described (Saviour, Lord, whose birth brings peace and heralds 'good news of great joy'). Finally, it is reflected in the shepherds (not Matthew's magi) who come to the manger: poor, despised, marginal Jewish figures, yet who bear a family resemblance to that great shepherd of Bethlehem, King David.

To do

Look carefully at Matthew's genealogy (Matthew 1.1–17), noting Jesus' pedigree, the careful pattern of three sets of fourteen generations, and the women who are mentioned. What conclusions can you draw about the purpose of this genealogy in Matthew's account? How does Matthew solve the problem that this is Joseph's genealogy, not Jesus'?

Further Reading

Raymond E. Brown, 1993, *The Birth of the Messiah*, updated edition; London: Geoffrey Chapman.

Raymond E. Brown, 1994, *The Death of the Messiah*, two volumes; London: Geoffrey Chapman.

Edwin D. Freed, 2001, *The Stories of Jesus' Birth: A Critical Introduction*, Sheffield: Sheffield Academic Press.

Herman Hendrickx, 1984, *The Resurrection Narratives of the Synoptic Gospels*, London: Geoffrey Chapman.

Pheme Perkins, 1984, *Resurrection*, London: Geoffrey Chapman.

8

Acts: Luke's Ongoing Story

Continuing the Journey

A few miles outside Rome, there is a well-preserved and much-photographed section of the ancient Appian Way, its Roman cobbles still intact. This road, which connected ancient Rome with the south, and eventually with Brundisium (Brindisi), is the road by which Paul reached the city, when he finally arrived in Rome as a prisoner (Acts 28.13–15). It is just one of many ancient Roman roads traversing the Mediterranean world, a number of which are trodden by characters in Luke's second volume, the Acts of the Apostles. But the real roads or ways in Acts are not those built of cobbles. Rather, Acts is concerned with the ongoing way or journey of the followers of Jesus after his ascension. Luke's Gospel described the great journey of Jesus from Galilee to Jerusalem, and hinted at the future with that mini-journey from Jerusalem to Emmaus. Acts will continue that journey, through a series of mini-journeys to and from Jerusalem (in Acts even Paul returns to Jerusalem), and another great journey which will take the gospel by a series of concentric circles, out from Jerusalem into the rest of Judea, then Samaria, and eventually to Rome. This is understood to be in accordance with Jesus' will:

> But you will receive power when the Holy Spirit has come upon you; and you will be my witnesses in Jerusalem, in all Judea and Samaria, and to the ends of the earth. (Acts 1.8)

In discussing Luke's Gospel, we noted a number of threads connecting his two volumes. These threads often reflect this conviction that in Acts the journey commenced by Jesus is continued by the Church. Like Elisha receiving a double-portion of Elijah's spirit, the disciples receive the Holy Spirit in order to be Jesus' witnesses after his departure (Acts 1—2; cf. 2 Kings 2.9–12). Empowered by the Spirit, they are able to move beyond Jerusalem – following a number of different roads – to continue the way. Indeed, it is not coincidental that in Acts the disciples describe themselves simply as 'the Way' (Acts 9.2; 16.17; 18.25–6; 19:9, 23; 22.4; 24.14, 22).

These threads are all the more important if, as many scholars believe, Luke started his task consciously intending to write both volumes, rather than composing Acts at a later date. The influential work of Henry Cadbury, *The Making of Luke–Acts*, has ensured that the two books are linked together in much scholarly discussion (as the hyphenated Luke–Acts implies).[93] More recently, however, some have argued for 'loosening the hyphen' between Luke and Acts, so as to read each volume in its own right.[94] Our own position on this question will inevitably affect the way we read Acts.

To do

Locate the following places and territories on a map in a Bible atlas or study Bible: Jerusalem; Judea; Samaria; Rome. Which location lies at the centre of the map you are consulting? Compare other maps to see whether the centre changes. On these maps, where might 'the ends of the earth' (Acts 1.8) be? Does Luke focus our attention too much westwards?

Acts of the Apostles and Others

From earliest times Luke's second book has been known as the 'Acts' ('of the Apostles'), a designation already used in the Hellenistic world of books recounting the deeds of great figures. Following the use of this term to describe Luke's second volume, a distinctive genre of later Christian apocryphal 'Acts' developed (for example, the Acts of Paul and Thecla; the Acts of John).

Identifying more precisely what kind of a book this is has been a dominant issue in recent study of Acts. Scholars have noted parallels between Acts and ancient novels (in its capacity to entertain through vivid descriptions of mass conversions, arrests, riots and a shipwreck). Others see links with succession narratives (the story of Jesus' followers continuing the story of Jesus recounted in the gospel), with historical monographs (Luke having long been regarded as the first church historian), and with the more theological or apologetic histories associated with Judaism, such as the Deuteronomistic History, or the works of Josephus (Luke is concerned to show the hand of God at work in the history of the followers of Jesus).

Whatever the case, the title 'Acts of the Apostles' is something of a misnomer. For Acts is a highly selective account of the deeds of the apostles of Jesus (whom Luke seems to equate with the Twelve, Matthias making up the full complement after Judas' death: Acts 1.15–26).[95] More precisely, it contains the acts of only some of the apostles: most of the Twelve are in fact not mentioned again after being listed at Acts 1.13. What happened to them? To answer this question we must rely on later traditions and legends, which have some of them evangelizing in territories (notably in the east) not mentioned in Acts. We search Luke's second volume in vain for the acts of Bartholomew, or Matthew, or Judas son of James.

Instead, the narrative of Acts tells the story of just three: Peter and John (though in fact when he appears with Peter, John is the silent partner), and one brief mention of the martyrdom of John's brother James (Acts 12.2). Peter is joined on one occasion by another James, but this is James the Lord's brother rather than one of the Twelve (Acts 15.13–21; cf. Galatians 2.1–10). Other non-apostles also play key roles: Stephen, Philip (a different Philip to the apostle), Barnabas, Silas (the Silvanus of Paul's letters) and Timothy.

Moreover, even Peter and John disappear from the scene after the first half, their stories incomplete. Thus Acts is only 'some of the acts of some of the apostles'. They give way to another non-apostle (at least by Luke's criteria): Saul of Tarsus. Saul, or Paul, is introduced briefly in the story of Stephen's martyrdom (Acts 8.1); his Damascus road experience is described in narrative sequence in Acts 9, and he becomes the key player (initially in partnership with Barnabas) from Acts 13 onwards. This makes the traditional title even more of a misnomer, for more than half the book describes the acts of a non-apostle.

> **Reflection**
>
> Reread the prologues to Luke (Luke 1.1–4) and Acts (Acts 1.1–2).
> What kind of books do these prologues suggest them to be? What
> elements strike you as important, and why? Do you think it neces-
> sary to read the two in the light of each other?

The Words of the Apostles

There is another reason why 'Acts of the Apostles' is a misnomer. Acts is as
much an account of the words of apostles and other early Christian leaders as it is of their deeds. Memorable speeches and sermons include that
delivered by Peter at Pentecost (Acts 2.14–36), the sermon which prompted
Stephen's martyrdom (7.2–53), and Paul's address to the philosophers in
Athens (17.22–31). There is hardly a chapter of Acts that does not contain a
speech or sermon of some kind. This is one of the ways in which Acts models
Luke's Gospel, which is a narrative of 'all that Jesus did and taught from the
beginning until the day when he was taken up to heaven' (Acts 1.1–2).

But how are we to account for the speeches in Acts? Are they based on
earlier sources preserving the memory of words actually spoken? Many have
been impressed by the way in which different characters speak in terms
appropriate to their cultural context. The early speeches of Peter, for example, seem to reflect an early adoptionist Christology, arguably contrasting
with Luke's own Christology (for example, Luke 1.35; 3.21–2):

> Therefore let the entire house of Israel know with certainty that God *has*
> *made* him both Lord and Messiah, this Jesus whom you crucified (Acts
> 2.36, italics mine).

This primitive-sounding kerygma can be found elsewhere in the New Testament (such as Romans 1.3–4). Similarly, the anti-Temple speech of Stephen
in Acts 7 is often thought to enshrine the theology of the Hellenist party
within the Jerusalem church (with similarities to the thought of the Letter
to the Hebrews).[96]

Others regard the speeches as Luke's own composition, in line with contemporary convention. The ancient historian Thucydides (fifth century BCE), explaining his procedure in his *History of the Peloponnesian War,* writes of putting on the lips of speakers words appropriate to the occasion rather than reporting verbatim (Thucydides, *History* 1.22). A similar strategy is employed by the second-century CE historian Lucian of Samosata:

> If some one has to be brought in to give a speech, above all let his language suit his person and his subject . . . It is then, however, that you can exercise your rhetoric and show your eloquence. (*How to Write History* 58)[97]

If Luke is employing a similar convention, then we are hearing the voice of Luke in the voices of Peter, Stephen and Paul (even if he draws upon some traditions in his composition). Just as in his Infancy Narrative he was capable of imitating Old Testament Greek, so he can compose appropriate speeches to express the development of early Christian preaching, and to reflect the requirements of different audiences.

To do

Compare the gospel message as presented in the following speeches: Acts 3.12–26; 17.22–31; 26.2–23. Note where they agree, and how they differ. How far are these differences due to different audiences and circumstances?

The Story of Acts

Attention to the speeches of Acts highlights Luke's potential for literary artistry. Recent interest in the literary dimension of New Testament books has highlighted wider literary features of Acts. First, one might mention the interweaving and development of themes in Luke's unfolding story:

- The emergence of a 'renewed Israel', gathered around the Twelve in Jerusalem, in fulfilment of prophecy and the prophetic word of Jesus. This renewed people is not restricted to Jews living in the holy land: those who hear the apostles at Pentecost are Jews and proselytes (Gentile converts to Judaism) from throughout the known world (you might wish to locate on a map the places listed at Acts 2.9–11).

- The gradual expansion of the disciples from pious Jews to include Samaritans and God-fearing Gentiles such as the centurion Cornelius. All this takes place even before the 'call' or 'conversion' of Paul, significantly altering the boundaries of the holy people of God.
- The crucial role of Peter in the conversion of Gentiles, a development understood as initiated by the Holy Spirit (Acts 10). Although Acts hints that concerted efforts to win over Gentiles may only have begun with the Hellenists in Antioch-on-the-Orontes (Acts 11.19–20), it is important for Luke that the seeds of this development be traced to the leader of the Twelve.
- The emergence of Saul of Tarsus (Paul) as a key player who will build on Peter's foundation in bringing the good news to the wider Mediterranean world. Paul's role as the dominant figure in the second half of Acts is prepared for skilfully: he is introduced in passing in the story of Stephen's martyrdom (8.1), and his emergence as a Christian witness is interwoven with the narrative of Peter and Cornelius.
- The repeated hostility of certain sections of the Jewish synagogue to the activity of Paul and his associates, presenting a motif of a divided Israel already prophesied by Simeon at the beginning of Luke's Gospel (Luke 2.34). This is underlined by a series of pronouncements by Paul (in Antioch-in-Pisidia, 13.46–7; in Corinth, 18.6; in Rome, 28.25–7), which speak of a turning to the Gentiles.
- The generally positive portrayal of Roman officials in the treatment of Paul and his companions, and in the reception of the gospel.

These thematic elements, and transitional stages, are supplemented by a series of distinctive Lucan summaries which punctuate the narrative. These give a sense of a growing movement, first as a reform movement within the Jewish community of Jerusalem (Acts 2.42–7; 4.32–5; 5.11–16; 6.7), and then more widely (9.31; 12.24; 16.5; 19.20; 28.30–1).

As mentioned when discussing Luke's Gospel, another literary feature is the patterning between Luke's two volumes. This presents the ministry of the apostles as the continuation of Jesus' pre-Easter ministry. It happens in individual stories, as well as on a wider level. An example of the former is the story of Peter's healing of a paralysed man at Lydda:

> There he found a man named Aeneas, who had been bedridden for eight years, for he was paralysed. Peter said to him, 'Aeneas, Jesus Christ heals you; get up and make your bed!' And immediately he got up. And all the residents of Lydda and Sharon saw him and turned to the Lord. (Acts 9.33–5)

There are striking similarities with the healing described at Luke 5.17–26. Here Jesus heals a paralysed man, commanding him to 'stand up and take your bed and go to your home' (Luke 5.24). The result is that the onlookers are amazed and glorify God, echoing the response of the residents of Lydda and Sharon to Peter's action.

On the broader scale, the period of preparation, in which the risen Lord appears to his disciples for forty days, and urges them to expect the gift of the Spirit (Acts 1.3–8; note the discrepancy with the timing of the ascension in Luke 24.51), echoes Jesus' forty days of preparation in the wilderness, before he returned 'in the power of the Spirit' to begin his public ministry (Luke 4.1–14). Similarly, the story of Paul's arrest in Jerusalem and subsequent trials (Acts 21—6) provides a narrative parallel to the passion of Jesus in the later chapters of Luke's Gospel. Paul is presented here as walking in the steps of his Lord, following his path of suffering (though not yet of death).

Finally, the narrative of Acts makes effective use of repetition. What older source critics might have regarded as evidence for multiple sources, is viewed by literary critics as an effective didactic tool. Three times, for example – though in quite different ways – Acts describes Paul's Damascus road experience (Acts 9.1–9; 22.6–21; 26.12–23). This repetition underscores the importance of this event for the unfolding story of Paul, as well as enabling different aspects of the same event to be explored.

Table 19: Acts and the Damascus Road.

Acts 9.1-9	Acts 22.6-21	Acts 26.12-23
Paul sees a light and hears a voice	Paul sees a light and hears a voice	Paul sees a light and hears a voice
Voice asks: 'Saul, Saul, why do you persecute me?'	Voice asks: 'Saul, Saul, why do you persecute me?'	Voice asks: 'Saul, Saul, why do you persecute me?'
Paul told to go into city	Paul to go to Damascus	Paul given more detailed commands, and given fuller account of his mission
Companions hear voice but see no one	Companions see light but do not hear voice	
Paul blinded	Paul unable to see because of light	

To do

Read the story of Dorcas/Tabitha in Acts 9.36–42, and compare it with Luke's story of Jairus' daughter (Luke 8.41–2, 49–56). Note the similarities between the two stories. How does reading the two together affect interpretation?

Luke the Historian

Yet if Luke is a compelling storyteller, how accurate is the story he relates? The portrayal of Luke as a historian is an ancient one, and contemporary scholars debate both whether Acts should be classified as historiography, and the extent to which its author did a good job. Our answer depends in part on whether we are judging Luke by ancient understandings of the historian's task, or rather different modern standards. Indeed, it is related in no small part to our own understanding of what history is.

In our discussion of Paul in Chapter 3, we noted some differences between Acts and Paul in details of his life and ministry. We concluded then that a nuanced approach was called for, recognizing agendas in both Acts and Paul, such that one should not always be preferred over the other. In particular, the issue of chronology is especially complex. Scholars have drawn attention to other historical 'errors'. In Gamaliel's speech in Acts 5.35–9, for example, Luke refers to Theudas and Judas the Galilean in the wrong chronological sequence. At the very least, he is capable of making mistakes.

But these mistakes do not invalidate the claim that Luke is attempting to write history of some kind. There are enough similarities between Acts and ancient historical works to make this a probable aim. However, the kind of history that Luke writes is a surprising one. We expect our history books to be full of the 'big players', the ruling classes, prominent political and religious figures, whose impact on the world stage is felt to be significant. Acts, however, presents a history which concentrates on marginal figures. Although the Roman emperor is mentioned, and Roman governors such as Felix and Porcius Festus and client kings such as Herod Agrippa have walk-on parts, they are not the characters who really make history. Centre stage is given instead to Jewish fishermen such as Peter and John, and Paul, a wandering tent-maker from Tarsus. Along with them are a long list of heroes of the faith, whose names would now be lost to posterity were it not for Luke's alternative history: they include Matthias, Barsabbas known as Justus, Prochorus, Nicolaus of Antioch, Ananias of Damascus, Tabitha of Joppa, Cornelius the centurion, Rhoda the maid, Simeon Niger, Lydia of Thyatira, and Dionysius the Areopagite.

Moreover, as a theological history (akin to the work of the Deuteronomistic Historian or the Chronicler), Acts is interested in how the hand of God has guided the history of the expanding group of followers of Jesus. Attention is paid to the movement of the Holy Spirit in directing the Church in often-unexpected directions. Figures like Peter and Stephen (Acts 4.8; 7.55), and sometimes the whole community (as at 4.31), are said to be 'filled with the Spirit' as they witness to Christ. The Spirit directs Philip to his meeting with the Ethiopian eunuch (8.29), prepares Peter for his encounter with Cornelius (10.19), and sets Barnabas and Paul apart for their mission-ary activity (13.2). At times, the Spirit even seems to thwart the intentions of missionaries for a higher purpose:

> They went through the region of Phrygia and Galatia, having been forbid-den by the Holy Spirit to speak the word in Asia. When they had come opposite Mysia, they attempted to go into Bithynia, but the Spirit of Jesus did not allow them; so, passing by Mysia, they went down to Troas. (Acts 16.6–8)

This theological concern is also reflected in Luke's portrayal of the early Jerusalem community as a faithful core of pious Israelites, and in Acts' account of the transition to a Gentile mission. Luke's overriding concern seems to be that expressed in the prologue to his gospel: to provide Theo-philus, and through him readers of Acts, with 'confidence', 'security' or 'certainty' (Greek *asphaleia*) about the message in which they have been instructed (Luke 1.4). A major plank of this is confidence in the God of Israel. Luke–Acts is concerned to show that this is not a God who changes his mind, by swapping allegiance from Israel to the Gentiles. Rather, this God has ful-filled his promises to Israel: the raising up of the Messiah-Prophet Jesus, and the gathering of witnesses from among pious Israelites, is testimony to this.

Reflection

What do you understand by 'history'? How far is it a description of 'what happened', albeit often derived from limited sources? How far is history itself an interpretative exercise? What implications might this have for our assessment of Acts?

Acts and the Church

Understood as history, Acts has often been viewed as the first history of the Church. As we have seen, this needs some qualification. First, if it was intended to be a companion volume to the Gospel of Luke, then its primary aim is to trace the ongoing story of Jesus and his followers into the post-Easter period. Second, given its likely dating (along with Luke, in the last quarter of the first century CE), it is looking back at the first few decades of the Church's life from a later period. This is not necessarily a bad thing: a sense of distance can sometimes provide a more even-handed perspective. Paul's somewhat tendentious autobiographical account in Galatians 1—2 is an example of where an earlier, first-hand version may lack the balance of a later, more reflective description.

On the other hand, Acts has often been accused of presenting a somewhat romantic account of the past apostolic age. Its description of the relationship between Paul, Peter and James, or the transition from a Jewish reform group to a Mediterranean-wide movement embracing both Jews and Gentiles, presents a relatively harmonious picture. How far Luke has 'papered over the cracks' of tensions and divisions remains a matter of considerable debate. Moreover, even if we take the 'we-passages' as referring to the experiences of the author (and therefore that Luke was a companion of Paul for certain parts of his ministry), he was not an eyewitness to many of the events described in his book. For much of the 'history' Luke describes, Acts is not a primary source but is dependent upon the testimony of others.

That being said, Acts provides us with significant information about the life and organization of the early Church. Indeed, without Acts much of this would remain unknown to posterity. It is from Acts that we learn of the earliest disciples in Jerusalem, and the prominent role of the Antiochene church in the Gentile mission. Acts tells us about the activity of 'the Seven', especially Stephen and Philip, and the prominence of James the Lord's brother within the Jerusalem church. Furthermore, even if Luke has downplayed the worst of the disagreements, he retains a certain realism by including the negative story of Ananias and Sapphira (Acts 5.1–11), and pointing to divisions among believers over the circumcision of Gentile converts (15.5).

A particular glimpse of the life of the community of believers in Jerusalem is provided in one of Acts' distinctive summaries:

> They devoted themselves to the apostles' teaching and fellowship, to the breaking of bread and the prayers. (Acts 2.42)

How far this reflects the actual situation in the 30s, and how far Luke's perspective towards the end of the century (or a mixture of both), remains a matter of debate. Whatever, the following features emerge:

- The *apostolic teaching* is regarded as important, because the apostles were the ones 'sent out' by Jesus. Increasingly as the first generation gave way to the second, the apostles became the crucial links with Jesus, heightening the significance of their teaching. Their priority was not a foregone conclusion, however: tensions between the followers (represented by the Twelve) and the family of Jesus (represented by James) may lie beneath Acts' harmonious picture.
- Fellowship, communion, *koinōnia*, is what connected disparate Christian communities (Jewish, Gentile, mixed), and even prominent figures who sometimes disagreed among themselves (Peter, James, Paul). It is the concern for *koinōnia* which kept channels of communication open between Pauline Gentile churches and the mother-church of Jerusalem. It is expressed concretely through the sharing of material goods (Acts 2.44–5).
- The *breaking of bread* is generally (though not universally) thought to refer to the Eucharist. If so, then such meals of the post-Easter community would be celebrations of Christ's risen presence as at Emmaus, looking back to the scandalous table-fellowship of Jesus' ministry as Luke recounts it, and breaking down social boundaries as Jesus' practice did.
- Finally, the *prayers*. Of course, there are some prayers distinctive to followers of Jesus found in the New Testament (the Lord's Prayer; the canticles of Luke's Infancy Narratives). But we are probably meant to understand that the disciples maintained the existing Jewish pattern of prayer, originally in the Jerusalem Temple (v. 46) and the synagogue. The picture painted by Acts is not one of great disruption, but of essential continuity.

Why Is Acts Where It Is?

One final question remains. Why is Acts located where it is in our New Testaments? After all, if Luke and Acts were intended to be read together (as the majority, though not all, of scholars think[98]), isn't the book's present context at best inappropriate, at worst misleading? Shouldn't our canonical order be: Matthew—Mark—Luke—Acts—John? To read the two volumes separately, if their author intended them to be read together, risks our failing to hear clearly the author's – or the narrative's – voice.

In fact, the evidence points to Luke and Acts being separate at a very early stage (this is noted by Mikeal Parsons in his appeal for loosening the connection between the two books).[99] No extant ancient codex contains the two side-by-side (though this could be related to their having originally been written on two separate scrolls, one scroll not long enough to contain both volumes). Even though different canonical orders for the New Testament have survived, none of these places Luke and Acts together. The push towards a four-gospel canon from the second century onwards seems to have overridden the requirement to preserve the link between Luke's two volumes. This represents a shift in the interpretation of Luke's Gospel: it is preserved as one of the four portraits of Jesus, his ministry, death and resurrection.

It also – through separation – reflects a shift in the interpretation of Acts. As a 'stand-alone' text rather than a sequel to Luke, and in its present canonical context, Acts now functions as a 'bridge' between the Gospels and Epistles. It is a bridge in a twofold sense. First, it provides the broad historical setting (the spread of the early Christian movement after the resurrection) within which the Epistles can be located. Second, at least in the Western ordering, it prepares the ground for a shift from Jesus to Paul as his apostle. This second sense of Acts' bridge function differs in some Eastern canonical lists, where Acts is immediately followed not by Paul's letters but by the seven Catholic Epistles.

To do

Read the last chapter of Acts (Acts 28), and then the opening chapter of Romans. In what ways does Acts serve as a good introduction for Romans and the other Pauline letters? How is your reading of Acts affected if it is followed immediately by James and the other Catholic Epistles?

Further Reading

Martin Hengel, 1980, *Acts and the History of Earliest Christianity*, ET Philadelphia: Fortress Press.

I. Howard Marshall, 1992, *The Acts of the Apostles*, New Testament Guides; Sheffield: Sheffield Academic Press.

Jaroslav Pelikan, 2006, *Acts*, SCM Theological Commentary on the Bible; London: SCM Press.

F. Scott Spencer, 2004, *Journeying through Acts: A Literary-Cultural Reading*, Peabody, Massachusetts: Hendrickson.

9

The Ongoing Pauline Tradition

Paul's Ongoing Legacy

As we have seen, the New Testament contains several different 'portraits' of Paul. Acts presents Paul as an intrepid missionary traveller and eloquent public speaker. Paul's own letters reveal him to be a passionate pastor and letter-writer, able to engage in fierce debate on occasion. But not even his own letters present a monochrome Paul, not least because his own ideas and perspectives developed and changed in response to particular situations.

But what of Paul's legacy outside Acts? How else was Paul remembered in the later New Testament period? This chapter will consider four additional letters attributed to Paul, but generally thought by scholars to have been written – at least in their present form – by Pauline disciples after his death. The four are Ephesians, a magnificent exposition of the Pauline vision, and 1 Timothy, 2 Timothy and Titus (known collectively as the 'Pastoral Epistles'). Two further letters sometimes treated by scholars as 'deutero-Pauline' (that is, from a second stage of the Pauline tradition) have already been discussed among Paul's authentic letters: Colossians and 2 Thessalonians.

I have deliberately said that these four are regarded as deutero-Pauline 'in their present form'. While many scholars consider them to be composed in their entirety by later disciples of Paul, there are other voices positing more complex scenarios. For example, John Muddiman has made a good case for

Ephesians being an expanded version of Paul's lost letter to the Laodiceans (Colossians 4.16).[100] Similarly, it is possible that the Pastorals contain fragments of genuine Pauline letters. In particular, the personal references in 2 Timothy and Titus have been so identified.[101]

But Paul's legacy in the New Testament is not confined to letters written in his name. A famous passage from 2 Peter hints at ambivalence towards him. On the one hand, he is 'our beloved brother Paul' whose letters seem to be accorded scriptural authority (2 Peter 3.15–16). On the other hand, there is a warning about the early misuse of Paul's letters: 'There are some things in them hard to understand, which the ignorant and unstable twist to their own destruction.' Similarly, the Letter of James has often been read as a challenge to Paul's teaching about justification by faith (for example James 2.18), or at least a need to refute misunderstandings of Paul's gospel.

This ambivalence feeds into later apocryphal traditions about Paul. For some (for example the Acts of Paul and Thecla), Paul is a great hero, presenting a radical, ascetic gospel message particularly appealing to women as an alternative to marriage. For others (including the Pseudo-Clementine writings), Paul is a demonized figure, responsible for betraying the Jewish vision of Jesus. Strands of both portraits are recognizable in people's attitude towards Paul today.

The Issue of Pseudonymity

Scholarly discussion of Ephesians and the Pastorals raises the issue of pseudonymity. The general scholarly position on these letters is that they are pseudonymous (from the Greek 'falsely named'). They are presented in the name of someone other than their real author, though not necessarily for deceptive purposes. In the case of these four 'Pauline' letters, they are attempts by later Pauline followers to apply Paul's vision, and claim his authority, for a later situation. Two issues are worth flagging up here. One is the claim of pseudonymity itself: how widespread and legitimate a practice was it held to be in the early Church? The second concerns the criteria used for making judgements about pseudonymity.

To begin with the first, evidence exists for the practice of pseudonymity among first-century Jews and in the wider classical world. Many Jewish apocalypses are given the names not of their historical authors, but of significant characters from Israel's past. So too are literary 'testaments', in which a dying figure is presented as preparing his children, or his followers, for life after his death. Hence we find several books attributed to Enoch, an Apocalypse of Abraham, an apocalyptic Book of Daniel, a Testament of Moses, and Testaments of the Twelve Patriarchs.

The difference between these Jewish pseudepigrapha and New Testament examples is that the latter claim the names not of ancient figures but of figures of the recent past, such as Peter or Paul. Nevertheless, they may reflect a distinctive Christian development, according similar authority to the (now deceased) apostolic generation. However, the ancient world was aware of the difference between deceptive pseudonymity (texts setting out to deceive readers about their real author) and transparent pseudonymity (such as Jewish apocalypses and testaments). The issue about the deutero-Paulines and other possibly pseudonymous texts is this: are they intended to deceive, or would their genre mean that ancient readers would have understood their true provenance?[102]

To turn to the second issue: we have already outlined in Chapter 3 the various criteria used to assess the authorship of letters attributed to Paul:

- *Stylistic:* attention to the distinctive style used by the author, with particular attention to the form of Greek used;
- *Linguistic:* looking for a concentration of words and phrases not found in the 'undisputed' Pauline letters;
- *Theological:* evidence for theological positions different from those of Paul, or for significant theological development;
- *Textual:* hints in the manuscript tradition which might support a different authorship.

We also noted some of the criticisms of these criteria. Attention to style, for example, needs also to consider evidence within the letter for the use of a scribe or amanuensis (as in 1 Corinthians 16.21; Colossians 4.18). Attention to rare words or phrases must take into account the relative shortness of all Paul's letters, and the need for particular issues – with their own distinctive vocabulary – to be addressed in certain letters. The theological criterion, as it has sometimes been applied, does not always allow for theological development in Paul's own thinking. In short, these criteria need to be applied judiciously, and to be understood as presenting a cumulative case.

Reflection

What do you think of claims that some Pauline letters are pseudonymous? Is this problematic? Does it challenge modern notions of individual authorship? In what ways might a later generation seek to preserve the memory, teaching and influence of a deceased leader or teacher?

Paul and Ephesians

The glorious vision of Ephesians – describing the unsearchable riches of God's love in Christ – has often been regarded as 'more Pauline than Paul'. If it is by Paul, then it is arguably more of a systematic presentation of his gospel than Romans, urging a rethink about the centre of Paul's theology. This, coupled with its rather impersonal tone, and the manuscript evidence for the omission of 'in Ephesus' at Ephesians 1.1, points to a circular letter rather than a typical Pauline response to a specific situation. For many, this impersonal character is part of the evidence for its being deutero-Pauline.

Among other arguments against Paul's authorship, scholars point to a preponderance of 'non-Pauline' vocabulary, such as 'the devil' (in place of Paul's typical 'Satan'), 'in the heavenlies' (used five times in Ephesians, and never in the undisputed Paulines), and 'the beloved' as a title for Christ. Others object that such statistics are ambiguous: some undisputed letters have a higher percentage of *hapax legomena* than Ephesians. There are significant stylistic differences between the long sentences typical of Ephesians and Paul's undisputed letters, and the author of the former has a fondness for coupling synonyms. As examples of the latter, the Greek literally reads: 'the intention of his will' (Ephesians 1.11), 'the strength of his might' (Ephesians 1.19), and 'the law of commandments in decrees' (Ephesians 2.15). Commentators also point to Ephesians' relationship with Colossians, explained by some (but not all) on the grounds of literary dependence. Further arguments centre on theological development: for instance, Ephesians' doctrine of the Church (for example, Ephesians 1.22–3; 2.20–2; 3.10; 5.24f.), built on the foundations of the 'apostles and prophets' (Ephesians 2.20; cf. 1 Corinthians 3.11), and the more universal scope of Christ's redemptive work, encompassing both heaven and earth (for example Ephesians 1.3–14; though see a similar perspective in Colossians).

One famous view (posited by E. J. Goodspeed) is that Ephesians was penned as a 'covering letter' to the Pauline corpus, written by a disciple involved in an early collection of Paul's letters. However, there is no evidence that it was ever placed at the head of the Pauline epistles. John Muddiman's nuanced position takes seriously that there are passages in Ephesians which Paul could not possibly have written (such as 1.22b–3; 3.5, 10; 5.32), and other passages which Paul could not but have written (such as 3.4, 8; 4.20–1; 6.18–22).[103] It looks to him a 'stand alone' text rather than something composed as an introduction to other letters.

To do

Compare the following passages from Colossians and Ephesians: Colossians 2.19 and Ephesians 4.15b–16; Colossians 3.16–17 and Ephesians 5.18b–20. Do they convince you that one of these letters is dependent upon the other?

The Vision of Ephesians

Whoever composed this letter, and for whatever purpose, it is generally regarded as presenting a magnificent vision of the Pauline gospel. Part of this appeal may be its hymnic, liturgical feel (for example Ephesians 1.3–14; 3.14–21; 5.14). Among the distinctive features of Ephesians are the following:

- *A heightened Christology:* it is Christ, rather than God, who achieves reconciliation (Ephesians 2.16), and who appoints apostles, prophets and evangelists (4.11; cf. 1 Corinthians 12.28; Colossians 1.20; 2.13–14). Emphasis is upon Christ's exaltation to God's right hand, God having already put all things under his feet (1.22; cf. 1 Corinthians 15.24–8).

- *A heightened ecclesiology:* the Church has a more universal scope than Paul's focus on local churches, and as Christ's Body is now distinguished from Christ the Head (Ephesians 1.22–3). It is built on the foundations of apostles and prophets (2.20–2) and has become the medium of God's revelation (3.10). Christ 'loves' the Church as his Bride, and gave himself for her (5.25; cf. Galatians 2.20).

- *A positive view of marriage:* it would be difficult to base a constructive theology of Christian marriage on what Paul has to say on the subject in 1 Corinthians: 'For it is better to marry than to be aflame with passion' (literally 'than to burn', 1 Corinthians 7.9). Ephesians presents a far more positive view, comparing the self-sacrificing love of husband for wife to Christ's sacrificial love for the Church (Ephesians 5.25–33). Indeed, given Christ's example, Ephesians' appeal to husbands may be far more radical than the language of subjection might suggest.

- *An appeal to unity:* this appeal particularly stresses the ending of hostility between Jew and Gentile, enabling those who were 'aliens from the commonwealth of Israel' to become 'citizens with the saints' (Ephesians 2.11–22). The need for such an appeal (primarily to Gentile Christians) may reflect the growing success of the Gentile mission, leading to marginalization of Christian Jews by their Gentile brothers and sisters (cf. Romans 11.17–24).

- *A redefinition of Israel's cultic imagery:* the imagery of the Temple (as in Paul's undisputed letters) has become an important image for the Christian community. Ephesians' use of this (Ephesians 2.11–22) is more far-reaching. Reconciliation has happened through the offering of a sacrifice ('by the blood of Christ'), which is effective for Gentiles as well as Jews. Like the high priest who had access to God's presence on Yom Kippur, Christians now have 'access in one Spirit to the Father'. The old Temple has been replaced by a new one, with Christ as its chief cornerstone, in whom 'the whole structure is joined together and grows into a holy temple in the Lord'.

> **To do**
>
> Consulting Bible encyclopaedias or websites, locate a plan of the Jerusalem Temple in the first century. Note especially the various courts, and the divisions between them. Now reread Ephesians 2.11–22 in the light of your research. How might this passage be illuminated by what you have discovered?

Paul and the Pastorals

Although grouped canonically with Philemon as letters addressed to individuals rather than communities, 1 and 2 Timothy and Titus are known collectively as the Pastoral Epistles. This is because (unlike Philemon) they are addressed to individuals designated by Paul as pastors of churches he founded. Their distinctive vocabulary, Greek style, and subject-matter mark them out as a discrete group within the wider Pauline corpus. Though attributed to Paul (1 Timothy 1.1; 2 Timothy 1.1; Titus 1.1), they are regarded by many scholars as pseudonymous.

We have reiterated above the arguments used to assess authorship, along with certain criticisms of them. Despite these criticisms, applied cumulatively they present a good case against Pauline authorship of the Pastorals. The Greek is generally considered to be of a 'higher' form than that of the other Paulines. For relatively short letters, these three have a strong concentration of 'un-Pauline' words and phrases, and lack many of the conjunctions that are telltale signs of Paul's writing style. Theologically, they lack the eschatological urgency of Paul, focusing instead on developing an ordered existence for the Church in the world, with instructions about 'bishops' or 'overseers' (Greek *episkopoi*), 'deacons' and widows. Textually, they are absent from the Chester Beatty Papyrus (P[46]: *c.*200 CE), at least in its present form, and not found in Marcion's canon. Indeed, there is no clear evidence for knowledge of these epistles before the second half of the second century. In addition, the historical situations they presuppose can only be fitted with difficulty into what is known about Paul's ministry. They require a further stage in his missionary activity after the Roman house-arrest of Acts 28.

If not by Paul, then they can be seen as an attempt to apply his teaching and authority to the different situation of Christian existence after his death. In particular, there is emphasis on sound doctrine (for example Titus 2.1), holding fast to 'what has been entrusted' (the 'deposit') and avoiding 'what is falsely called knowledge' (1 Timothy 6.20). This suggests that the Pastorals have a particular concern to protect against rival understandings of the gospel, claiming Paul as their authority. The warning against 'what is falsely called knowledge' (Greek *gnōsis*) has led some to locate the Pastorals against the background of second-century Gnosticism (although that presupposes a very late dating).

To do

Read all three Pastoral Epistles, noting down any personal references the author provides to events in Paul's life or people associated with him. From your knowledge of Paul's ministry, can you see any problems with fitting them into a chronology of his life?

Revisiting the Pastorals

Scholarly discussion of the Pastorals often results in a negative assessment of these three letters. But is such negativity fair? On the one hand, we should not deny the difficulties many have found with the Pastorals, seeing in them a blunting of Paul's radical edge, presenting a perspective on Paul's teaching (for example regarding women, or the relationship between church and world) which can be used to justify unjust practices and institutions. This real criticism will be explored further below.

But we would not be doing justice to these letters if we ignored other, more positive features. I will mention a selection here:

• Not all scholars are convinced that the three should be treated as a group. As we have noted, some scholars have argued that the Pastorals contain fragments of authentic Pauline letters. Thus they are more than simply post-Pauline creations. Others point to differences in genre: 2 Timothy has the characteristics of Paul's 'last will and testament', as his earthly life draws to its close. This is summed up classically in 2 Timothy 4.6–7: 'As for me, I am already being poured out as a libation, and the time of my departure has come. I have fought the good fight, I have finished the race, I have kept the faith.'

- The overarching concern of these letters is to preserve Paul's legacy for a different situation. This is clear in their desire to refute false teaching, particularly through authoritative teachers. Timothy, for example, despite his youth (1 Timothy 4.12), is to 'fight the good fight of the faith', defending the deposit passed on to him (6.12, 20). Titus has been left behind in Crete to appoint elders there, thus providing continuity with Paul (Titus 1.5).

- This means stressing certain aspects of Paul's teaching rather than others. The Pastorals' tendency towards 'social respectability' can be understood as a development of Paul's doctrine of 'good citizenship' (as at Romans 13.1–7). Though sometimes viewed negatively, this aspect of the Pastorals presents a positive attitude to the world. The Church does not stand over against the world, but affirms what is good in society. Indeed, the vision of the Church in the Pastorals draws heavily on Graeco-Roman institutions, notably the household. The Church is now the 'household of God' (1 Timothy 3.15). This has its dangers: it can blunt the Church's counter-cultural edge. On the other hand, it balances more world-renouncing tendencies in Christianity. Moreover, it could be seen as having an evangelistic purpose, drawing in those committed to the order of Graeco-Roman society. It preserves, for a new situation, Paul's conviction that the gospel is to be proclaimed to all the Gentiles.

- Sociological approaches to the Pastorals (notably that of Margaret Mac-Donald)[104] have challenged as simplistic the view that they represent a degeneration from an original Pauline charismatic radicalism to a straitjacketed institutionalization ('early Catholicism' viewed in a negative sense). Rather, argues MacDonald, institutionalization as a process would have begun as early as Paul's day. She utilizes a sociological model which points to the necessity of this process in any group in order for it to survive and continue to exert influence: from community-building (Paul's authentic letters) to community-stabilizing (here she locates Colossians and Ephesians) to community-protecting (exemplified by the Pastorals).

Has Paul been Betrayed?

One question is often bubbling under the surface of discussion of the deutero-Pauline letters: has Paul been betrayed? Has the radical, liberating, charismatic edge of Paul's gospel of freedom somehow been tamed, as later Pauline writers accommodate themselves – and the gospel – to societal norms? Has Paul's message, along with the people who convey it – become institutionalized?

One issue often serves to illustrate this concern: the role of women. This is particularly relevant to the Pastorals (though feminist critics have also raised questions about the bride–bridegroom language of Ephesians). The crucial, and much-debated passage comes at the end of 1 Timothy 2:

> Let a woman learn in silence with full submission. I permit no woman to teach or to have authority over a man; she is to keep silent. (1 Timothy 2.11–12)

The language is reminiscent of an authentic Pauline letter, 1 Corinthians 14.33b–6, where women or wives are told to 'be silent in the churches' and not permitted 'to speak' or 'to chatter' (Greek *lalein*). These verses are often treated as a gloss or interpolation (partly on textual grounds), though one can make sense of them as part of the wider argument of 1 Corinthians 11—14 (dealing with liturgical order in Corinth). What in 1 Corinthians seems to be addressing a specific issue – wives interrupting the liturgy to ask questions of their husbands (verse 35) – has become in 1 Timothy a general principle, and now explicitly rules out teaching.

For some, there is no contradiction between 1 Corinthians and 1 Timothy. Both clearly teach the quite different positions of men and women in society, or the Church, or the marriage relationship. For others, the 1 Timothy passage is difficult to reconcile with 1 Corinthians 11.2–16, which presupposes a liturgical role for both men and women in praying and prophesying publicly. The position of the Pastorals is regarded as a retrograde step from Paul's vision of 'no longer male and female' (Galatians 3.28), as early Christianity conforms to established societal norms.

Others still see a specific context for 1 Timothy's denial of a woman's teaching role. The clue lies in the reference to a woman being 'saved through childbearing' (1 Timothy 2.15). Such a saying would make sense, in the context of Ephesians' positive view of marriage, as a refutation of more ascetical views of Paul's gospel (easily derived from 1 Corinthians 7). We have later evidence for just such a view in the second-century Acts of Paul and Thecla. This describes how Thecla, a young woman betrothed to a man called Thamyris, renounces marriage in favour of virginity after hearing Paul's teaching, including these words:

> Blessed are the bodies of the virgins, for they shall be well pleasing to God, and shall not lose the reward of their purity. For the word of the Father shall be for them a work of salvation in the day of his Son, and they shall have rest for ever and ever. (Acts of Paul and Thecla 6)[105]

After being converted and baptized, Thecla is told by Paul: 'Go and teach the word of God' (Acts of Paul and Thecla 41).

It is possible that the Pastorals are responding to a similar scenario, in which the teaching role of Pauline women is linked to a prizing of virginity and shunning of marriage, with its consequences for society's stability. The Pastorals would then be seeking to provide an alternative vision of a Christian society, in which marriage performed a positive role. They would be critiquing an overly ascetical view of Paul, which had already caused difficulty in Corinth years before. But affirming one aspect of the Pauline vision for the future may lead to other voices being sidelined or even silenced. Whether the cost of 1 Timothy's response has been too great remains a matter of continuing debate.

Further Reading

J. Christiaan Beker, 1992, *Heirs of Paul*, Edinburgh: T. & T. Clark.
Margaret Davies, 1996, *The Pastoral Epistles*, New Testament Guides; Sheffield: Sheffield Academic Press.

Neil Elliott, 1995, *Liberating Paul: The Justice of God and the Politics of the Apostle*, Sheffield: Sheffield Academic Press, chapter 2.

John Muddiman, 2001, *The Epistle to the Ephesians*, Black's New Testament Commentaries; London and New York: Continuum.

Frances Young, 1994, *The Theology of the Pastoral Epistles*, New Testament Theology; Cambridge: Cambridge University Press.

10

The Letter to the Hebrews

Locating Hebrews on the Map of Early Christianity

'Who wrote the Letter to the Hebrews? In truth, God knows.' So wrote Origen, the great biblical exegete of the early Church (as quoted by Eusebius, *Historia Ecclesiastica* 6.25.11–14). Origen's statement highlights the uniqueness of Hebrews: it stands alone among the New Testament epistles for its powerful rhetoric, its intricate yet coherent argument, and its distinctive proclamation of Christ as the great high priest. Though long attributed to Paul (particularly in the East), the consensus view among scholars is that it is not by him (see Table 20). Indeed, it does not even claim to be by Paul, unlike all the letters in the main Pauline corpus. A host of other early Christian figures have been proposed as its author: Barnabas (for example by Tertullian); Luke (according to Clement of Alexandria, translating Paul's original into Greek); Apollos (first suggested by Martin Luther); Clement of Rome; Priscilla; even the Virgin Mary. Perhaps Origen's own assessment offers the sagest advice.

Nevertheless, agnosticism about its authorship does not prevent us trying to locate Hebrews on the map of first-century Christianity. Some connection with the Pauline tradition might be implied by the reference to 'our brother Timothy' at Hebrews 13.23 (although Timothy may have been known

---

Table 20: Paul and the Author of Hebrews.

Paul writes the following about his dependence on his predecessors:

> Paul an apostle – sent neither by human commission nor from human authorities, but through Jesus Christ and God the Father, who raised him from the dead. (Galatians 1.1)

> But when God . . . was pleased to reveal his Son to me, so that I might proclaim him among the Gentiles, I did not confer with any human being, nor did I go up to Jerusalem to those who were already apostles before me, but I went away at once into Arabia, and afterwards I returned to Damascus. (Galatians 1.15–17)

The author of Hebrews writes of his dependence on his predecessors:

> It was declared at first through the Lord, and it was attested to us by those who heard him. (Hebrews 2.3)

---

more widely). Others point out the links between Hebrews and the speech of Stephen in Acts 7, regarding both as representing a radical, anti-Temple viewpoint associated with the 'Hellenists' or Greek-speaking Jewish Christians from Jerusalem (see Acts 6.1). For example, both Stephen and Hebrews focus on Israel's wilderness wanderings under Moses, and interpret the wilderness tabernacle as modelled on a (heavenly) pattern revealed to Moses on the mountain (Acts 7.44; Hebrews 8.5; cf. Exodus 25.40). Both Stephen's speech and Hebrews imply a critique of the earthly Temple and its cult.

An alternative view sees links with strands of Judaism and Jewish Christianity influenced by Platonic philosophy (notably the Middle Platonism of Philo of Alexandria). One example is Hugh Montefiore's proposal, building on Luther and C. Spicq, that Hebrews was written by Apollos to the Corinthians.[106] According to Acts 18.24–6, Apollos was a Jew from Philo's city of Alexandria, 'an eloquent man, well-versed in the scriptures', who knew the baptism of John and was instructed more fully in the Christian way by Paul's associates Priscilla and Aquila. The author of Hebrews is certainly eloquent, and knows the Greek Old Testament well. There are also links in phraseology between Hebrews and 1 Corinthians (for example the claim that the addressees are ready only for milk, not solid food: Hebrews 5.12; 1 Corinthians 3.2), which Montefiore believes to be Paul's response to Apollos' letter.

Still others see links in theme, vocabulary and techniques with the Qumran scrolls, and propose that the first recipients of Hebrews were converted priests of the Essene branch of Judaism, now needing reassurance that following Christ was to their benefit.[107]

Reflection

Do you think it important to establish who wrote Hebrews? If you have a view on its authorship, where does this come from? After reading Hebrews again, see whether your view has changed.

Ways into Reading

However, historical questions are not the only questions to be asked of Hebrews. It also raises important literary and theological issues. Yet many modern readers are put off by the intricacy and apparent complexity of the argument, or the unfamiliarity of the imagery (at least for those who do not spend their spare time studying the details of Jewish sacrifice in Leviticus!). Without some helps to find a 'way in' to the text, one may feel that one cannot see the trees for the branches, or even the branches for the twigs, let alone the wood for the trees! The following are some suggestions for getting into the literary and theological sophistication of the text:

- *The literary genre:* What kind of book is Hebrews? Although generally referred to as a letter, Hebrews lacks conventional epistolary features, at least at the beginning (it ends as a letter does, at Hebrews 13.18–25). Many scholars think it is best regarded as a *homily* or sermon, albeit sent from a distance rather than delivered orally by the author. Our author describes his work as 'a word of exhortation' (Hebrews 13.22, a phrase also used of Paul's synagogue sermon at Antioch-in-Pisidia, Acts 13.15).

- *The rhetoric:* sermons and homilies are generally preached in order to draw out the implications of scripture for the audiences, and to elicit a particular response. The art of persuasion (rhetoric) was highly prized in the ancient world, and rhetorical criticism of the New Testament seeks to uncover the rhetorical techniques used by the New Testament authors. Hebrews is particularly noted for its 'deliberative rhetoric', aimed at persuading an audience to take, or dissuading them from taking, a particular course of action in the future. It also uses 'epideictic rhetoric', which uses praise and blame to achieve a desired effect. Given its appeal to the emotions, however, particularly its use of threats and fear as well as encouragement and praise, some commentators find the author's rhetorical technique morally objectionable. For others, it is justifiable on the grounds that 'desperate circumstances call for desperate measures'.

- *A theological point of entry:* Hebrews can be understood as a sustained exploration of the early Christian claim that 'Christ died for our sins in accordance with the scriptures' (1 Corinthians 15.3). This early claim that Christ's death was 'for our sins' interprets the cross as some kind of sacrifice. Ancient audiences would ask: if Christ's death is a sacrifice, who is the priest offering this sacrifice? Hebrews presents a sustained argument from the Old Testament that Christ is that priest, and that his sacrifice is sufficient to replace all the sacrifices offered by Israel's priesthood. It is essentially unpacking what is implicit in 1 Corinthians 15.3.

- *The argument:* despite our author's tendency to pursue subsidiary arguments, there is in fact one sustained argument running throughout. Readers of Hebrews should hold onto that, and try to follow what that main argument is (plotting a basic structure to the argument which can be revised on subsequent readings). Indeed, it is a good policy to read Hebrews all in one go, or better, to have someone else read it out to you (recalling the fact that the first recipients of Hebrews were an audience rather than a set of readers). In particular, remembering that Hebrews argues 'from the lesser to the greater' (if this is the case with so-and-so, which is inferior, how much more will be the case with the salvation in Christ, which is shown to be superior) will help you remain on track.

- *The conceptual background:* one key debate in the study of Hebrews concerns the philosophical/theological background of the author, which determines the way in which he views and describes the world. As noted above, some regard the author as influenced by Plato's philosophy, particularly as mediated through the first-century Jewish writer Philo. On this way of reading Hebrews, emphasis is placed on a spatial contrast between heaven, the realm of ultimate reality, and earth, which is an imperfect, changeable reflection of the real thing (building on Plato's notion of the realm of Forms or Ideas). The really real world is not this physical, visible world, but the invisible world. Thus the great contrast in Hebrews is between the true, perfect sanctuary in heaven, where Christ ministers forever as high priest, and the earthly sanctuary of Israel's priests, which is imperfect, a pale shadow of the real thing. An alternative view locates the background in Jewish eschatology with its more temporal focus (the contrast between the present evil age, and the age to come when God's world will be what it was intended to be), and particularly in Jewish apocalyptic, which was able to combine this temporal axis with the more spatial axis of heaven/earth. In this reading, Hebrews' main contrast is between the old sanctuary of the Levitical priests, and that which it foreshadowed, the new temple currently located in heaven ('in the mind of God').[108] The difference can be illustrated by two translations of the same passage. The Revised Standard Version (RSV, partially followed by the NRSV) uses Platonic terms to translate certain Greek words:

> They [the Levitical priests] serve a copy and shadow of the heavenly sanctuary. (Hebrews 8.5)

An alternative translation of Hebrews 8.5, however, would give a sense more akin to Jewish apocalyptic eschatology:

> They offer worship in a pattern and foreshadowing of the heavenly things . . .

Either way, what both readings have in common is a conviction that the unseen, spiritual realm – populated by myriad angels, and where Christ is exalted – is more real, more powerful and somehow more authentic than our limited perspective on the world.

To do

Compare different English translations of Hebrews 9.23–4 and 10.1. Try and decide where they stand in the debate about Platonic/Philonic or Jewish apocalyptic background to Hebrews. What different nuances do the translations give to the passages in question?

The Priestly Messiah

Many readers of the New Testament – particularly Christian readers – assume that Jews of the first century placed all their hopes on a kingly Messiah (from the Hebrew meaning 'anointed'), one who would lead an army against the Roman occupiers and restore the royal dynasty of David. As we saw in Chapter 1, Jewish messianic hopes were rather more diverse. The 'Letter to the Hebrews' gives us a glimpse of this diversity continuing into earliest Christianity. For although the author of Hebrews certainly believes Christ to be a king of the line of David, he is first and foremost a priestly Messiah: 'a merciful and faithful high priest in the service of God' (Hebrews 2.17). In contrast to most other New Testament writers (though not the author of Revelation: see Revelation 1.12–20), who present Christ as just a royal Messiah, or the Qumran scrolls, which envisage two Messiahs, one a king and one a priest (1QS 9.10–11; 1QSa 2.12–15), the author of Hebrews stresses that Christ is a priest-king. This is not a straightforward claim to make, however, and requires a number of steps:

- *Genealogy:* to be a priest in Israel required being a male of the tribe of Levi. The author of Hebrews knows that Christ came from the tribe of Judah, and therefore could not be a priest of this kind (Hebrews 7.14).
- *Scriptural exegesis:* our author finds a solution in Psalm 110, possibly originally a coronation psalm for Israel's king, but widely considered by early Christians to refer to Jesus' ascension ('The Lord says to my lord, "Sit at

my right hand . . . "', Psalm 110.1). At verse 4, the psalmist has this to say of the king: 'You are a priest for ever according to the order of Melchizedek.' The king, in other words, is also a priest, though not of the Israelite line of Levi.

- *Figure of Melchizedek:* Melchizedek first appears in the Old Testament in Genesis, as a mysterious priest-king of Salem (that is pre-Israelite Jerusalem), whom Abraham encounters (Genesis 14.18–20; cf. Hebrews 7.1–10). Psalm 110 may allude to an early form of sacral kingship associated with Melchizedek, still preserved by Judah's kings in the biblical period.

- *Christ as eternal priest:* the psalm speaks of the king as 'a priest for ever'. Christ's qualification to be an eternal priest of Melchizedek's order would appear to be twofold. First, Hebrews seems to speak at 1.2–3 of the Son as pre-existent, like divine Wisdom. Second, through his resurrection Christ now lives an imperishable life, and stands as high priest in the eternal, heavenly sanctuary (Hebrews 7.24; 13.20).

Having established Christ's high priestly credentials, the author can develop this distinctive Christology in striking ways. What does this mean in practice about his understanding of Christ, and how might this impinge on the lives of his Christian audience, and indeed on audiences hearing Hebrews ever since?

- *It brings together the human and divine dimensions of Christ's person:* Hebrews understands Christ as the perfect candidate for high priesthood, given that he is both one of us and one who belongs to heaven. As divine Son, he mediates divine blessings to God's people; as human being, he is able to offer sacrifice on behalf of his human brothers and sisters, and intercede on their behalf. Some of the most beautiful passages in Hebrews emphasize the importance of Christ's humanity:

> Since, then, we have a great high priest who has passed through the heavens, Jesus, the Son of God, let us hold fast to our confession. For we do not have a high priest who is unable to sympathize with our weaknesses, but we have one who in every respect has been tested as we are, yet without sin. Let us therefore approach the throne of grace with

boldness, so that we may receive mercy and find grace to help in time of need. (Hebrews 4.14–16)

- *It emphasizes the dignity of humanity:* by presenting Christ as our great high priest, Hebrews insists that the work of salvation was carried out through one of our own race, our own flesh and blood. To cite the old patristic adage: 'That which he has not assumed, he has not healed.' Moreover, in being exalted to heaven, Hebrews believes that Christ has taken his – and our – human nature with him. As one Ascensiontide hymn has it:

> Thou hast raised our human nature
> In the clouds to God's right hand;
> There we sit in heavenly places,
> There with thee in glory stand. (Christopher Wordsworth, 1807–85)

- *It offers an understanding of Christ which deals with human sin and failure:* religious sacrifice offers a means of dealing with sin, which fractures not only the vertical relationship between God and his people, but also the horizontal relationship of God's people one with another. Hebrews presents an understanding of Christ's work in sacrificial terms, which fulfils that human need in a religious tradition that has abandoned animal sacrifice.
- *It draws upon two different types of Jewish sacrifice to express different aspects of Christ's work:* the first is the Day of Atonement (Yom Kippur) sacrifice where the Levitical high priest goes into the Holy of Holies with the blood which reconciles God to God's people. Christ's entry once for all through the veil of the heavenly sanctuary is understood as replacing that annual Day of Atonement sacrifice. However, in the Old Testament, a sacrifice was also offered to inaugurate a new covenant or alliance between two parties. Drawing on the 'new covenant' passage from the prophet Jeremiah (Jeremiah 31.31–4; cf. Hebrews 8.8–12), Hebrews understands Christ's death as a sacrifice initiating a new covenant, which renders the old covenant obsolete (Hebrews 8.13).
- *It offers an example for the audience to embrace:* although Hebrews insists that Christ's sacrifice was offered once for all and cannot be repeated or

added to, there are aspects of Christ's priestly and sacrificial ministry which the text urges readers to imitate. As well as being a unique sacrifice, it is also an exemplary sacrifice. Christ is set forward as the example of a sacrificial life, which learns obedience through suffering (Hebrews 5.8).

Understanding Sacrifice

But it is precisely this notion of sacrifice which makes Hebrews so difficult for many contemporary readers. Sacrifice – in its concrete expression of offering animals to God or to the gods – is hardly central to the experience of most twenty-first-century humans, even those who are religious. For many, it sounds a barbaric practice, envisaged as an activity intended to appease an angry deity. Others, rightly shocked by the way in which human beings – especially daughters, wives and mothers – have been encouraged to 'sacrifice themselves' for others, shudder at even the most metaphorical use of sacrificial language.

Yet in the ancient world, sacrifice was a day-to-day reality. Jews went on pilgrimage to the Temple in Jerusalem, where sacrifices were offered to Israel's God. Greek and Roman cities were dominated by temples to the various deities, whose primary rites were sacrificial. The earliest Christians – whether living in Jewish Palestine or in cities such as Antioch, Ephesus, Corinth or Rome – inhabited a world in which offering sacrifice was the norm. In urban markets, the bulk of meat for sale was sacred meat (what Paul calls 'food sacrificed to idols', as at 1 Corinthians 8.1), the surplus from the sacrificial animals after the god's portion had been burned and the priests' share taken.

In the contemporary world, however, 'sacrifice' language is much less central. We speak of sacrifice as a metaphor: parents making sacrifices for their children; soldiers laying down their lives as a sacrifice. The action described is only too real; its description as a 'sacrifice' remains metaphorical. Catholic and Orthodox Christians, it is true, understand the Eucharist as a sacrifice. However, even this does not require that animals be slaughtered during a Catholic Mass or Orthodox Liturgy.

How can contemporary readers begin to engage with Hebrews' language of sacrifice? A first move might be to reflect on what humans do when human relationships are fractured. It is a common human experience – expressed differently in different cultures – to want something concrete to be done in order to repair what has been fractured. This normally requires someone – one of the estranged parties –taking the initiative, perhaps offering a gift which symbolizes themselves as a sign of sorrow, reconciliation, or forgiveness. It reflects a basic human need for something to be done to put things right.

In some contexts this is done vicariously, by someone else or something else. At the heart of animal sacrifice lies precisely this kind of vicarious understanding: an animal, or a bird, which is costly to me depending on my financial situation, takes my place. However, sacrificial animals have no awareness of the broken relationship – normally a relationship between human beings and God or the gods – and their part in restoring it. They can be an external substitute for internal transformation.

The sacrifice of Christ in Hebrews represents a movement away from such an external understanding of sacrifice (the offering of animals or other gifts, which cost in financial terms) to the internal (a costly offering of self, which springs from the human heart). It is precisely this internal dimension which makes Christ's sacrifice so effective:

> For it is impossible for the blood of bulls and goats to take away sins. Consequently, when Christ came into the world, he said,
>
> > Sacrifices and offerings you have not desired,
> > but a body you have prepared for me;
> > in burnt offerings and sin offerings you have taken no pleasure.
> > Then I said, 'See, God, I have come to do your will, O God'
> > (in the scroll of the book it is written of me).
> > (Hebrews 10.4–7)

However, we misunderstand if we think that sacrifice is always to do with righting wrongs. In Israel's cult, there are thanksgiving offerings as well as sacrifices for sin. There is the offering of the 'first fruits' of the flock or the harvest: a joyful offering to God of what God has given, in hope that he will give more of the same. In short, there is an element in sacrifice of free, joyful giving of one's self, and of what one has, in gratitude to God and for the benefit of others. Hence as well as understanding Christ's death as a sacrifice 'for sin', and a sacrifice which initiates a new covenant relationship between God and his people, Hebrews also exploits other dimensions of sacrifice. Human suffering (probably specifically suffering under persecution) is interpreted as a sacrificial participation in Christ's sacrifice (Hebrews 13.12–13). Joyful worship of God, in early Christian house churches quite unlike temples in other respects, is understood as a 'sacrifice of praise' (Hebrews 13.15). Sharing material goods with others, such as giving alms, is presented as a sacrifice pleasing to God (Hebrews 13.16), for it requires the giving of oneself.

Reflection

What does the word 'sacrifice' mean to you? In what contexts would you use it, or have you heard it used? Are any of these religious contexts? Do you find the idea offensive, or appealing, or both? What reasons might you have for this? What place might a notion of sacrifice have in Christian theology?

Following the Two Jesuses

But Hebrews not only presents Jesus as a great high priest. The earlier chapters have argued that Christ is also superior to other mediator figures in Israel's story: the angels, who were believed to have delivered the Law to Moses on Mount Sinai, and who ministered as priests in the heavenly Temple (Hebrews 1.5—2.18); Moses himself, the great mediator and redeemer figure (Hebrews 3.1–6).

However, there is another figure whose significance might be overlooked by readers working from an English Bible: Joshua. Joshua son of Nun was an assistant of Moses, sent into the land of Canaan to spy out the territory in preparation for Israel's entry (for example Numbers 13.1–16; Deuteronomy 1.38). Joshua's name in the Greek Septuagint is *Iēsous* (Jesus). Early Christians hearing Hebrews read out in Greek would have difficulty distinguishing between the two. Our author plays on the parallels between Joshua/Jesus son of Nun and Joshua/Jesus Son of God. The former was a pioneer in going ahead to spy out the land of Canaan. The latter is also a 'pioneer' (Hebrews 2.10; 12.2) in that he has gone ahead of God's people into the 'promised rest' of heaven:

> For if *Iēsous* had given them rest, God would not speak later about another day. So then, a sabbath rest still remains for the people of God. (Hebrews 4.8–9)

> Since, then, we have a great high priest who has passed through the heavens, *Iēsous*, the Son of God, let us hold fast to our confession. (Hebrews 4.14)

If the first Joshua/Jesus is a type of the second, then there is also a parallel (and a contrast) between the wilderness generation under Joshua and the contemporary people of God who look to Jesus. Hebrews presents a dynamic picture of the Church as the wandering people of God, progressing on their journey towards the promised rest of heaven, looking ahead (and up) to where they are going rather than back to what they might be missing. The Church is not yet perfect, but a people on the move, following Jesus who has gone before them:

> Therefore, since we are surrounded by so great a cloud of witnesses, let us also lay aside every weight and the sin that clings so closely, and let us run with perseverance the race that is set before us, looking to *Iēsous* the pioneer and perfecter of our faith, who for the sake of the joy that was set before him endured the cross, disregarding its shame, and has taken his seat at the right hand of the throne of God. (Hebrews 12.1–2)

> **To do**
>
> Read the list of those who lived 'by faith' in Hebrews 11 (the 'cloud of witnesses' of 12.1). Try and work out which Old Testament figures and events are being described (you might get a bit lost in verses 33–8, and need to consult a commentary). Are there any significant omissions? Is there anything surprising? What function do these examples serve?

The Purpose of Hebrews

One important historical question remains: Is it possible to say why Hebrews was first written? Precise identification of the historical first recipients is not possible, given that none are named directly. Nevertheless, it is possible to glean from the text a fairly good picture of the readers:

- They are second-generation Christians rather than original followers of Jesus (Hebrews 2.3), originally properly enlightened (probably a synonym for baptism, 6.4) and taught the basics of the faith (5.12).
- Given the intricate discussion of Jewish cultic matters throughout Hebrews, they are most likely Greek-speaking Christian Jews.
- They seem to be located somewhere in Italy (the most obvious reading of 13.24: 'Those from Italy' but now living abroad, where the author is located, send greetings back to the recipients). Rome is a good candidate.
- They have experienced sufferings and 'afflictions' for their faith in the past, including the seizing or plundering of their own possessions (10.32–4); they have also visited fellow sufferers in prison (10.34; 13.3, 23). If they are in Rome, there may be an allusion to Nero's persecution in the early 60s.
- Now they have become 'dull in understanding' (5.11), in danger of losing confidence in their Christian confession and growing weary (10.35; 12.3).
- Some of their group are no longer meeting together with fellow Christians, and the addressees are urged not to neglect to do so themselves (10.25).

Indeed, they are bidden to 'remember' their leaders (13.7, possibly leaders of the past who suffered martyrdom), and 'obey' their leaders in the present (13.17).

- At least from the author's perspective, they are in danger of being carried away by 'all kinds of strange teachings', especially about 'foods' (13.9). Jewish food-laws may well be at issue.
- They need to be assured that they still have 'an altar' (13.10), connected to Christ who was sacrificed 'outside the city gate' just as the sacrificial animals were burned outside the camp (13.11–12).

Hebrews' distinctive priestly Christology, then, may point us to the heart of the problem: they need convincing that Christ's death can achieve what the Levitical sacrifices were believed to have achieved. Moreover, against a climate of suffering and even persecution, their Christian confession may have lost something of its gloss. Their leaders seem to have tried everything to convince them otherwise, but in vain. Perhaps the author of Hebrews – clearly a respected figure – is their last resort: if he cannot win the addressees over by his powerful rhetoric and force of argument, then no one can!

The Reception of Hebrews

The fact that Hebrews was preserved for posterity may be an indication that it succeeded in its aims. But the significance of Hebrews did not end with its original historical purpose. Reception history – study of how a biblical text has been received throughout history – points to Hebrews' rich ongoing influence.[109]

Eastern icons of Christ the enthroned high priest, and Western crucifixes showing the victorious Christ dressed as Priest and King, present the distinctive priestly Christology of Hebrews in a vivid visual fashion. Both reveal the profound influence of the theology of Hebrews on the devotional lives of ordinary Christians across the centuries. They point to the accessibility of this image of a high priest who is both one of us and able to do for us what we cannot do for ourselves.

But Hebrews' emphasis on Christ as priest and sacrifice has also had

an important impact on theological debate. It has proved a veritable bat-
tle-ground, with quite different Christian understandings of the nature of
the ordained ministry and the Eucharist claiming support in the text. For
some, the image of Christ the high priest lays the foundation for an understanding of a Christian ministerial priesthood participating in Christ's one
high-priesthood. A more Protestant position has read Hebrews as abolishing
the need for any human mediatorial priesthood. There has been a similar
Catholic–Protestant divide over understanding the Eucharist as a sacrifice.
Protestants tend to point to Hebrews' stress on the once-for-all nature of
Christ's offering, while Catholic Christians, along with their Orthodox
brothers and sisters, highlight the ongoing effects of Christ's sacrifice, made
present for the worshippers during the Mass or Divine Liturgy.

This eucharistic interpretation of Hebrews is reflected in a number of
English hymns. The nineteenth-century Anglican hymn writer William
Bright (1824–1901) penned the following words:

> Once, only once, and once for all,
>   His precious life he gave;
> Before the Cross in faith we fall,
>   And own it strong to save.

His hymn goes on to compare the moment when 'the priest of Aaron's line
within the holiest stood' with the ongoing intercession of Christ, 'who once
atonement wrought, our Priest of endless power'. The final verse of this hymn
expresses that Catholic conviction that, at the Eucharist, the past sacrifice
of Christ on the cross is made present in order that the worshippers might
receive its benefits:

> And so we show thy death, O Lord,
>   Till thou again appear,
> And feel, when we approach thy board,
>   We have an altar here.

Similarly, 'Alleluia, Sing to Jesus' by W. Chatterton Dix (1837–98) climaxes
with Hebrews' description of Christ the great high priest passing into the
heavenly Temple:

Thou within the veil hast entered,
    Robed in flesh, our great High Priest;
Thou on earth both Priest and Victim
    In the Eucharistic Feast.

But the priestly Christology of Hebrews and its view of Christ's death as a sacrifice is not Hebrews' only contribution to Christian theology and experience. Its dynamic vision of God's wandering people journeying towards the promised land has also influenced the Christian imagination. John Bunyan's *Pilgrim's Progress* is a famous example. In the mid-twentieth century, this aspect of Hebrews became particularly important for Roman Catholic ecclesiology (theology of the Church). The Second Vatican Council's Dogmatic Constitution on the Church (*Lumen Gentium*, 1964) puts it in these terms:

As Israel according to the flesh which wandered in the desert was already called the Church of God (2 Esdras 13.1; cf. Numbers 20.4; Deuteronomy 23.1 ff.), so too, the new Israel, which advances in this present era in search of a future and permanent city (cf. Hebrews 13.14), is called also the Church of Christ . . .[110]

Further Reading

Luke Timothy Johnson, 2006, *Hebrews: A Commentary*, New Testament Library; Louisville and London: Westminster John Knox.

Marie E. Isaacs, 1992, *Sacred Space*, Sheffield: Sheffield Academic Press.

Andrew T. Lincoln, 2006, *Hebrews: A Guide*, London and New York: T. & T. Clark.

Barnabas Lindars, 1991, *The Theology of the Letter to the Hebrews*, New Testament Theology; Cambridge: Cambridge University Press.

11

The Catholic Epistles

Where Does the Centre Lie?

The shape and contents of the New Testament might give the impression that the figure of Paul overshadowed all others (with the possible exception of Peter) in earliest Christianity. Works attributed to Paul comprise 13 of the 27 New Testament books, while more than half of the Acts of the Apostles is concerned with his travels and ministry. As well as presenting him as the great letter-writer of the early Church, the New Testament portrait allows a view of him as the chief architect of the Gentile mission, and therefore the one to whom millions of Christians are indebted for their faith. Christianity without Paul, in other words, would be unthinkable for many.

But how universal is this portrait? Travelling more widely in the Christian world, to some of its great pilgrimage centres, might suggest a rather differ-ent picture. Even in the city of Rome, the traditional site of his martyrdom and burial, Paul does not stand alone. In many ways he is outshone by the figure of Peter, 'prince of the apostles', whose shrine forms the centre of the great Vatican basilica bearing his name.

However, in the birthplace of the Christian faith, Jerusalem, another name dominates: that of James 'the brother of the Lord' (see Acts 15.13–21; Galatians 1.19; 2.9). James is remembered in Christian tradition as the first bishop of that city, and accounts of his death as a martyr are preserved in both Jewish (Josephus) and Christian authors. The Armenian Cathedral in Jerusalem is dedicated to him, and claims to contain his tomb, along with the head of another James, James the apostle, brother of John. Elsewhere, other early Christian leaders made their own impact: John the apostle in Ephesus, for example, or Thomas in India.

This chapter will introduce another seven New Testament letters, which preserve something of this non-Pauline heritage. Two of these letters (James and Jude) are attributed to members of Jesus' blood-family. The remainder are presented as the work of two prominent members of the Twelve, Peter (two letters) and John (three). Because they are found in our New Testaments after Paul, they are often neglected, even by Christians. However, in some ancient canonical lists, they – and not Paul's letters – are located at the centre of the New Testament, immediately after Acts. Historically speaking (if not necessarily chronologically so), this makes sense, for James, Peter, John and Jude were active before Paul ever arrived on the scene.

Reflection

What is your image of earliest Christianity? Who were the prominent leaders, and how central a role do you think Paul played? Does the presence of the Catholic Epistles in the New Testament force you to rethink this?

What Makes a Catholic Epistle 'Catholic'?

Why are these seven New Testament letters called the Catholic Epistles? The phrase 'Catholic Epistles' as a description of this group is in use by the fourth century at the latest. Both Eusebius (c.275–339) and Athanasius (c.293–373) know them by this designation. Earlier sources reveal that the adjective 'catholic' had already been used of some of the individual letters (for example 1 Peter and 1 John), as well as 'non-canonical' texts intended for wider circulation. The word 'catholic' means 'universal', and thus the seven Catholic Epistles are so called because they are understood to have been composed for the Church at large, for general circulation, as opposed to specific congregations or individuals (as for Paul's letters).

Closer study might suggest that some of these letters are not quite so 'universal' in their composition. As we shall see, James was almost certainly written with congregations of Jewish Christians in mind, rather than for the whole Church, Jewish and Gentile. 2 and 3 John are addressed to specific individuals (or to an individual and a specific church, if the term 'elect lady' at 2 John 1 refers to a congregation rather than a woman). Nevertheless, for the most part, they have the character of encyclical letters, addressed to a number of different churches in different locations (in contrast to Paul's Corinth, Thessalonica, etc.):

> James, a servant of God and of the Lord Jesus Christ, to the twelve tribes in the Dispersion: Greetings. (James 1.1)

> Peter, an apostle of Jesus Christ, to the exiles of the Dispersion in Pontus, Galatia, Cappadocia, Asia and Bithynia. (1 Peter 1.1)

> Simeon Peter, a servant and apostle of Jesus Christ, to those who have received a faith as precious as ours through the righteousness of our God and Saviour Jesus Christ: may grace and peace be yours in abundance in the knowledge of God and of Jesus our Lord. (2 Peter 1.1–2)

> Jude, a servant of Jesus Christ and brother of James, to those who are called, who are beloved in God the Father and kept safe for Jesus Christ, may mercy, peace, and love be yours in abundance. (Jude 1.1–2)

In the case of a writing like James, we may owe its preservation in the canon to its transformation from a circular letter to Christian-Jewish synagogues into an epistle of relevance to all Christians, including Gentiles. In the case of 1 Peter, its encyclical nature overrides its original focus on Christian communities located specifically in Asia Minor (admittedly a huge geographical area!).

James, Jewish Christianity and 'Westocentrism'

The first of the seven is attributed to James. Although this name is shared by several New Testament characters (it is the common Jewish name Jacob), its implied author is almost certainly James 'the brother of the Lord', prominent leader of the Jerusalem church. The only other main contender, James the son of Zebedee, was martyred relatively early (by Herod Agrippa I in the early forties, according to Acts 12.2). Although modern scholarship has tended to regard James as pseudonymous (written in James's name after his death), more recent commentators have shown a greater willingness to treat the letter as relatively early and penned by James himself.[111]

For those with an interest in earliest Christian history, James is fascinating for at least two reasons. First, it provides a rare glimpse into issues facing non-Pauline Jewish Christianity in the first century. The implied audience of James are from the twelve tribes of the Jewish diaspora (James 1.1), they meet in synagogues (2.2), and the author provides teaching on the appropriate interpretation of the Jewish Law (which, at least on the surface, presents a quite different stance to Paul: for example 2.14–26). It may be that the intended recipients were Jewish communities of believers in Jesus evangelized from Jerusalem (1 Corinthians 9.5 testifies to 'the brothers of the Lord' engaging in missionary activity).

Second, close attention to James's greeting challenges the 'westocentrism' of so much New Testament scholarship. If we take the reference to 'the twelve tribes in the Dispersion' (Greek *diaspora*) seriously, then this letter was originally intended for Christian Jews living in the east as well as the west. As Richard Bauckham has shown,[112] the western diaspora was primarily made up of descendants of the southern tribes of Judah, Benjamin and Levi. James's 'twelve tribes' probably include descendants of the northern exiles, located in northern Mesopotamia and Media, especially Adiabene. Bible maps which centre New Testament Christianity on Asia Minor (Turkey) may need to be redrawn to bring in significant territory to the east (and also to the south, for there was a significant Jewish community in Egypt).

Largely due to its dismissal by Luther as an 'epistle of straw', James's recent reception history (particularly in the West) has been rather chequered. Discussion has tended to focus on James's relationship to Paul, and to the Pauline teaching on justification by faith. This is unfortunate, given that the 'faith and works' discussion only accounts for a tiny section of the letter. Older commentators, and more recent writers on the epistle, provide a more rounded picture. Among the issues worth exploring are the following:

- *The relationship between James and Jesus:* Particular focus here is on James's use of the teaching of Jesus. Although James has little explicit Christology, leading to the (ideologically loaded) claim that it is a 'Jewish' rather than a 'Christian' text, there are significant echoes of Jesus' teaching, especially as found in Matthew's Sermon on the Mount (Matthew 5—7: see Table 21). Interestingly, James never explicitly states that this is Jesus' teaching. Rather, he has absorbed it into the substance of his exhortation to fellow Christian Jews, making Jesus' teachings his own, in a manner akin to Jesus ben-Sira's use of the book of Proverbs.
- *The Law and followers of Jesus:* not surprisingly, the Jewish James has much to say positively about the Jewish Law, the Torah. 'Doing' the Law is strongly enjoined upon believers. However, as in the Sermon on the Mount, the Torah seems to be interpreted in the light of Jesus' teaching, with the commandment to love neighbour at its heart (James 2.8). This might help explain the meaning of James's phrase *nomos basilikos*, generally translated 'royal law' (2.8). An alternative translation might be 'law of the kingdom', that is, as interpreted by the kingdom preaching of Jesus.
- *God's preference for the poor:* given its harsh denunciation of riches, and prophetic critique of discrimination against the poor (as at 2.1–7; 5.1–6), it is not surprising to find James at the heart of contemporary liberationist and political readings of the Bible. A good example of this is Elsa Tamez's *The Scandalous Message of James*, written out of a Costa Rican context of extreme poverty.[113] Heard from the perspective of the poor and oppressed, James emerges as a politically subversive document, siding firmly with those at the bottom of the pile.

To do

Compare what James says about 'faith' and 'works' (James 2) with Paul's teaching (for example, Romans 3.27—4.12; Galatians 2.15—3.14). Do James and Paul disagree with one another? Or are they using the same terms differently? Do you think one is written as a direct response to the other?

Table 21: James and Jesus' Teaching.

James	*Matthew*
But be doers of the word, and not merely hearers who deceive themselves. (James 1.22)	Everyone then who hears these words of mine and acts on them will be like a wise man who built his house on rock. (Matthew 7.24)
Can a fig tree, my brothers and sisters, yield olives, or a grapevine figs? (James 3.12)	Are grapes gathered from thorns, or figs from thistles? (Matthew 7.16)
Your riches have rotted, and your clothes are moth-eaten. Your gold and silver have rusted, and their rust will be evidence against you, and it will eat your flesh like fire. You have laid up treasure for the last days. (James 5.2–3)	Do not store up for yourselves treasures on earth, where moth and rust consume and where thieves break in and steal; but store up for yourselves treasures in heaven, where neither moth nor rust consumes and where thieves do not break in and steal. (Matthew 6.19–20)
Above all, my beloved, do not swear, either by heaven or by earth or by any other oath, but let your 'Yes' be yes and your 'No' be no, so that you may not fall under condemnation. (James 5.12)	But I say to you, Do not swear at all, either by heaven, for it is the throne of God, or by the earth, for it is his footstool, or by Jerusalem, for it is the city of the great King. And do not swear by your head, for you cannot make one hair white or black. Let your word be 'Yes, Yes' or 'No, No'; anything more than this comes from the evil one. (Matthew 5.34–7)

Two Petrine Letters

If James preserves the memory of a significant member of Jesus' blood-family, 1 and 2 Peter testify to the importance of one particular member of Jesus' chosen Twelve, the fisherman Simon Peter. Again, issues of authorship surface. Certainly, the differences between the two make it unlikely that both spring from the same pen, and 2 Peter (about whose authenticity there were doubts from earliest times) bears possible hints of pseudonymity. Unlike 1 Peter, it uses the archaized form 'Simeon Peter', and presents itself as a sequel to the first letter (2 Peter 3.1). It is also almost certainly dependent upon Jude, odd if composed by Peter himself. A stronger case can be made for the authenticity of 1 Peter, particularly if we take seriously the author's claim that it was written 'through Silvanus' (1 Peter 5.12). Silvanus' involvement as scribe weakens the objection that a Galilean fisherman would be incapable of writing such polished Greek.

But undue focus on authorship detracts from the more significant aspects of these two letters. I will begin with 1 Peter. Though addressed like James to 'the Dispersion' (1 Peter 1.1), the wider context makes clear that *diaspora* is used metaphorically: the implied readers are Christians from a pagan background (1.18; 2.10; 3.6; 4.3–4), located in various provinces of Asia Minor. 1 Peter is early evidence for titles and privileges traditionally associated with Israel being transferred to a predominantly Gentile Church. The particular titles are those given to Israel at the Exodus, pointing to Peter's Christian addressees as also a people on the move, heading towards their own promised land:

> But you are a chosen race, a royal priesthood, a holy nation, God's own people, in order that you may proclaim the mighty acts of him who called you out of darkness into his marvellous light. (1 Peter 2.9)

> but you shall be for me a priestly kingdom and a holy nation. (Exodus 19.6)

This is a sensitive and controversial issue, particularly for Jewish–Christian dialogue. Is it right, and in what sense, for Christians to claim titles originally given to their Jewish brothers and sisters?

Two further theological features of 1 Peter are worth mentioning. First, its description of Christian addressees sheds interesting light on its ecclesiology. Christians are described as 'exiles' (or 'refugees', 1.1), and 'aliens' (2.11), both highlighting their lack of rootedness in this world and their surrounding culture. This may be as a direct result of their Christian confession. They no longer belong to their society, their family, their home, as they did before.[114] Against this background, 1 Peter speaks of the Church in terms which denote profound belonging and stability. Not only do they now belong to God's people (as at 2.10); they are also part of a new building, stones of a 'spiritual house' or temple (2.5).

The second feature is 1 Peter's Christology, which is intricately linked with the theme of innocent suffering. Whether slaves suffering unjustly at the hands of their masters, or Christians experiencing social exclusion for their faith, set in the context of the suffering of Jesus, such negative experiences find meaning in Christ's sufferings. For 1 Peter, Christ is the sacrificial lamb (1.19), the innocent one who 'like a lamb that is led to the slaughter' did not open his mouth (Isaiah 53.7). Set within this context, 1 Peter addresses the suffering of believers (quoting from Isaiah 53.9):

> For to this you [slaves] have been called, because Christ also suffered for you, leaving you an example, so that you should follow in his steps.
> 'He committed no sin,
> and no deceit was found in his mouth.'
> When he was abused, he did not return abuse; when he suffered, he did not threaten; but he entrusted himself to the one who judges justly. He himself bore our sins in his body on the cross, so that, free from sins, we might live for righteousness; by his wounds you have been healed. For you were going astray like sheep, but now you have returned to the shepherd and guardian of your souls. (1 Peter 2.21–5)

Nevertheless, particularly in its exhortation to Christian slaves to endure unjust treatment, 1 Peter is not without its critics. Is there not a time for Christians actively to oppose evil and unjust behaviour? 1 Peter's perspective needs to be set alongside a text such as Revelation, which offers a rather different perspective on the suffering of innocent followers of the Lamb (for example Revelation 6.9–11).

To do

Read 1 Peter 2.4–12, noting especially the references to 'stones' and architectural allusions. What image of the Church emerges? For what kind of people would such an image speak most powerfully?

---

2 Peter, like several other New Testament writings, is concerned with false teaching, presenting the authoritative warning of the apostle Peter. Though use of stock polemical language makes it difficult to be precise about this teaching, it seems to be of a libertine, even antinomian type (for example 2 Peter 2.2–3, 10, 19). 2 Peter 3 suggests that their ethical teaching is directly related to their End-time beliefs. They seem to have been frustrated about the delay of the Parousia (not unique among early Christians), and their apparent conclusion that the Lord was not returning in judgement might have encouraged their libertine attitude. The world has remained the same since the beginning! There is no judgement still to come!

The author's response to their eschatological position is twofold. First, he denies that the world has remained unchangeable, pointing back to the Old Testament story of Noah's flood, which transformed the world through divine judgement (3.5ff.). So, he claims, a world conflagration has been prepared for the end. Second, he presents a theological position based on Psalm 90.4. What appears to be an unacceptable delay is no delay from God's perspective; from the human perspective, it allows time for repentance:

> But do not ignore this one fact, beloved, that with the Lord one day is like a thousand years, and a thousand years are like one day. The Lord is not slow about his promise, as some think of slowness, but is patient with you, not wanting any to perish, but all to come to repentance. But the day of the Lord will come like a thief, and then the heavens will pass away with a loud noise, and the elements will be dissolved with fire, and the earth and everything that is done on it will be disclosed. (2 Peter 3.8–10)

How literally one understands the imagery here will dramatically affect one's overall interpretation of this passage.

If 2 Timothy is Paul's 'testament', then 2 Peter serves the same function for Simon Peter. This letter shares many of the characteristics of the Jewish 'Testament' genre (for example, Testaments of the Twelve Patriarchs; John 14—17; Acts 20): Peter is expected to die soon, and before he does he commits his teaching to his disciples for posterity. Though still 'in the body', he knows that his death (literally 'the putting off of my tent') is soon to take place. The purpose of setting his teaching down in writing is that 'after my departure you may be able at any time to recall these things' (2 Peter 1.13–15). This gives his perspective on the expected 'false teaching' greater authority.

The Memory of Simon Peter

Having looked at both Petrine letters, what picture of Peter and his ongoing authority emerges in them? A number of 'facets' of Peter's memory come to the fore, all of which have contributed to the 'afterlife' of Simon Peter in Christian history and theology:

- Peter as apostle to Gentiles no less than to Jews (1 Peter 1.1–2). This claiming of Peter for the non-Jewish world may be surprising, given Peter's association with the mission to the circumcised (Galatians 2.7). But it may reflect something of Peter's historical role outside Jewish Palestine (see Acts 10), urging a rethink of Paul's role as *the* apostle to the Gentiles.
- Peter as pastor or shepherd of the flock (1 Peter 5: a facet also found in John 21, raising questions about the relationship between 1 Peter and the Johannine tradition). Christ is the 'chief shepherd', and Peter is one shepherd among many, urging fellow elders to tend the flock entrusted to them.
- Peter as martyr, whose death is at hand (2 Peter 1.14). In John 21, Peter's shepherding is in imitation of the good shepherd, who lays down his life for the sheep. Christ foretells the death by which Peter would glorify God. So too at 2 Peter 1.14, Christ has made clear to him that his death is imminent. This is a facet of Peter particularly exemplified in Rome, where the sites of two martyrdoms and burials – those of Peter and Paul – are marked and venerated.
- Peter as 'bridge-builder': 1 Peter seems to draw upon and hold together

a number of diverse New Testament strands, including the Pauline and Johannine. Similarly 2 Peter draws heavily upon the Palestinian Jewish Jude, and also speaks warmly of 'our beloved brother Paul' (2 Peter 3.15–16). Might both provide a glimpse of Peter's historical role within the early Church, as holding the mediating position between Paul, James, and other voices?

To do

Select two or three portraits of Peter, or artistic portrayals of scenes from Peter's life, by different artists (for example at www.wga.hu or www.nationalgallery.org.uk). What facet of Peter is each of them attempting to convey? How far does the artist's context shed light on the portrayal?

The Ongoing Johannine Tradition

When we turn to the three letters attributed to John, we are suddenly in familiar territory. Their distinctive style and vocabulary – such as beginning, testimony, truth, light, darkness, love, the Father and the Son – suggests not only that they belong together, but that they come from the same stable as the Fourth Gospel (or perhaps, to continue the Johannine metaphor, the same sheepfold!). This does not necessarily mean that their author (called 'the Elder') is also the beloved disciple or even the evangelist: scholars remain divided over this question. But it locates these writings in the same early Christian tradition or community.

Although these three are called the Johannine 'letters' or 'epistles', 1 John lacks the characteristics of a letter (both at the beginning and at the end). It is more akin to a sermon or theological treatise, with an introduction evoking the gospel's prologue:

We declare to you what was from the beginning, what we have heard, what we have seen with our eyes, what we have looked at and touched with our hands, concerning the word of life – this life was revealed, and we have seen it and testify to it, and declare to you the eternal life that was with the Father and was revealed to us . . . (1 John 1.1–2)

2 and 3 John, on the other hand, are letters proper. The latter is addressed to a male Christian, 'the beloved Gaius' (3 John 1), warning him of another Christian, Diotrephes, who 'does not acknowledge our authority' (so the NRSV, though the Greek literally reads 'does not receive us', 3 John 9). Is this a clash of authority figures, or an issue of Christian hospitality? The identity of the 'elect lady' to whom, along with her 'children', 2 John is addressed, is more controversial. Is she a female Christian, perhaps a leader of a congregation? Or does the feminine singular denote a corporate identity: a local church (cf. 2 John 13; 1 Peter 5.13)?

Although different in their genres, 1 and 2 John seem closest in the issue they appear to address: a schism among Christians in the circles of the Elder ('Johannine Christians') over Christology. What precisely those who part company with the Elder (the 'secessionists') believe about Christ is open to debate, but it certainly involves a downplaying of Christ's humanity. A classic text for identifying their christological position is 1 John 4.1–3a:

Beloved, do not believe every spirit, but test the spirits to see whether they are from God; for many false prophets *have gone out into the world*. By this you know the Spirit of God: every spirit that confesses that *Jesus Christ has come in the flesh* is of God, and every spirit that does not confess Jesus is not from God. (italics mine)

The reference to those who 'have gone out into the world' is probably to the secessionists (it may be that the 'secessionists' regarded the Elder and his followers as having 'gone out' from them!). Some understand their position as Docetism (the early heresy that Christ only *appeared* to be human). They deny Christ's true incarnation. For others, more precisely, they see no significance in Christ's fleshly existence. It is through the Son's coming into the world, rather than his historical ministry, or his dying on the cross, that humans are saved.

Similarly, 2 John presupposes a christological disagreement relating to Christ's coming. Is this precisely the same as that in 1 John? The NRSV thinks so, for it translates 2 John 7: 'Many deceivers have gone out into the world, those who do not confess that Jesus Christ *has come in the flesh . . .*' (italics mine). However, the Greek literally means 'Jesus Christ coming in flesh' (a present participle for 'coming', as opposed to a perfect tense in 1 John 4.2). An alternative is that 2 John is referring not to Christ's past coming – his incarnation – but to the 'fleshly' reality of his future coming – the Parousia. This may still point to a devaluing of Christ's human existence: if Christ comes again, it will not be 'in flesh'.

Whatever nuance we give to these references, they certainly point to the close relationship between Christology and ethics. If Christ is not truly human, or his humanity is not significant for salvation, then our life in the flesh is not of significance, nor are the lives of our fellow human beings. Hence, we have no real need of concern for this world and those in it. In response, the Johannine epistles underscore the importance of the love commandment: to love the brethren.

One possible scenario for the production of these letters (classically expressed by Raymond Brown in his *Community of the Beloved Disciple*)[115] is that the Elder is responding to what he regards as misunderstanding of the Fourth Gospel (or the gospel tradition it preserves). For all its brilliance, John's Gospel represents theological trends which – without certain checks and balances – might lead to the kind of theological positions the Elder appears to be responding to:

- *Christology:* as we have seen, a devaluing of Christ's human existence seems to lie at the heart of the schism. Arguably, the exalted vision of Jesus in the gospel could lead to a position whereby Christ's divinity is in danger of subsuming his humanity. The Elder's position is to stress the salvific significance of Christ's true humanity, including his human death (as at 1 John 2.2; 5.6).
- *Ecclesiology:* it is possible to read the Fourth Gospel (with its emphasis upon the Christian's personal relationship with Christ, like a branch to the vine) as privileging the individual Christian over the community. Some see little overt doctrine of the Church in John. This might account for the Elder's stress upon loving one another (for example, 1 John 3.10–17; 2 John 5–6; 3 John 6).

- *Eschatology:* the so-called 'realized eschatology' of John's Gospel (the conviction that believers already 'have' eternal life, as at John 3.18; 5.24; 6.54) could result in a downplaying of what is still to come in the future. Although the Elder shares this perspective, 1 John betrays a shift in emphasis towards the 'not yet': 'what we will be has not yet been revealed' (1 John 3.2).
- *Pneumatology:* the gospel's emphasis on personal inspiration by the Spirit-Paraclete undercuts the need for human teachers within the community (including the Elder!). 1 John in particular, while sharing this basic outlook (for example 1 John 2.27), emphasizes the need to test the spirits (1 John 4.1). Not all come from God!

Reflection

What do you make of the polemical language in these letters, particularly as directed against the 'secessionists'? Do you find it reassuring, or embarrassing, or objectionable? How might you account for your response? What place should there be for such polemic within religious discourse?

Jude the Obscure

The title of Thomas Hardy's famous novel seems a highly appropriate one for the New Testament Letter of Jude. It is indeed obscure, particularly for the modern reader unfamiliar with the subtle allusions to Old Testament characters and Jewish traditions. Though a mere 25 verses (only Philemon, 2 John and 3 John are shorter in length), the density of its strange imagery and obscure language makes it one of the hardest New Testament writings to get a handle on. See Table 22 for some of the Old Testament characters used as types for the first-century teachers Jude is warning against.

Table 22: Old Testament Types of Jude's 'Opponents'.

3 Old Testament types (groups: Jude 5–7)

1. Wilderness generation (Numbers 16)
2. Watchers or fallen angels (Genesis 6; 1 Enoch 6—19)
3. Cities of the Plain (Genesis 19)

3 Old Testament types (individuals: Jude 11)

1. Cain (Genesis 4.8)
2. Balaam (Numbers. 22; 31.16; Deuteronomy 23.5; Nehemiah 13.2)
3. Korah (Numbers 16)

The implied author is named as 'Jude, a servant of Jesus Christ and brother of James' (Jude 1). Almost certainly we are to identify him as the Judas (or Judah, after one of the twelve patriarchs) among the Lord's brothers (as for example Mark 6.3). Thus this letter gives us another glimpse into non-Pauline Christian Judaism, either based in or with strong links to Jerusalem. This is all the more significant if – as a growing number of scholars are prepared to consider – Jude is relatively early and authentic rather than a late, pseudonymous example of 'early Catholicism'. Like 2 Peter and other New Testament epistles, Jude seems to be responding to a rival view of the faith. Though Jude's stock polemical language makes positive identification difficult, these seem to be antinomian visionaries.

In terms of the argument of the letter, Richard Bauckham has proposed a helpful strategy, to prevent the reader from getting bogged down in its more obscure details (particularly its scriptural exegesis in verses 5–19).[116] Bauckham urges readers to concentrate not on the polemical 'name-calling' nor the exegetical section, but on those sections which focus on the letter's addressees:

> Beloved, while eagerly preparing to write to you about the salvation we share, I find it necessary to write and appeal to you *to contend for the faith that was once for all entrusted to the saints.* (Jude 3, italics mine)

> But you, beloved, *build yourselves up on your most holy faith*; pray in the
> Holy Spirit; *keep yourselves in the love of God*; look forward to the mercy
> of our Lord Jesus Christ that leads to eternal life. And *have mercy on some
> who are wavering*; *save others* by snatching them out of the fire; and *have
> mercy on still others with fear*, hating even the tunic defiled by their bodies.
> (Jude 20–3, italics mine)

There are some variant readings in the Greek of verses 22–3. Nevertheless,
these two passages suggest that the purpose of Jude is (a) to encourage the
addressees to hold onto and build up the faith they have received, and (b)
to remedy the situation by merciful action towards those who either have
embraced the alternative vision, or are in danger of doing so.

Of the range of other issues raised by Jude, I note three here. The first is
the theme of judgement. The main point of the 'polemical' section of verses
4–19 is that, given antecedents in Israel's history, these new teachers will not
escape judgement. Judgement as a theological motif is problematic for many
Western Christians, and understandably so, given the way in which it has
often been presented. Yet it is a more common feature of the New Testament
than is often admitted. Moreover, as liberationist exegesis has reminded us,
judgement is a two-edged sword. It is the flip-side of salvation: understood
as God's action to put right what is wrong, overcoming injustice.

Second, Jude raises questions about the boundaries of the biblical canon.
On one occasion the author explicitly quotes – as a prophetic text –1 Enoch
(Jude 14, quoting 1 Enoch 1.9). Beyond this clear quotation, Jude contains
several other allusions to this esoteric book.[117] Though highly regarded in the
early Church, and still read as scripture by the Ethiopian Orthodox Church,
1 Enoch is generally treated by Christians as pseudepigraphical. Moreover, it
is generally thought that Jude's reference to Michael disputing with the devil
over the body of Moses (Jude 9) alludes to the lost ending of the Testament
of Moses. These pseudepigraphical allusions remind contemporary readers
not only of the more fluid definition of prophetic texts in the New Testament
world, but also of the importance of such texts for entering into the 'worlds'
of Jesus and his earliest followers.

Third, despite its brevity, Jude's christological references are worth exploring. First, he apparently interprets Enoch's one who comes 'with ten thou-

sands of his holy ones' (in 1 Enoch, the 'eternal God') as the returning Christ ('the Lord'). Second, as Bauckham has shown, Jude uses four christological titles which may give a glimpse of earliest Jewish Christianity: Messiah/Christ, the Lord (perhaps derived from the Aramaic *mare*), 'our Lord' (Jude 4; cf. 1 Corinthians 16.22; Revelation 22.20), and Master. The identification of Jesus as 'the Lord' (in Jude 14) begs the question: is he also to be identified with 'the Lord' who saved Israel at the Exodus in verse 5? The title Master (Greek *despotēs*, Jude 4) is particularly interesting. This is otherwise virtually unknown as a title for Christ before the late second century; yet the relatives of Jesus were known in early Palestinian Christian tradition as *hoi desposunoi* (Julius Africanus in Eusebius, *Historia Ecclesiastica* 1.7.14). Is this an indication of Jude's origin in those Jewish Christian circles where the family of Jesus were so called?

To do

Look up the references given in Table 22 to characters and stories alluded to in Jude 5–7 and 11. What are the similarities between them? In what ways do these help you understand Jude's argument?

Further Reading

Richard Bauckham, 1990, *Jude and the Relatives of Jesus in the Early Church*, Edinburgh: T. & T. Clark.

Bede the Venerable, 1985, *Commentary on the Seven Catholic Epistles*, Kalamazoo, Michigan: Cistercian Publications.

Andrew Chester and Ralph P. Martin, 1994, *The Theology of the Letters of James, Peter and Jude*, New Testament Theology; Cambridge: Cambridge University Press.

Luke Timothy Johnson, 2004, *Brother of Jesus, Friend of God: Studies in the Letter of James*, Grand Rapids, Michigan/Cambridge: Eerdmans.

Judith Lieu, 1991, *The Theology of the Johannine Epistles*, New Testament Theology; Cambridge: Cambridge University Press.

Pheme Perkins, 2000, *Peter: Apostle for the Whole Church*, Edinburgh: T. & T. Clark.

12

Revelation: Guide to the End of the World?

A Fascinating and Disturbing Book

Ask most people what they know about the book of Revelation, and you are likely to receive answers containing phrases such as the following: 'the end of the world'; 'cosmic destruction'; 'a terrifying, nightmarish book', 'the decisive battle between good and evil', 'a roadmap to Armageddon'. Such answers point to the popular fascination – both within and outside the churches – with what is probably the most difficult New Testament book. Few people are ambivalent about Revelation; many will willingly venture an opinion on it.

More surprisingly, Christians themselves seem sharply divided over this book (and have been from the earliest centuries). For many, particularly in the USA, Revelation sets out a detailed description of End-time. Indeed, a large number believe it is being played out as we speak on a map of the Middle East, and such interpretations have a powerful impact on the political realm. For many others, it is so obscure, or so dangerous, that it is best ignored, or challenged by other less disturbing biblical texts, or reserved for the wise and spiritually mature. It rarely occurs in the lectionaries (books of biblical passages organized for public reading) of many mainstream churches. Indeed, it is never read publicly during the Liturgy of the Orthodox Church. But, as the reception history of Revelation reveals, it has also provided inspiration, hope and challenge to Christians of very diverse cultures and backgrounds.

What is it about the book of Revelation (or the Apocalypse of John as it is also called, from its Greek title *apokalupsis*) that provokes such strong and divergent reactions? Among the possible reasons are the following:

- its elusive and ambiguous character, which leaves it open to a range of divergent interpretations;
- its often violent imagery, which raises significant moral and theological questions;
- the certainty it seems to offer about God's plan for the world;
- its attractiveness to lovers of puzzles, mysteries and enigmas;
- its visual character, which has been exploited by artists as diverse as Michelangelo, Sandro Botticelli, Diego Velázquez, and Hans Feibusch;
- its subversive, anti-imperial message (which may account for the ambivalent attitude of Eusebius, close associate of the Emperor Constantine).

Reflection

What images do you have of the book of Revelation? What are these the result of? Personal reading or study? Teaching you have received? Films you have watched? Paintings you have seen? Note your initial reactions, and revisit them after you have worked through this chapter to see whether they have been confirmed or challenged.

What Kind of Book is This?

Fundamental to any act of interpretation – especially pronounced when it comes to interpreting Revelation – is the question of a text's genre. What kind of book is it? Establishing its genre is an important step towards deciding the ground rules for responsible interpretation. The opening section of the Apocalypse suggests that it is an example of three overlapping literary genres:

- *Apocalypse:* 'The revelation of Jesus Christ, which God gave him to show his servants what must soon take place' (Revelation 1.1).
- *Prophetic book:* 'Blessed is the one who reads aloud the words of the prophecy, and blessed are those who hear and keep what is written in it: for the time is near' (Revelation 1.3).
- *Letter:* 'John to the seven churches that are in Asia: Grace to you and peace from him who is and who was and who is to come, and from the seven spirits who are before his throne, and from Jesus Christ, the faithful witness, the firstborn of the dead, and the ruler of the kings of the earth' (Revelation 1.4–5).

I shall suggest some implications of these three aspects in reverse order. First, as a letter, it was originally addressed to 'the seven churches that are in Asia', Asia being the Roman province of that name in what is now western Turkey. This means that, whatever mysteries are revealed in this book, it had a particular message to those first-century Christian communities. Historical-critical scholars have wanted to emphasize this ancient context within which the human author wrote, and the situation of his ancient addressees in cities such as Ephesus and Smyrna. The so-called 'letters to the seven churches' (better regarded as seven 'prophetic messages') in Revelation 2—3 are particularly important here.

To do

Read Revelation 2—3, trying to detect the specific issues addressed in each of the seven churches (remember that we are only hearing Revelation's viewpoint, and even this is clothed in highly symbolic language). Locate the cities of the seven churches on a map, in either an atlas or a study Bible, noting their geographical relationship to each other, and to Patmos, where the implied author is located.

Next, as a work of prophecy, this is a book claiming to mediate God's word to his people. Though in the popular mind prophecy is regularly regarded as 'prediction', looking into the future akin to clairvoyance, the prophets of the

Old Testament are perhaps better seen as proclaiming a message from God to and for their own generation. They are not so much foretellers as *forthtellers*. Prophets speak to their contemporaries in order that they might change their lives and avert impending disaster.

A number of implications follow from Revelation's prophetic claim. First, John is identifying his book with Old Testament antecedents. Indeed, his is the only book of the New Testament which explicitly sets itself up as on a par with Jewish scripture (compare Revelation 22.18–19 with Deuteronomy 4.2). Particular similarities have been noted with Ezekiel and Daniel. Second, treating John's apocalypse as prophecy should warn against viewing it as a fatalistic prediction of God's predetermined plan. Prophecy calls for a change of heart, and presumes that a change of heart can issue in a very different future. Barbara Rossing has likened Revelation's terrifying visions to the warning of the 'Ghost of Christmas Yet to Come' in Charles Dickens' *A Christmas Carol*, who reveals to Scrooge not what *will* be, but only what *may* be.[118] Third, those who take the prophetic dimension of Revelation seriously are not content with asking historical-critical questions about the message addressed to John's first-century audiences. They have wanted to ask another hermeneutical question: What does this book have to say to readers in our own or indeed any age?

Finally, this is a 'revelation' or 'apocalypse', from the Greek word meaning 'unveiling' or 'uncovering'. It is debated whether John is using the word *apokalupsis* in Revelation 1.1 to describe a distinctive literary genre. Nevertheless, Revelation can be categorized along with other similar Jewish and Christian texts from this period which fairly soon came to be called 'apocalypses'. Apocalypses are narrative works which describe a revelation given to a privileged human being, whether by angelic visitation, heavenly journey or during a dream, often clothed in dramatic, even fantastic symbols. Monsters and other animals speak; angels wage war; women turn into cities; numbers and colours have symbolic significance.

What all these literary apocalypses have in common, however, is not that they speak about the end of the world. Rather (as the Greek word *apokalupsis* or 'unveiling' suggests), they are books which claim to reveal mysteries normally hidden from mortals.[119] In the light of such revelations, the visionaries – and those who read their literary works – are challenged to view the world in a different light. Taking seriously the apocalyptic nature of Revelation raises this question: How does it confront us with a different way of seeing, such that we are forced to reassess our view of reality?

The apocalyptic character of John's Apocalypse raises a further question. Did John see what he claims to have seen? Is his book merely a literary creation, or is it based upon actual visionary experience? This is not as straightforward as might at first appear, for mystics and visionaries necessarily convey what they believe they have seen in language and forms inherited from their own religious and cultural tradition. Those who write them down may well be influenced – consciously or unconsciously – by their literary predecessors (hence the similarities between Revelation, Old Testament prophetic books, and Jewish apocalypses). Nevertheless, John's book gives us reasons for wanting to take his claim seriously:[120]

- many of its visions have a fluid, dream-like quality;
- the author resorts to piling up similes, as if attempting to describe the indescribable;
- John sometimes describes himself as participating in his visions;
- there are significant parallels with other visionary texts, including hints that John has prepared himself for visionary experience (as at Revelation 1.10; 10.9).

Two implications follow from this. First, if John is in some sense conveying what he believes he saw and heard, then the quest for authorial intention becomes less important than historical critics have wanted to claim. John is not simply setting out to convey his 'point of view' in his book (though that inevitably comes through in how he writes). His primary concern is to convey his visionary experience, even if he does not fully understand what that means. Second, this type of literature calls for the use of our imaginations. Perhaps this is the greatest difficulty that interpreters in the contemporary West have in reading a book like Revelation, for our imaginative muscles have become rather flabby and need rigorous training in order to become effective again.

Table 23: Possible Structural Division of Revelation.

Rev. 1.1—3.22	Prologue and Seven Messages
Rev. 4.1—8.1	Seven Seals
Rev. 8.2—11.18	Seven Trumpets
Rev. 11.19—15.4	Seven Visions of the Church in the World
Rev. 15.5—19.10	Seven Bowls and Babylon
Rev. 19.11—22.21	Seven Visions of the End, New Jerusalem and Epilogue

The Primary Historical Setting

If Revelation is not a straightforward historical text, it nevertheless emerges out of a particular historical context. The implied author John tells us that, when he had the visions he describes, he was 'on the island called Patmos because of the word of God and the testimony of Jesus' (Revelation 1.9). Patmos is a small island, part of the Dodecanese group of islands in the eastern Aegean, approximately 40 miles from the coast of Turkey. Moreover, his visionary message is sent in literary form to the seven churches of Asia, situated in seven cities on the mainland. What can we glean of this setting, what we might call the 'primary historical setting' of the Apocalypse?

There are in fact two contexts or settings: that of John, and that of the seven congregations. Both of them are somewhat ambiguous. To begin with John's, the reason given in Revelation 1.9 for his being on Patmos is open to more than one interpretation:

- He went there in order to receive God's word, perhaps as some kind of retreat.
- He went there as part of his missionary activity, perhaps impelled by God's word to preach there.
- He fled there to escape persecution.
- He was exiled there by the authorities (later traditions claim that he was

exiled either from Asia itself, normally from Ephesus, or from Rome at the order of the emperor).

Given the use elsewhere in Revelation of the preposition 'on account of' (Greek *dia*, with the sense of 'as a result of'), and the wider context in Revelation 1.9 of hostility, the final interpretation is the most likely. This places him in a long line of Jewish exiles who believed they had a prophetic message for God's people (notably Ezekiel and Daniel, both of whose books have made a strong impact on Revelation). But his island exile has its own particular significance: an environment of physical separation from the seven churches on the mainland, and one which highlights the potentially hostile environment of 'the sea' (regularly mentioned negatively throughout John's book).

To do

Consult commentaries, Bible dictionaries and websites in order to discover as much as possible about Patmos in the first century. What kind of environment would John have discovered there? What impact might this have had upon what he saw, and how he describes it? How might the fact of being on an island have affected him?

The second context is that of the seven churches. Commentators have often highlighted difficulties both internal (for example the Nicolaitans, 'Balaam', 'Jezebel') and external (hostility from 'the synagogue of Satan') for the various congregations. One particular issue divides interpreters, however: Is Revelation primarily addressing first-century Christians who are facing persecution, whether from Roman authorities, perhaps related to their refusal to participate in the imperial cult, or from local Jewish authorities? The persecution theory is often connected with the traditional dating of Revelation to the last years of Domitian's reign (died 96 CE). However, an alternative position dates the book to the late 60s, either during or soon after the death of Nero, while a number of scholars have challenged the ancient view that Domitian systematically persecuted Christians.[121] Or is this a prophetic book largely directed at comfortable Asian Christians too closely identified with

Roman culture and commerce, aimed at shocking them out of their compla-
cency into maintaining a more faithful witness? Evidence can be found in
support of both positions.

A Rich Reception History

But attending to the first-century context of John and his original audiences
is only one aspect of interpreting Revelation. The imaginative quality of this
book, and the ambiguous nature of many of its images, means that its reception history has been especially rich. Two fine recent accounts of Revelation's
reception history are Arthur Wainwright's *Mysterious Apocalypse* and the
Blackwell Bible Commentary volume on Revelation by Judith Kovacs and
Christopher Rowland.[122]

One way to categorize the different approaches to the Apocalypse throughout its reception history is through the metaphor of seeing. The standard
historical-critical approach described above, and found in many modern
commentaries, envisages John essentially looking across the water to the
seven churches on the mainland. His visions primarily contain a message of
urgent importance for them. The task of the interpreter is to identify their
first-century historical situation and John's intention in writing (we have
already noted the implications of the book's visionary character for priori-
tizing authorial intention). Particular elements in Revelation's visions can be
decoded as symbolic descriptions of first-century figures and institutions:
the beast from the sea is a particular Roman emperor, such as Nero; Babylon the Great is imperial Rome; the rider on the white horse carrying a bow
represents the archer cavalry of the Parthians, Rome's greatest threat on its
eastern borders.

Other strands of interpretation share the historical-critical concern for
decoding the visions, but regard them as describing not so much John's own
day as subsequent historical events. For them, John is privileged to be able to
see into the future. But which future? Some interpreters treat Revelation as
unveiling events of world history, or church history, between John's day and
their own. Other interpreters believe that Revelation focuses primarily on
the ultimate future, the events leading up to the End of the World (reflected

in the popular perception of what Revelation is all about).

A further line of interpretation challenges the tendency to treat Revelation's visions as codes to be cracked. It envisages John not so much as seeing precise events in the future, but as looking into the heart of the world of every age. Revelation is treated as a lens through which one is invited to view and judge the world in which one lives. It takes seriously the polyvalence of John's imagery, which makes it more difficult to be tied too closely to any particular historical personage or event, even if elements of John's own day may be detected in it. It acknowledges that Revelation rarely offers precise interpretations of details of its visions, in contrast to apocalypses such as Daniel and 4 Ezra (Revelation 1.20 and 17.9–10 are among the exceptions). Hence, the significance of Babylon in Revelation 17 cannot be exhausted by highlighting the connections with imperial Rome of John's own day. In this pattern of interpretation, Babylon does not equal Rome. Rather, Rome is the concrete manifestation in John's day of the oppressive, arrogant city Babylon. Readers are invited to ask where Babylon is to be encountered in their own day.

Some Recent Trends

Recent trends in New Testament study have raised other issues. Increased attention to the role of the contemporary reader in the act of interpretation has posed the question: What do we bring to the text? This includes the recognition that there may be aspects of the text which contemporary readers would wish to challenge (an issue which feminist critics have particularly raised). How trustworthy is John's account of alleged visionary experience, or his claim to speak God's word? How far does this text demonize unfairly the author's religious and political enemies, and justify his unacknowledged prejudices?

More literary approaches have asked whether there is a coherent story being told throughout the book, articulating a narrative vision which the implied readers are invited to embrace. Social-scientific criticism has asked about the social realities behind the seven churches, or their portrayal by John. Liberationist and other political readings, such as those of Pablo Richard in

Latin America and Allan Boesak in Apartheid South Africa, have questioned the naivety of Western liberals who balk at the violence of the text. On the contrary, they claim, Revelation is a declaration of good news for the victims of injustice, and a necessary challenge to those implicated in structures of oppression.[123] For certain feminist critics, Revelation is itself implicated in some of these very structures, in its androcentric portrayal of women.[124]

Finally, given its visual character, Revelation is probably the most visualized of all New Testament writings. Scenes from its visions have been immortalized in stone sculptures and illuminated manuscripts, in woodcuts and tapestries, in icons and on canvases. A growth area in the study of Revelation is precisely this history of its reception in the work of artists. An excellent website on art relating to the Apocalypse, with links to other sites, is maintained by Felix Just SJ: http://catholic-resources.org/Art/Revelation-Art.htm.

By way of illustration, here are some examples, taken from various historical periods, of how readers of Revelation have received its vision of the great prostitute Babylon (Revelation 17):

- The city of Rome under the emperors, or the Roman empire itself (both by ancient commentators such as Tertullian, during actual Roman persecution, and by contemporary historical-critical scholars).
- Historical Jerusalem (an interpretation favoured by a number of modern Protestant interpreters, though not widespread in earlier periods).
- A warning to Christians against the seduction of luxury and wealth (as in Cyprian of Carthage, or Albrecht Dürer's late fifteenth-century woodcut, based on an earlier portrayal of a rich Venetian woman).
- The false, apostate Church as opposed to the true Church, the New Jerusalem (building on the interpretations found in Tyconius and in Augustine's *City of God*).
- The oppressive and unjust City, which can be located in any age and any number of different geographical locations (an interpretation revived by modern liberationist interpreters).
- The papacy, or the Roman Catholic Church (seeds of this emerging in the late Middle Ages, and developed in anti-Catholic Protestant polemic since the Reformation).[125]

To do

Find two or three different paintings (or other illustrations such as sculptures or woodcuts) representing the same scene from the book of Revelation.[126] How do the different artists portray their chosen scene? Do they offer anything surprising? What can you learn from their pictures of their own interpretative strategy?

Reading Revelation as Story

Literary approaches, especially narrative criticism, have become increasingly important in the past two decades or so in scholarly interpretation of the gospels. They offer holistic readings of narratives which counterbalance the tendency of historical criticism to dissect the text. But such literary approaches are also illuminating when applied to Revelation, for this too is a kind of narrative text (although its narrative, being visionary, is perhaps rather more cyclic and repetitive than linear).

First, they pay attention to the symbolic world that Revelation describes. Revelation presents a three-tiered universe (heaven, earth and the realm under the earth) which describes the present fragmentation of God's creation. Only in heaven is God currently acknowledged as God, whereas the forces of evil and chaos dominate the underworld (occasionally emerging from the sea or 'abyss'). The earth is a battleground where God's people currently struggle to be faithful, while many others ('the earth-dwellers') are led astray by the demonic forces. However, this is not an equal battle, nor is its ultimate outcome in any doubt. Before the end of John's story, the chaotic sea will disappear, and the separation of heaven and earth will be overcome (Revelation 21.1–5).

Reflection

Revelation has much to say (particularly in chapters 12—16) about the 'dark side': Satan, fallen angels, the beasts, 'demonic spirits'. What sense do you make of these characters? How might such language reflect and speak to contemporary human experience? Does it raise any theological difficulties?

However, one striking dimension of Revelation's world (its 'apocalyptic' dimension) is that the veil separating heaven and earth is very thin, and seeing what is going on in heaven sheds light on what is occurring on the earth. Central to seeing correctly is Revelation's repeated vision of God's throne-room, the source of true power (first-century audiences would be reminded of descriptions of the emperor's court in Rome). Ordinary Christian readers – including those first audiences who would have formed a tiny minority of the population of a city like Ephesus – are caught up into an alternative world and alternative heavenly liturgy, which is somehow truer than the world of sight and sense, proclaimed by the imperial propaganda.

Reading Revelation as narrative also involves listening for the underlying story. Intertextual echoes and allusions within the narrative point to it being the story of a New Exodus. Like the original Exodus story, which describes how the Israelites were led out of slavery in Egypt, Revelation's story also describes a journey of liberation for God's people. They are saved by the death of a Lamb (Revelation 5.6), who frees them from their sins by his blood (1.5). Symbolized (as Israel so often was) as a mother, they are led into the wilderness, and nourished there (12.6), though pursued by a dragon who recalls the Egyptian Pharaoh (Ezekiel 29.3; 32.2). Having crossed a sea of glass (echoing the Sea of Reeds), the redeemed sing the Song of Moses and the Lamb (15.2–4). Like the original Exodus story, which describes the bloody slaughter of the Egyptian oppressor, Revelation's New Exodus is indeed a very violent story. But both stories are told from the perspective of the vulnerable underdog, and proclaimed in story and liturgy rather than on a literal battlefield.

Table 24: Key Characters in Revelation's Narrative.

Good	Evil
God, 'seated on the throne'	Satan, the dragon
angels	devil's angels
Christ, the Lamb	beast from the sea
John	beast from the earth/false prophet
woman clothed with the sun	Babylon
New Jerusalem	'those who dwell on the earth'
martyrs/faithful witnesses	'kings of the earth'
144,000	Nicolaitans
twenty-four elders	'Balaam' of Pergamum
four living creatures	'Jezebel' of Thyatira

To do

Read through Revelation 13.1—14.5. Identify the different characters, and where they fit on the God/Satan grid. With the help of a concordance or commentary, try and discover where else these characters appear in the book. Are any of them difficult to fit on the grid?

Playing with Numbers

Like much else in Revelation, numbers have symbolic significance. The most obvious number, due to its frequent repetition, is seven. There are seven churches (symbolized by seven lampstands) to which seven messages are addressed (Revelation 2—3). The remainder of the book is structured around the number seven: notably seven seals (Revelation 6.1—8.1), seven trumpets (Revelation 8.2—11.18) and seven bowls (Revelation 15.5—16.21). Seven beatitudes are scattered throughout the book. Moreover, some commentators detect two further sequences of seven visions (though these are implicit rather than explicitly numbered). Seven seems to be significant as the number of completion or perfection, as the sum of three (the number associated with the divine) and four (the number of the created universe).

Other numbers also play a symbolic role (see Table 25). The number 12 (produced by multiplying three by four), associated with the tribes of Israel, is reflected in the crown adorning the woman at Revelation 12.1, and built into the dimensions of the heavenly Jerusalem (21.12, 14, 21). Three-and-a-half (half of the perfect number seven) is also found, symbolizing a limited time period: for example, 'three-and-a-half days' at 11.9, 11. Scattered throughout Revelation are variants of three-and-a-half years: 42 months (11.2; 13.5), 'a time, times and half a time' (12.14), and 1,260 days (11.3; 12.6).

Table 25: Symbolic Numbers in Revelation.

2	Number of valid witness
3	Number of God
4	Number of the universe
6	Number of imperfection (less than 7)
7	Number of perfection (3 + 4)
12	Number of completion (3 x 4; multiples of 12 are also important: 144 and 144,000)

Multiples of these numbers are also significant. One of the most famous is 144,000. In Revelation 7.1–8 John hears about the sealing of 'the servants of our God', who number 144,000, an equal number chosen from each of the twelve tribes of Israel. Taken literally, this is a number of exclusion (as understood for example by the Jehovah's Witnesses). But there are good grounds for taking this number symbolically, particularly when we attend to the relationship between what John hears and what he sees. At Revelation 7.4, John describes what he *hears*:

And I heard the number of those who were sealed, one hundred and forty-four thousand, sealed out of every tribe of the people of Israel. (Revelation 7.4)

Yet what John actually *sees* is rather different:

After this I looked, and there was a great multitude that no one could count, from every nation, from all tribes and peoples and languages, standing before the throne and before the Lamb, robed in white, with palm branches in their hands. (Revelation 7.9)

Understood symbolically, the number 144,000 is the numerical equivalent of that which 'no one could count'. It is formed by the square of twelve (a number of completion), multiplied by a biblical number of a great multitude (a thousand: for example Exodus 20.6; Deuteronomy 1.11). Hence, from an apocalyptic point of view, it is a number not of exclusion but of inclusion, a greater number than which cannot be thought of.

Surely the most famous number in Revelation, however, is 666 (though some may be disappointed to discover that one ancient alternative reading is 616). Revelation 13.18 reads as follows:

This calls for wisdom: let anyone with understanding calculate the number of the beast, for it is the number of a person. Its number is six hundred and sixty-six.

In every generation since John wrote, commentators have taken up his challenge and attempted to identify the beast from its number. History is littered with the debris of previous identifications: Emperor Julian the Apostate, Pope Innocent IV, Patriarch Nikon of Moscow, Bill Gates. Nor has the modern age lost its enthusiasm for such an enterprise: a recent Google search for the 'number of the beast' yielded over a million webpages!

What do New Testament scholars make of the number of the beast? There are two basic approaches. The first is to identify 666 (or 616 if the alternative minority reading is preferred) as the name of an individual. The normal strategy is to understand John as engaging in the ancient practice known as gematria. In both Hebrew and Greek, letters of the alphabet had numerical equivalents (for example, a = 1, b = 2, and so on up to 10, then multiples of ten, then hundreds). People's names could be given a number by calculating the numerical sum of the letters of the name in question (for example, the number of the name *Paulos*, Greek for Paul, is 80 + 1 + 400 + 30 + 70 + 200 = 781).

In the case of Revelation, things are more complicated, since we are given the solution (666, or 616, which could be the sum of a number of different combinations of letters), and have to work back to the name. However, most scholars who adopt this line of interpretation believe that the number matches the name of a Roman emperor. Working with the Hebrew numerical system (even though John writes in Greek), this would be Nero Caesar (666 if one uses the longer form *Neron*, 616 for the shorter *Nero*). Those who use the Greek system note that the variant form 616 is the number of *Gaios Kaisar*, that is the emperor Gaius (Caligula).

The second approach is to take seriously the symbolic nature of numbers elsewhere in the Apocalypse. Six is the number of imperfection, being one less than the perfect number seven. 666 is thus appropriately the number of that beast which is always imperfect yet strives for perfection, presenting itself as the object of divine worship. The two approaches – the symbolic and the specific name – are not necessarily mutually exclusive.

A Revelation of Jesus Christ

All this interest in 666 has led some to conclude that Revelation is primarily a revelation of evil, about Satan, the beast or the Antichrist. Yet the opening words of the book suggest very different priorities: this is a 'revelation of Jesus Christ' (Revelation 1.1). The genitive 'of' is ambiguous: is it a revelation about Jesus Christ, or a revelation which Jesus gives? Despite the ambiguity, Revelation certainly does tell us quite a lot about John's visionary apprehension of who Jesus Christ is. No less than Matthew, Mark, Luke and John, it is concerned with 'the gospel', the good news of what God has done in Jesus. But it does so in symbolic, often elusive ways. I will conclude with four of these symbolic descriptions of Christ.

First, in his opening vision, John sees Jesus as the heavenly 'one like a Son of Man' (Revelation 1.12–20). This is a vision best heard read aloud. John describes an awesome vision, which causes him to fall at the figure's feet 'as if dead'. He sees the human, crucified Christ as a heavenly being, whose description echoes Daniel's description of exalted angels, and even of God himself (the white-haired Ancient of Days). As significant, however, is the description of his clothing ('clothed with a long robe and with a golden sash across his chest'), and his location 'in the midst of the lampstands' (Revelation 1.13). Like the author of Hebrews, John of Patmos sees Jesus as the high priest.

Second, and perhaps the most famous of Revelation's christological images, is Christ as the Lamb. John sees a Lamb 'standing as if it had been slaughtered' (Revelation 5.6). This juxtaposition of verbs of power ('standing') and weakness ('slaughtered') are important to hold together. He is presented as a sacrificial victim, and also as the Passover Lamb whose blood saves God's people from death. But he is also all-powerful (he has the perfect number of seven horns) and all-seeing (he has seven eyes). This image typifies Revelation's extraordinary vision of a Saviour whose power lies precisely in allowing himself to be killed.

Third, Christ is envisaged as the male child born of the woman clothed with the sun (Revelation 12). In apocalyptic vision, however, this is no simple retelling of Christ's birth from Mary at Bethlehem. Rather, his being born and caught up to God seems to describe the whole sequence of his birth, death and resurrection. Moreover, the woman of whom he is born is more than Mary; she is the personification of God's persecuted people, the race out of which the Messiah was born. Christ is revealed as one of us, emerging out of the human race, and specifically out of the Jewish nation. However, there is more: the story of a pregnant woman pursued by a dragon echoes pagan myths – which certain emperors made their own – describing how peace and order was established out of chaos. John's vision raises the question: Where does true peace come from? Through the bloody conquests of Roman emperors? Or through the child crucified by Roman imperial power?

Finally, John sees Christ as a mighty warrior, riding on a white horse (Revelation 19.11–16, white being the colour of victory). His description of what he sees echoes the book of Wisdom's description of the Word of God descending from heaven (Wisdom 18.14–16, interpreted as the Destroying Angel of the Passover), as well as a rather gory vision from Isaiah 63. Many readers find the military imagery distasteful, and indeed its reception history has its dark side. However, two issues need to be borne in mind. First, Revelation's military language takes utterly seriously the presence of evil and disorder in the world, which needs to be defeated. Second, the *kind* of battle described may not be what at first appears. The rider, for example, wears a robe 'dipped in blood' (19.13). But it seems to be his blood, rather than that of his enemies.

To do

Read out loud (or get someone else to read for you) the four passages just described. Note down your reactions to the reading experience. What features of the visions strike you? To which do you respond positively, and to which negatively? What questions do these passages raise for you? What possible answers might there be?

Further Reading

Richard Bauckham, 1993, *The Theology of the Book of Revelation*, New Testament Theology; Cambridge: Cambridge University Press.

Ian Boxall, 2002, *Revelation: Vision and Insight*, London: SPCK.

Gilbert Desrosiers, 2000, *An Introduction to Revelation*, London and New York: Continuum.

Christopher Rowland, 1993, *Revelation*, Epworth Commentaries; London: Epworth Press.

13

The New Testament Canon

The Emergence of the Canon

The term canon is derived from the Greek word *kanōn*, meaning a 'reed' or 'measuring rod'. The New Testament canon describes that authoritative list of New Testament writings acknowledged by the churches, providing a yardstick by which Christian teaching and practice could be judged. Yet this canon seems to have emerged only gradually in its present form. Although many of the New Testament books are in use and being quoted from an early stage, the earliest surviving list of all 27 books together is an Easter festal letter of Athanasius, written in 367 CE.

Evidence suggests that the earliest Christians saw little need for an expanded Bible beyond what we now call the Old Testament (which most read and cited in the Septuagint version). With a few exceptions (such as 1 Timothy 5.18; 2 Peter 3.16), when the New Testament speaks of 'the scriptures' it is referring to the Jewish scriptures. These are the scriptures cited regularly by Paul, for example, and regarded by the evangelists as being fulfilled in the life and death of Jesus.

Nevertheless, distinctly Christian traditions were emerging alongside these ancient scriptures. The tradition about Jesus seems to have been circulating orally (and perhaps also in some written form) for several decades prior to the writing of the gospels. Letters from Paul and others, written to particular Christian communities in response to local issues, were being preserved and circulated more widely even during the New Testament period (for example Colossians 4.16). From the start, Revelation presented itself as a work of prophecy, mediating the true word of God (Revelation 1.3; compare 22.18–19 with Deuteronomy 4.2). By the second century if not earlier, these writings (both apostolic letters and the gospels or 'memoirs of the apostles') were regularly read alongside the Jewish sacred writings in Christian liturgical assemblies. The seeds had been sown for an authoritative collection of Christian writings.

But the formation of different parts of the canon may well have occurred separately, rather than as part of a single process. Part of the explanation may be practical. If New Testament books were originally written on scrolls, rather than the book-like codex which Christians soon adopted, then individual texts may have been in circulation independently of each other. Even with the adoption of the codex, constraints of size meant that some would have contained only gospels, or the gospels and Acts, while others collections of Paul's letters.

Moreover, different circumstances may have been catalysts for the emergence of different groupings of texts. Followers of Paul may have initiated a preliminary collection of his surviving letters very early, and independently of any desire to bring together extant gospels. Indeed, 2 Peter's reference to the letters of 'our beloved brother Paul' presupposes just such a collection. There might be an echo of an early desire to collect Paul's letters at 2 Timothy 4.13, where Timothy is urged to bring 'the books, and above all the parchments'. This process may have involved revisiting the churches associated with Paul to discover what was in their possession, editing letters to the same congregations (such as 2 Corinthians) and 'writing up' less substantial fragments (for example the letter to the Laodiceans). This rather untidy process may have meant that not all churches had exactly the same set of texts.

Nevertheless, certain figures are generally regarded as significant in the formational process of the New Testament canon. One such was the second-century figure Marcion, though the extent of his role is debated. For some, he was the first to provide a distinctively Christian canon, consisting of a version of Luke (purged of what he regarded as judaizing interpolations) and ten Pauline epistles (all except the Pastorals). It was thus as a response to Marcion that the orthodox, though in a rather haphazard manner, began to develop their own canon (with the four-gospel canon being the first to emerge).[127] Others credit Marcion with a less creative role.

Although manuscript evidence points to the four-gospel canon preceding Irenaeus of Lyons, his argument in favour of it in *Against Heresies* 3.11 is important. Drawing on the vision of the four creatures in Ezekiel and Revelation, he presents a bold case for the 'fourfold gospel', each evangelist's work bearing characteristics of one of the creatures. As a response to Marcion (if not to the wider Gnostic groups with their multiplicity of gospels and 'revelations'), Irenaeus' vision of the canon can be viewed as an inclusive one. Four gospels side-by-side, and in occasional tension, is where the truth is to be found. This raises the question: is Mark, or John, canonical in its own right, or only in relation to the other three?

We have already mentioned the significance of Athanasius' festal letter, providing a definite list of our New Testament books (differing somewhat from earlier canonical lists, such as the Muratorian canon). Not that Athanasius' letter marked an end to controversy. The Syrian church, for example, continued to favour Tatian's Diatessaron over the fourfold gospel into the fifth century. Debate also continued about certain of the Catholic Epistles, while Revelation continued to have a chequered history for several centuries to come.

Reflection

What do you understand by the 'New Testament canon'? Is it something fixed, or open to change (by addition or subtraction)? Do you think of it as primarily exclusive, or primarily inclusive?

Features of the New Testament Canon

In our discussion of the New Testament books in previous chapters, we have been influenced (consciously or unconsciously) by canonical decisions. The grouping of particular texts together, and the related tendency to interpret them in relation to each other, is often determined by the shape of the New Testament canon. Among the most significant features of the canon in our discussion so far are the following:

- A *four-gospel canon* (famously argued for by Irenaeus): this became the mainstream position amid a number of alternatives: selecting one gospel as the definitive version (Marcion's position); allowing a multiplicity of gospels (as in Gnosticism's plethora of gospel texts, from the Gospel of Thomas to the Gospel of Truth); harmonizing all four into one (a good example of this is Tatian's Diatessaron); preferring the oral tradition to written gospels. The early adoption by Christians of the book-like codex may be due to a desire, earlier than Irenaeus, to have all four gospels bound together. Although in contemporary discussion of the non-canonical gospels the four-gospel canon is often understood exclusively (excluding texts like the Gospel of Thomas or the Gospel of Mary), one way of reading Irenaeus is as promoting an inclusive canon: preventing a narrow, monochrome vision of the gospel and of the person of Christ.
- A *collection of Paul's letters*: as noted already, it is unclear how precisely the Pauline corpus evolved (though evidence from the Chester Beatty Papyrus and Marcion may suggest that the Pastorals were latecomers to this collection). Nevertheless, placing these letters together enables texts with quite narrow interests due to localized concerns (such as the polemical Galatian controversy) to be 'broadened' out by other perspectives on Paul. Not all would see this positively; arguably Paul has been 'tamed' by the Pastorals being read canonically as 'Pauline'. On the other hand, this process can work the other way too: setting socially conservative aspects of the Pastorals within a broader and potentially more radical context.
- *Acts*: we have flagged up in our discussion of Acts what some have seen as deficiencies in the canon as it stands. For it encourages a reading of Acts as a separate entity from Luke's Gospel, or as the preface to Paul's letters. On the other hand, while not a scenario which Luke envisaged, this canonical treatment of Acts as prefacing the Pauline corpus, and therefore providing a lens through which to read the Paul of the letters, is not inappropriate for a book which promotes a very definite portrait of Paul.
- *The Catholic Epistles*: grouping these quite disparate texts together, and

calling them 'Catholic' or 'universal', may have rescued some of them from obscurity. Whatever the specific occasion of their composition, they now have a universal appeal, speaking more widely to the churches. Moreover, as a group if not as individual letters, they represent a significant voice to supplement that of Paul.

But what criteria were at work in the canonical process, besides a pragmatic concern to preserve these writings for posterity? On what grounds were these 27 preserved rather than others? Why is the Didache not included, or the Shepherd of Hermas, or the Gospel of Thomas? Is the present shape of the New Testament canon simply evidence for the survival of the fittest? Some think so, making the point that the dominant ideology can often afford to be inclusive (hence the relative diversity of the canon), though 'taming' marginal voices in the process. On the other hand, the canonical process is a recognition (already flagged up by Paul in Galatians) that not all versions of the Christian gospel are equally valid. Among the criteria that seem to be at play in early discussions of the canon are the following:

- *Apostolic origin:* the attribution of texts to apostles is one important criterion, perhaps highlighting a particular concern for the apostolic teaching. This criterion seems to be broader than concern for apostolic authorship, for two gospels (Mark and Luke) are attributed to followers of apostles (Peter and Paul respectively), rather than apostles themselves.
- *Antiquity:* how old are the texts under discussion during debates about the canon? Are they ancient, or relatively recent? This accounts for the Muratorian canon's exclusion of the Shepherd of Hermas: it was known to be of recent origin.
- *Use:* attention to the use to which these writings were put in the churches, and how widely they were used, seems to be a concern in the canonical debates.

To do

Reread the four gospel accounts of the discovery of the empty tomb. How might you read these four accounts as 'the fourfold gospel', rather than four divergent accounts, or four accounts to be harmonized? What features come to the fore in such a reading?

Canonical Order

Athanasius' important festal letter referred to above is also interesting for the order in which it lists the New Testament books (which differs from their normal order in published New Testaments):

> Again it is not tedious to speak of the [books] of the New Testament. These are, the four Gospels, according to Matthew, Mark, Luke, and John. Afterwards, the Acts of the Apostles and Epistles (called Catholic), seven, viz. of James, one; of Peter, two; of John, three; after these, one of Jude. In addition, there are fourteen Epistles of Paul, written in this order. The first, to the Romans; then two to the Corinthians; after these, to the Galatians; next, to the Ephesians; then to the Philippians; then to the Colossians; after these, two to the Thessalonians, and that to the Hebrews; and again, two to Timothy; one to Titus; and lastly, that to Philemon. And besides, the Revelation of John. (Letter 39.5)[128]

As we have already noted in relation to the Catholic Epistles, canonical order makes a difference to how the books are read and interpreted. It may, for example, affect the shape of our 'canon within the canon' (the tendency of all readers to privilege particular authors or books as more 'central'). The differences in Athanasius' list are twofold. First, he is one of those who places the Catholic Epistles immediately after Acts, thus giving the 'first generation' of James, Peter, John and Jude greater prominence. They have taken the central place normally accorded to the Pauline letters. Second, the location of Hebrews has shifted from after Philemon to before 1 and 2 Timothy. This reflects the tradition, widespread in the East, that Paul was its author. Hence it is listed immediately after letters of Paul to the churches, and before his letters to individuals.

Nor is this the only canonical order to be preserved. Although Matthew–Mark–Luke–John is the normal order of the gospels, alternative orders can be found (for example Matthew–John–Mark–Luke in the Codex Claromantanus). The position of Acts moves around in various lists: for example to after Paul's letters; or to just before Revelation (but never immediately after Luke, despite the Luke–Acts consensus).[129]

To do

Try and track down other alternative canonical lists. Note down the differences in order between them. What difference do these differing orders make to interpretation?

Other Canonical Issues

The phenomenon of the New Testament canon raises other issues for New Testament scholarship. First, implications of canon for reading and interpretation have been especially important in one particular interpretative approach. This is canonical criticism, associated with Brevard Childs. Childs' main concern is how the New Testament writings should be used within the community of faith, as scripture.[130] This concern, he believes, has been too often neglected by the narrowly historical focus of much biblical criticism. He urges attention to the final form of the text (rather than hypothetical sources and earlier editions, or the intention of the historical author), and on a text's location within the canonical collection. Both of these, he claims, are of hermeneutical significance.

In his canonical reading, Childs speaks of texts being gradually 'loosened' from the original historical context and audiences. They not only have a more universal appeal; they are also no longer treated in splendid isolation, but can be read in the light of other texts. Others object that this imposes an artificial unity on quite disparate writings. Critics of Childs also point to the difficulty of arriving at the 'final form' of the text. Is it a particular English translation? If the original Greek, then which ancient manuscript, or modern critical edition, is to be chosen? What is the 'final form' of Mark? The version ending at Mark 16.8, or containing the Longer Ending, or the alternative Shorter Ending?

The second issue is both historical (concerning Christian origins) and theological (concerning the legitimacy of a diversity of views). Is the diversity in the New Testament canon a problem? Or alternatively, how is it possible to speak of a single 'canon', given the diversity of positions represented within it?

From a historical perspective, the influential Tübingen hypothesis, associated with the nineteenth-century German scholar Ferdinand Christian Baur, has highlighted the presence of conflict within the New Testament writings. Baur's distinctive Hegelian reading of the New Testament found an original Jewish Christian 'thesis' (represented by 'Petrinists', Peter, James and others), challenged by a Pauline 'antithesis', and eventually (through the harmonizing Acts) achieving a 'synthesis' in the early Catholic Church. A recent version, with some refinements, of the Tübingen hypothesis is Michael Goulder's *A Tale of Two Missions*.[131]

Baur's Tübingen hypothesis has been criticized by many as too simplistic, and too heavily influenced by his Hegelian philosophy, as well as confessional rivalries between Catholic and Protestant Theology faculties in Tübingen (presenting the Protestant 'Paulines' as challenging the Catholic 'Petrines'). Nevertheless, Baur has established beyond reasonable doubt the presence of disagreement and division within the early Church. This disagreement has left its mark on the canonical writings, as well as on other early Christian writings beyond the boundaries of the New Testament canon.

To return to the theological question: if the canon is perceived as straitjacketing theological diversity, then it may be problematic. But there is an alternative view: that, while maintaining legitimate boundaries, a New Testament canon which contains four different gospels rather than one Diatessaron, and which enables James and Jude to be read alongside Romans and Galatians, may be capable of holding differing voices in creative tension without stifling debate.

Further Reading

Brevard Childs, 1985, *The New Testament as Canon: An Introduction*, Philadelphia: Fortress Press.

James D. G. Dunn, 1990, *Unity and Diversity in the New Testament*, 2nd edition; London: SCM Press.

Harry Gamble, 1985, *The New Testament Canon: Its Making and Meaning*, Philadelphia: Fortress Press.

Bruce M. Metzger, 1987, *The Canon of the New Testament: Its Origin, Development and Significance*, Oxford: Clarendon Press.

Notes

Chapter 1 The Worlds Which Produced the New Testament

1 Luke Timothy Johnson, 1999, *The Writings of the New Testament: An Interpretation*, revised edition; London: SCM Press.

2 On these issues, see e.g. Christopher Rowland, 2002, *Christian Origins*, 2nd edition; London: SPCK.

3 E.g. Martin McNamara (ed.), *The Aramaic Bible*, Collegeville: Liturgical Press.

4 R. H. Charles, 1913, *Apocrypha and Pseudepigrapha of the Old Testament*, Oxford: Clarendon Press; James H. Charlesworth, 1983 and 1985, *The Old Testament Pseudepigrapha*, London: Darton, Longman and Todd; H. F. D. Sparks, 1984, *The Apocryphal Old Testament*, Oxford: Clarendon Press.

5 Geza Vermes, 1997, *The Complete Dead Sea Scrolls in English*, London: Penguin Books; Florentino García Martínez, 1996, *The Dead Sea Scrolls Translated: The Qumran Texts in English*, Leiden: E. J. Brill.

6 The extensive body of Philo's works is most easily consulted in the Loeb edition: F. H. Colson and G. H. Whitaker (eds), 1929–53, *Philo*, London: William Heinemann.

7 Josephus' works are available in the Loeb edition: H. St J. Thackeray, R. Marcus and L. H. Feldman (eds), 1926–65, *Josephus*, London: William Heinemann.

8 The standard English edition is H. Danby, 1933, *The Mishnah*, Oxford: Oxford University Press.

9 For this see *Jewish War* 2.162–6. Note also Luke 13.31.

10 A detailed account of the role of the Temple and its various sacrifices can be found in E. P. Sanders, 1992, *Judaism: Practice and Belief*, London: SCM Press, pp. 47–145. A useful collection of primary texts with commentary is C. T. R. Hayward, 1996, *The Jewish Temple: A Non-Biblical Sourcebook*, London and New York: Routledge.

11 See K. C. Hanson and Douglas E. Oakman, 1998, *Palestine in the Time of Jesus*, Minneapolis: Fortress Press, ch. 4.

12 See e.g. Richard A. Horsley with John S. Hanson, 1985, *Bandits, Prophets, and Messiahs: Popular Movements in the Time of Jesus*, Minneapolis: Winston Press; Sean Freyne, 1980, *Galilee from Alexander the Great to Hadrian, 323 B.C.E. to 135 C.E.*, Notre Dame, Indiana: University of Notre Dame Press, pp. 208–47.

13 One reaction to this Hasmonaean development may be the expectation at Qumran of *two* Messiahs, one a priest and one a king.

14 On this see Will Deming, 2004, *Paul on Marriage and Celibacy*, 2nd edition; Grand Rapids, Michigan/Cambridge: Eerdmans.

Chapter 2 What Can We Know about Jesus?

15 See e.g. John Dominic Crossan, 1988, *The Cross that Spoke*, San Francisco: Harper and Row.

16 As argued strongly in Richard A. Burridge, 2004, *What are the Gospels? A Comparison with Graeco-Roman Biography*, 2nd edition; Grand Rapids, Michigan/Cambridge: Eerdmans (first edition published 1992). See chapter 5 in the *SCM Studyguide to New Testament Interpretation*.

17 A good summary of the quests can be found in N. T. Wright, 1996, *Jesus and the Victory of God*, London: SPCK, chapters 1–3.

18 Martin Kähler, 1964, *The So-Called Historical Jesus and the Historic, Biblical Christ*, ET Philadelphia: Fortress Press, p. 102.

19 John P. Meier, 1991, *A Marginal Jew: Rethinking the Historical Jesus*, volume 1: *The Roots of the Problem and the Person*, New York: Doubleday, pp. 21–31.

20 Q (from the German *Quelle* = 'source') is the hypothetical source drawn upon independently by Matthew and Luke, according to the Two-Source theory of relationships between the synoptic gospels. For further information on this, see chapter 5 in the *SCM Studyguide to New Testament Interpretation*.

21 'Triple-tradition' is shorthand for passages with a parallel in all three synoptic gospels (Matthew, Mark and Luke); 'double-tradition' refers to passages paralleled in Matthew and Luke only (i.e. non-Marcan material).

22 Wright, *Jesus and the Victory of God*, p. 132.

23 On Hanina, and similar characters such as Honi the Circle-Drawer, see Geza Vermes, 1973, *Jesus the Jew*, London: Collins, pp. 69–78.

24 George Tyrrell, 1909, *Christianity at the Crossroads*, London: Longmans, Green and Co., p. 44.

25 Gerd Theissen and Annette Merz, 1998, *The Historical Jesus: A Comprehensive Guide*, London: SCM Press, p. 11.

26 James D. G. Dunn, 2005, *A New Perspective on Jesus: What the Quest for the Historical Jesus Missed*, Grand Rapids, Michigan: Baker Academic, especially pp. 46–56 and pp. 89–101. Dunn's thesis is discussed further in the companion volume to this, *SCM Studyguide to New Testament Interpretation*, chapter 3.

27 Luke Timothy Johnson, 1996, *The Real Jesus*, New York: HarperCollins. See also his 1999 *Living Jesus: Learning the Heart of the Gospel*, New York: HarperCollins.

Chapter 3 Studying Paul

28 I use the term 'authentic' here because there are some New Testament letters attributed to Paul which many scholars believe were composed by his disciples after his death. On this, see Chapters 4 and 9.

29 E.g. John A. T. Robinson, 1976, *Redating the New Testament*, London: SCM Press; 1985, *The Priority of John*, London: SCM Press; James G. Crossley, 2004, *The Date of Mark's Gospel*, London: T. & T. Clark International.

30 Jerome Murphy-O'Connor, 1996, *Paul: A Critical Life*, Oxford: Clarendon Press; 2004, *Paul: His Story*, Oxford: Oxford University Press.

31 On this see N. T. Wright, 2005, *Paul: Fresh Perspectives*, London: SPCK.

32 Christine Kondoleon, 2000, *Antioch: the Lost Ancient City*, Princeton, New Jersey: Princeton University Press and Worcester Art Museum.

33 Jerome Murphy-O'Connor, 2002, *St Paul's Corinth. Texts and Archaeology*, 3rd revised and expanded edition; Collegeville: Michael Glazier.

34 Helmut Koester (ed.), 1995, *Ephesos: Metropolis of Asia*, Harvard Theological Studies; Valley Forge, Pennsylvania: Trinity Press International.

35 Karl P. Donfried and Peter Richardson (eds), 1998, *Judaism and Christianity in First-Century Rome*, Grand Rapids, Michigan/Cambridge: Eerdmans; Peter Lampe, 2003, *From Paul to Valentinus: Christians at Rome in the First Two Centuries*, London: T. & T. Clark International.

36 A further reference in Dio Cassius, *History* 60.6.6, in the context of recounting events of 41 CE, may be referring to a different episode, since the Jews were not expelled.

37 William Sanday and Arthur C. Headlam, 1895, *The Epistle to the Romans*, International Critical Commentary; Edinburgh: T. & T. Clark, p. lv.

38 For a flavour of the debate, compare A. N. Wilson, 1997, *Paul: The Mind of the Apostle*, London: Sinclair-Stevenson, with Tom Wright, 1997, *What Saint Paul Really Said*, Oxford: Lion.

39 John Ashton, 2000, *The Religion of Paul the Apostle*, New Haven and London: Yale University Press.

40 See, for example, D. E. H. Whiteley, 1964, *The Theology of St Paul*, Oxford: Basil Blackwell; Herman Ridderbos, 1975, *Paul: An Outline of His Theology*, Grand Rapids, Michigan: Eerdmans; James D. G. Dunn, 1998, *The Theology of Paul the Apostle*, Edinburgh: T. & T. Clark.

41 Wright, *Paul: Fresh Perspectives*, especially chapters 5–8.

42 See Rudolf Bultmann, 1952, *Theology of the New Testament*, volume 1, ET London: SCM Press, pp. 187–352.

43 Richard B. Hays, 1989, *Echoes of Scripture in the Letters of Paul*, New Haven and London: Yale University Press. See also his 2005 collection of essays, *The Conversion of the Imagination: Paul as Interpreter of Israel's Scripture*, Grand Rapids, Michigan/Cambridge: Eerdmans. Hays gives the following definition of intertextuality: 'the imbedding of fragments of an earlier text within a later one' (*Echoes of Scripture* p. 14).

44 On this see Morna D. Hooker, 2003, *Paul: A Short Introduction*, Oxford: Oneworld, pp. 90–5.

45 Compare Richard B. Hays, 1983, *The Faith of Jesus Christ*, Chico: Scholars Press, with Dunn, *Theology of Paul the Apostle*, pp. 379–85.

46 For different views, see Krister Stendahl, 1977, *Paul Among Jews and Gentiles*, London: SCM Press, pp. 7–23; Alan F. Segal, 1990, *Paul the Convert*, New Haven and London: Yale University Press.

47 E. P. Sanders, 1977, *Paul and Palestinian Judaism*, London: SCM Press; 1983, *Paul, the Law and the Jewish People*, London: SCM Press.

48 James D. G. Dunn, 1990, *Jesus, Paul and the Law*, London: SPCK, pp. 183–241. For a partial critique of the 'new perspective' associated with Sanders and Dunn, see e.g. Stephen Westerholm, 2004, *Perspectives Old and New on Paul*, Grand Rapids, Michigan: Eerdmans.

49 For a carefully argued case that Paul knows a great deal about Jesus' life and teaching, see David Wenham, 1995, *Paul: Follower of Jesus or Founder of Christianity?* Grand Rapids, Michigan/Cambridge: Eerdmans; 2002, *Paul and Jesus: the True Story*, London: SPCK.

Chapter 4 Introducing Paul's Letters

50 A good introduction is George A. Kennedy, 1984, *New Testament Interpretation through Rhetorical Criticism*, Chapel Hill, North Carolina/London: University of North Carolina Press.

51 A. Katherine Grieb, 2002, *The Story of Romans: A Narrative Defense of God's Righteousness*, Louisville and London: Westminster John Knox Press.

52 Some scholars argue that reception history and *Wirkungsgeschichte* are describing different, though overlapping, enterprises: the first focusing upon how a text is received, and particularly upon those receiving it, the second on the (negative and positive) effects a text has in different ages and cultures.

53 For further discussion of the difficulties with the Acts account, see Earl J. Richard, 1995, *First and Second Thessalonians*, Sacra Pagina; Collegeville, Minnesota: Michael Glazier, pp. 3–7.

54 Richard, *First and Second Thessalonians*, pp. 8–10.

55 See Karl P. Donfried and I. Howard Marshall, 1993, *The Theology of the Shorter Pauline Letters*, New Testament Theology; Cambridge: Cambridge University Press, pp. 84–7.

56 For a summary of such rhetorical analysis of 2 Thessalonians, see Donfried and Marshall, *Theology of the Shorter Pauline Letters* pp. 83–4.

57 On the 'body' in 1 Corinthians, and connections between the individual and corporate body, see Dale B. Martin, 1995, *The Corinthian Body*, New Haven and London: Yale University Press.

58 Jerome Murphy-O'Connor, 2002, *St Paul's Corinth: Text and Archeology*, 3rd edition: Collegeville: Michael Glazier, pp. 177–98.

59 Wayne Meeks, 1983, *The First Urban Christians*, New Haven and London: Yale University Press; Gerd Theissen, 1982, *The Social Setting of Pauline Christianity*, ET Edinburgh: T. & T. Clark.

60 E.g. John Ashton, 2000, *The Religion of Paul the Apostle*, New Haven and London: Yale University Press, pp. 113–42.

61 *1 Clement* cited from Kirsopp Lake (ed.), 1925, *The Apostolic Fathers*, Loeb Classical Library; London: William Heinemann, pp. 89–91.

62 For a concise discussion of these issues, see Raymond E. Brown, 1997, *An Introduction to the New Testament*, New York and London: Doubleday, pp. 610–15.

63 Though see the quite different assessment of Neil Elliott, 1995, *Liberating Paul: The Justice of God and the Politics of the Apostle*, Sheffield: Sheffield Academic Press, pp. 31–52.

64 As in e.g. James D. G. Dunn, 1998, *The Theology of Paul the Apostle*, Edinburgh: T. & T. Clark.

65 Early tradition and other evidence suggests that Christianity in Rome prior to Paul's visit was a strongly Jewish form, which may have been introduced into the city through specific synagogues. On this see e.g. Peter Lampe, 2003, *From Paul to Valentinus: Christians at Rome in the First Two Centuries*, London: T. & T. Clark International.

66 Although there are scholars who maintain that Romans 16 was originally

addressed to Ephesus, Romans itself being seen as a circular letter to a number of churches, most scholars would probably hold to the integrity of Romans 1–16. On this see e.g. Harry Gamble, 1977, *The Textual History of the Letter to the Romans*, Studies and Documents 42; Grand Rapids: Eerdmans.

67 See Markus Barth, 1983, *The People of God*, JSNTSS 5; Sheffield: JSOT Press.

68 Richard J. Cassidy, 2001, *Paul in Chains: Roman Imprisonment and the Letters of St Paul*, New York: Crossroad.

69 Jerome Murphy-O'Connor, 1976, 'Christological Anthropology in Phil. 2.6–11 ', *Revue Biblique* 83, pp. 25–50; James D. G. Dunn, 1989, *Christology in the Making*, 2nd edn.; London: SCM Press, pp. 114–20.

Chapter 5 The First Three Gospels

70 Wilhelm Wrede, 1971, *The Messianic Secret*, ET Cambridge and London: James Clark.

71 For different views, see William R. Telford (ed.), 1995, *The Interpretation of Mark*, 2nd ed.; Edinburgh: T. & T. Clark, pp. 89–104, 169–95.

72 W.D. Davies, 1964, *The Setting of the Sermon on the Mount*, Cambridge: Cambridge University Press.

73 E.g. J. Andrew Overman, 1990, *Matthew's Gospel and Formative Judaism*, Minneapolis: Fortress Press; Anthony J. Saldarini, 1994, *Matthew's Christian-Jewish Community*, Chicago and London: Chicago University Press.

74 For a critique of simplistic accounts of the 'Jamnian' generation, see Richard A. Horsley, 1995, *Galilee: History, Politics, People*, Valley Forge, Pennsylvania: Trinity Press International, pp. 94–5.

75 On this see Richard Bauckham (ed.), 1998, *The Gospels for All Christians*, Edinburgh: T. & T. Clark.

Chapter 6 John: The Spiritual Gospel

76 Translation from *Nicene and Post-Nicene Fathers*, vol. 1, p. 261.

77 E.g. C. H. Dodd, 1963, *Historical Tradition in the Fourth Gospel*, Cambridge: Cambridge University Press.

78 Rudolf Bultmann, 1971, *The Gospel of John: A Commentary*, ET Philadelphia: Westminster Press.

79 On this, see e.g. John Ashton, 1991, *Understanding the Fourth Gospel*, Oxford: Clarendon Press, especially Part II.

80 Martin Hengel, 1989, *The Johannine Question*, ET London: SCM /Philadelphia:

Trinity Press International, p. 1. It was the nineteenth-century scholar David Friedrich Strauss who likened John to Christ's seamless robe.

81 Ashton, *Understanding the Fourth Gospel*, p. 137.

82 Ruth Edwards, 2003, *Discovering John*, London: SPCK, p. 112, citing Lowry.

83 J. Louis Martyn, 1968, *History and Theology in the Fourth Gospel*, New York: Harper and Row.

84 Raymond E. Brown, 1979, *The Community of the Beloved Disciple*, London: Geoffrey Chapman; Ashton, *Understanding the Fourth Gospel*.

85 Richard Bauckham (ed.), 1998, *The Gospels for All Christians*, Edinburgh: T. & T. Clark.

86 For a recent assessment of the state-of-play in Johannine studies, see John R. Donahue (ed.), 2005, *Life in Abundance: Studies of John's Gospel in Tribute to Raymond E. Brown*, Collegeville, Minnesota: Liturgical Press.

Chapter 7 From the Cradle to the (Empty) Grave

87 E.g. Etienne Trocmé, 1983, *The Passion as Liturgy*, London: SCM Press.

88 Raymond E. Brown, 1994, *The Death of the Messiah*, London: Geoffrey Chapman, especially volume 1, pp. 4–35; John Dominic Crossan, 1995, *Who Killed Jesus?* New York: HarperCollins.

89 On these and other questions related to the Resurrection Narratives, see the following collections of essays: Paul Avis (ed.), 1993, *The Resurrection of Jesus Christ*, London: Darton, Longman and Todd; Stephen Barton and Graham Stanton (eds), 1994, *Resurrection: Essays in Honour of Leslie Houlden*, London: SPCK. Wider theological implications are explored in Stephen Davis, Daniel Kendall SJ and Gerald O'Collins SJ, 1997, *The Resurrection: An Interdisciplinary Symposium on the Resurrection of Jesus*, Oxford: Oxford University Press.

90 Accessible introductions to the Infancy Narratives include Herman Hendrickx, 1984, *The Infancy Narratives*, London: Geoffrey Chapman; Edwin D. Freed, 2001, *The Stories of Jesus' Birth*, Sheffield: Sheffield Academic Press; the classic major work is Raymond E. Brown, 1993, *The Birth of the Messiah*, updated edition, London: Geoffrey Chapman.

91 A more detailed summary of the similarities and differences is provided by Freed, *The Stories of Jesus' Birth*, pp. 57–9.

92 Suggestions include Isa. 11.1, which talks about the messianic Branch (Hebrew *nētzer*), and Judg. 16.17, where Samuel describes himself as a nazirite.

Chapter 8 Acts: Luke's Ongoing Story

93 Henry J. Cadbury, 1958, *The Making of Luke–Acts*, London: SPCK (first edition 1927).

94 See the survey by F. Scott Spencer, 2004, *Journeying through Acts: A Literary-Cultural Reading*, Peabody, Massachusetts: Hendrickson, pp. 17–19.

95 The exceptions are at Acts 14.4, 14, though the term here might refer to Paul and Barnabas' role as 'apostles' or emissaries of the Antiochene church.

96 Against the view of discrete 'Hellenist' and 'Hebrew' groups with their distinctive theologies, see Craig C. Hill, 1992, *Hellenists and Hebrews*, Minneapolis: Fortress Press.

97 Cited from Raymond E. Brown, 1997, *An Introduction to the New Testament*, New York and London: Doubleday, p. 318, n. 94.

98 For an alternative view, see Mikeal C. Parsons and Richard I. Pervo, 1993, *Rethinking the Unity of Luke and Acts*, Minneapolis: Fortress Press.

99 Parsons and Pervo, *Rethinking the Unity of Luke and Acts*, pp. 8–13, 21–2.

Chapter 9 The Ongoing Pauline Tradition

100 John Muddiman, 2001, *The Epistle to the Ephesians*, Black's New Testament Commentaries; London and New York: Continuum, pp. 24–32.

101 On the authorship question, see Margaret Davies, 1996, *The Pastoral Epistles*, New Testament Guides; Sheffield: Sheffield Academic Press, chapter 4.

102 On these issues, see e.g. Muddiman, *The Epistle to the Ephesians*, 41–7; Jeremy Duff, '2 Peter' in *The Oxford Bible Commentary*, p. 1271.

103 Muddiman, *The Epistle to the Ephesians*, pp. 2–3.

104 Margaret Y. MacDonald, 1988, *The Pauline Churches: A Socio-historical Study of Institutionalization in the Pauline and Deutero-Pauline Writings*, Cambridge: Cambridge University Press.

105 Translation from Edgar Hennecke and Wilhelm Schneemelcher (eds), 1965, *New Testament Apocrypha*, vol. 2, Philadelphia: Westminster Press, p. 355.

Chapter 10 The Letter to the Hebrews

106 Hugh Montefiore, 1964, *A Commentary on the Epistle to the Hebrews*, Black's New Testament Commentaries; London: A. & C. Black, pp. 9–31.

107 E.g. Y. Yadin, 1958, 'The Dead Sea Scrolls and the Epistle to the Hebrews', *Aspects of the Dead Sea Scrolls: Scripta Hierosolymitana* 4, pp. 36–55.

108 For further discussion of this, see C. K. Barrett, 1956, 'The Eschatology of the Epistle to the Hebrews', in W. D. Davies and David Daube (eds), *The Background of the New Testament and its Eschatology*, Cambridge: Cambridge University Press; L. D. Hurst, 1990, *The Epistle to the Hebrews: Its Background of Thought*, Cambridge: Cambridge University Press.

109 For examples of patristic commentary on Hebrews, see Erik M. Heen and Philip D. W. Krey (eds), 2005, *Hebrews*, Ancient Christian Commentary on Scripture; Downers Grove, Illinois: InterVarsity Press; there is some reflection on Hebrews' ongoing significance in Andrew T. Lincoln, 2006, *Hebrews: A Guide*, London and New York: T. & T. Clark, pp. 107–20.

110 *Lumen Gentium* 9; quoted from Austin Flannery OP (ed.), 1988, *Vatican Council II: The Conciliar and Post Conciliar Documents*, rev. edn, Dublin: Dominican Publications, p. 360.

Chapter 11 The Catholic Epistles

111 E.g. Luke Timothy Johnson, 1995, *The Letter of James*, Anchor Bible; New York: Doubleday.

112 Richard Bauckham, 1999, *James*, New Testament Readings; London: Routledge, p. 15.

113 Elsa Tamez, 2002, *The Scandalous Message of James*, rev. edn, New York: Crossroad.

114 For an interesting analysis of these terms, see John H. Elliott, 1981, *A Home for the Homeless*, London: SCM Press.

115 Raymond E. Brown, 1979, *Community of the Beloved Disciple*, London: Geoffrey Chapman, pp. 93–144.

116 Richard Bauckham, 1990, *Jude and the Relatives of Jesus in the Early Church*, Edinburgh: T. & T. Clark, pp. 179–234.

117 Christopher Rowland, 'Jude', in *The Oxford Bible Commentary*, p. 1286.

Chapter 12 Revelation: Guide to the End of the World?

118 Barbara R. Rossing, 2004, *The Rapture Exposed: The Message of Hope in the Book of Revelation*, Boulder, Colorado/Oxford: Westview Press, pp. 82–4.

119 On this see Christopher Rowland, 1982, *The Open Heaven*, London: SPCK.

120 To explore further the wider mystical tradition of which John may be part, see Ithamar Gruenwald, 1980, *Apocalyptic and Merkavah Mysticism*, Leiden: E. J.

Brill; Rowland, *The Open Heaven*, esp. pp. 214–47; Ian Boxall, 2002, *Revelation: Vision and Insight*, London: SPCK, pp. 30–6.

121 On the reassessment of Domitian, see Leonard L. Thompson, 1990, *The Book of Revelation: Apocalypse and Empire*, Oxford: Oxford University Press.

122 Arthur W. Wainwright, 1993, *Mysterious Apocalypse*, Nashville: Abingdon Press; Judith Kovacs and Christopher Rowland, 2004, *Revelation: The Apocalypse of Jesus Christ*, Blackwell Bible Commentaries; Malden, Massachusetts and Oxford: Blackwell.

123 Pablo Richard, 1995, *Apocalypse: A People's Commentary on the Book of Revelation*, Maryknoll, New York: Orbis; Allan A. Boesak, 1987, *Comfort and Protest*, Edinburgh: St Andrew Press.

124 E.g. Tina Pippin, 1992, *Death and Desire: The Rhetoric of Gender in the Apocalypse of John*, Louisville: Westminster/John Knox Press.

125 For further on this, see Ian Boxall, 2001, 'The Many Faces of Babylon the Great: *Wirkungsgeschichte* and the Interpretation of Revelation 17', in Steve Moyise (ed.), *Studies in the Book of Revelation*, Edinburgh: T. & T. Clark, pp. 51–68.

126 Useful reference books include: Frederick van der Meer, 1978, *Apocalypse: Visions from the Book of Revelation in Western Art*, London: Thames and Hudson; Nancy Grubb, 1997, *Revelations: Art of the Apocalypse*, New York, London and Paris: Abbeville Press. And see Felix Just SJ: http://catholic-resources.org/Art/Revelation-Art.htm.

Chapter 13 The New Testament Canon

127 E.g. Hans von Campenhausen, 1972, *The Formation of the Christian Bible*, ET Philadelphia: Fortress Press.

128 Translation from *Nicene and Post-Nicene Fathers*, volume 4, p. 552.

129 For more details, see Lee Martin McDonald, 2007, *The Biblical Canon: Its Origin, Transmission, and Authority*, Peabody: Hendrickson, Appendix C.

130 E.g. Brevard Childs, 1985, *The New Testament as Canon: An Introduction*, Philadelphia: Fortress Press. For a critique of Childs, see Mark Brett, 1991, *Biblical Criticism in Crisis?* Cambridge: Cambridge University Press, pp. 142ff.

131 Michael Goulder, 1994, *A Tale of Two Missions*, London: SCM Press.

Index of Bible References

Index of Subjects

Index of Names